Teacher Certification Exam

Principal
Study Guide

Written By:
XAM

Contributors:
Dr. Ada Burnett
Dr. Gloria Poole
Dr. Warren Hope
Dr. Janet Guyten
Ms. Marilyn Rainear MS.

To Order Additional Copies:
Xam, Inc.
99 Central St.
Worcester, MA 01605
Toll Free   1-800-301-4647
Phone: 1-508 363 0633
Email: winwin1111@aol.com
Web   www.xamonline.com
EFax   1-501-325-0185
Fax: 1-508-363-0634

You will find:
- Content Review in prose format
- Bibliography
- Sample Test

XAM, INC.
Building Better Teachers

"And, while there's no reason yet to panic, I think it's only prudent that we make preperations to panic."

MANKOFF

OSAT: Principal
ISBN: 1-58197-244-X

TABLE OF CONTENTS - Competencies

Subtest 1 School Management

Competency 1   leadership
Competency 2   organizational management and development
Competency 3   human resource management

Subtest 2 School Communications

Competency 4   communications

Subtest 3 School Operations

Competency 5 curriculum public school
Competency 6 school finance
Competency 7 school law
Competency 8 technology

TABLE OF CONTENTS – Competencies with skills

Subtest 1 School Management

Competency 1 Leadership

- Skill A Know basic leadership theories
- Skill B Know basic theories of human motivation
- Skill C Know effects of group dynamics in managing productive interaction of
- school personnel.
- Skill D Identify basic concepts of the change process
- Skill E Recognize the importance of external influences that impact the school.
- Skill F Know the components, stages, and appropriate applications of macro and
- micro planning systems.

Competency 2 Organizational management and development

- Skill A Know of the need to be responsible for all school events.
- Skill B Recognize the importance of forcefulness and self confidence in decision
- making.
- Skill C Know the need for a set of values for the school
- Skill D Know the need for gathering information before arriving at an
- understanding of an event or problem.
- Skill E Recognize the relationships among sources of information; generate
- hypotheses based on this information.
- Skill F Recognize the need for concern for the image of the school via impressions
- created by students and staff; manage impressions through public
- realations.
- Skill G Recognize the importance of feedback in monitoring progress.
- Skill H Recognize the need for planning in goal accomplishment.
- Skill I Recognize the need for delegating authority and responsibility in
- accomplishing organizational goals.
- Skill J Recognize the effects of behavior and decisions on people and groups
- inside or outside of organizations.

Competency 3 Human resource management

- Skill A Know the principal's role in the selection of staff
- Skill B Identify induction process activities
- Skill C Know staff development programs
- Skill D Know appraisal procedures for school district personnel
- Skill E Know the organization and use of materials found in a personnel file
- Skill F Know the procedures for termination of school employees
- Skill G Know the objectives and administration of collective bargaining
- Skill H Know the purpose of reward systems in attracting and retaining qualified
  - personnel

Subtest 2 School Communications

Competency 4 Communications

- Skill A Know public information management
- Skill B Know effective communication strategies
- Skill C Know the effect one's behavior and decisions have on others
- Skill D Know the relationship between interpersonal influence and effective
- communication.
- Skill E Know the relationship between self-concept and effective communication
- Skill F Write in a logical, clear style using appropriate grammar and structure.

Subtest 3 School Operations

Competency 5 Curriculum public school

- Skill A Know the principles of curriculum development
- Skill B Identify and organize resources to achieve curricular and instructional
- goals.
- Skill C Employ principles of curruculum implemention by establishing goals and
- motivating staff.
- Skill D Know methods and principles of program evaluation.
- Skill E Determine school needs and use principles of implementing and evaluating
- curricular and instructional innovations.
- Skill F Know of prevalent conceptions of schooling.
- Skill G Know research on instructional effectiveness
- Skill H Know of student performance evaluations and appropriate practices in
- student performance evaluations.
- Skill I Know the main components of performance measurement systems.

Competency 6 School finance

- Skill A Know Florida's funding plan for public schools. (Your state equivalent.)
- Skill B Analyze the process of planning, developing, implementing, and evaluating
- school budgets.
- Skill C Apply knowledge of school finance concepts.
- Skill D Know of the processes of financial accounting, auditing and reporting.
- Skill E Explain the precedence and purposes for funding public education.

Competency 7 School law

- Skill A Know of federal constitutional provisions that apply to public education
- Skill B Know of federal statutory and regulatory provisions that influence public
- education.
- Skill C Know of state constitutional, statutory, and regulatory provisions
- governing Florida's public schools.
- Skill D Know of tort and contract liability as related to the operation of Florida's
- public schools.

Competency 8 Technology

- Skill A Evaluate computer hardware components that are appropriate to the
- management of a school
- Skill B Evaluate computer software that is available for assisting in the
- management of a school.
- Skill C Determine the appropriate application of technology in the learning
- process.
- Skill D Know of the use of technology in instructional design.
- Skill E Make policies and decisions that appropriately govern the use of school
- technological resources.
- Skill F Know the definitions, function, and application of computer
- software/hardware terminology.

Subtest 1 – School Management

1. Leadership

The school principal is recognized as the most important person for effecting change and bringing to fruition the goals and objectives of a school. The kind and quality of leadership exercised by those invested with the authority to supervise school operations makes a difference in the lives of students, the community, and ultimately the nation. Hence, the role of the principal and the competencies that an individual brings to this position are key elements in creating dynamic and effective school organizations.

COMPETENCY A: Demonstrates knowledge of basic leadership theories.

> **Skill 1:** Demonstrates knowledge of the historical development of leadership perspectives and orientations.

> **Skill 2:** Summarizes current concepts of leadership.

Our earliest knowledge and understanding of leadership are revealed in what is known as the "great man studies." The great man approach to understanding leadership revolved around information and descriptions of business leaders, politicians, and military men. However, the great man studies did not provide a consistent set of attributes, which could be packaged, for emulation. The "Trait Approach" to understanding leadership focused on the personality traits of leaders. Other approaches to understanding leadership were highlighted in the "Situational Approach" which postulated leadership as a result of understanding the idiosyncrasies and character of a specific group.

Research from Ohio State University placed leadership in two dimensions, task and consideration. This two-factor view of leadership increased understanding of leadership behavior. Finally, another approach to understanding leadership emerged, known as the "Contingency Approach." The Contingency Approach specified that the kind of leadership to be exerted depended upon a number of variables: personality, task, group dynamics, and the situation.

Many theorists have proposed frameworks in an attempt to understand the dynamics that take place in organizations. Educational Administration has borrowed extensively from organizational theorists to form a foundation. Early organizational theorists were more concerned with how well people performed given tasks in the enterprise rather than with the well being of the individuals in the organization.

These theories and beliefs about organizations and individuals were soon challenged by another set of theories and beliefs, which focused on the quality of relations and the importance of people in the organization. This evolutionary pattern continued, followed by critical analysis of the formal and informal structures existing in organizations. The conceptualization of organizations as a system, with internal and external influences further contributed to the base of knowledge for educational administration and leadership.

Ours is a rapidly changing world, which impacts the way organizations function. Moreover, changing situations require leaders of organizations to assess their abilities and understand the characteristics needed to effectively lead their organization (Lewis, 1993). It is apparent that school administration parallels that of business organizations and other enterprises in American society. The responsibilities of fiscal management, curriculum development, physical plant management, employee supervision, and personnel administration all require an administrator who possesses broad skills and knowledge (Rebore, 1998).

COMPETENCY B: Demonstrates knowledge of basic motivational theories.

Skill 1: Demonstrates understanding of basic motivational theories.

Motivation is defined by Baron (1992) as a force that energizes, sustains, and channels behavior toward a goal. Theorists maintain that there are two types of motivation. One is intrinsic motivation, which results from an individual's internal drive state and provides impetus toward goal attainment. The second is extrinsic motivation, meaning that the orientation toward goal achievement is influenced by incentives and rewards external to the individual. Providing for the needs, desires, and likes of individuals in an organizational setting influences motivation and impacts the objectives of the organization. Motivating individuals is a complex process of trying to facilitate desired motivational patterns (Hoy & Miskel, 1996). A number of theories have developed to explain what influences individuals to work enthusiastically, to want to engage in professional growth, to contribute to goal attainment in organizations, and to act responsibly.

Organizations have goals and objectives, which they seek to achieve. For the most part, those goals and objectives are achieved through people. The question of how to get people motivated to achieve those goals and objectives expeditiously and effectively is at the heart of motivational theories. Theories of motivation are grouped into the categories of Behavioral, Cognitive, and Humanistic. The behavioral approach to motivation suggests that motivation depends upon the effectiveness of reinforcers. The utilization of specific reinforcers to influence behavior then becomes an important element in the behavioral approach.

Cognitive theory suggests that there are two personal factors to consider in relation to motivation (Eggen & Kauchak, 1997). Those factors are expectations and beliefs. When there is the expectation that one can succeed at a task and value to achieving that task is attached, then a feeling of self-efficacy emerges. In organizations then, leaders may ask what can be done to help bring about emotions of self-efficacy in its members. The Humanistic perspective views motivation as attempts by people to reach their potential (Eggen & Kauchak1997). Motivation proceeds from internal mechanisms acting to cause individuals to achieve, grow and develop, and reach their potential.

Incentives and rewards are used by an organization to influence individuals' motivation to be productive members in the organization. Of importance in any work environment are the environmental factors present, those things that tend to make the workplace enjoyable and those things that tend to make the workplace distasteful. Administrators' attentions to the factors, which will permeate the workplace and, subsequently, have impact on the motivation of organizations' members to accomplish tasks, have a bearing on the fulfillment of organizational goals. Because individuals have needs, desires, likes and dislikes and these are related to their motivation, an understanding of this and how it relates to work is important for the leadership function.

COMPETENCY C: Demonstrates knowledge of group dynamics in managing the productive interaction of school faculty and support personnel.

> **Skill 1:** Identifies the elements of groups as social systems.
>
> **Skill 2:** Interprets and critiques the structure and dynamics of informal organizations.
>
> **Skill 3:** Specifies problem-solving techniques and strategies.
>
> **Skill 4:** Demonstrates knowledge of decision making process and structure possibilities.
>
> **Skill 5:** Demonstrates knowledge regarding the dynamics of creative conflict resolution.

Schools are social systems. As a social system, it consists of four key elements: the structural, the individual, the cultural, and the political (Hoy & Miskel, 1997). Structure is recognized as the formal bureaucratic expectations promulgated by the organization to achieve its goals.

The individual is conceived in terms of personal needs and the capabilities required in order to exist in the organization and to contribute to fulfilling its goals. Culture is defined as the shared work expectations. And, politics is the system of power relations that emerge from the context of the organization's interacting parts. These interdependent parts contribute to the operations of the school. The behavior of the organization is directly related to the interaction of these elements. As a social system, schools are also open systems, meaning that they are influenced by organizations and structures external to the immediate school environment.

The conceptualization of schools as a social system suggests that conflict is possible. There are, within an organization, at least two roles for individuals: one, the role that the individual carves according to personal idiosyncrasies, and two, the role that the organization imposes because of the specified goals that are to be accomplished. The bureaucratic roles imposed by the organization upon the individual can be inconsistent with the roles the individual perceives as a member in the organization and with the personal role the individual desires to have.

Coexisting with the formal organization is the informal organization. Members of an organization bring with them a number of characteristics such as values, needs, and motives (Hoy & Miskel, 1987). These attributes play out in the atmosphere of the organization. The informal organization is a network of interpersonal relations that form over a period of time due to the interaction of members within an organization. As individual opportunities to engage in social settings emerge, group members begin to behave according to desirable and acceptable norms that grow out of group interactions. Hoy and Miskel (1987) identified three important functions of the informal organization. Those functions are to serve as a vehicle for communication, to serve as a means of cohesion, and to protect the integrity of individuals. Groups in organizations develop personalities, mores, customs, and traditions to sustain them in the organizational environment. These elements give identity to the group and define group behavior.

Inevitably, problems occur in schools. How those problems are addressed and the quality of the problem-solving episode determines the longevity of the proposed solution and the probable reoccurrence of the same or similar difficulty. Hersey and Blanchard (1988) identified four group problem-solving modes. They are the (a) Crisis Mode, (b) Organizational Problem Solving Mode, (c) Interpersonal Problem Solving Mode, and (d) Routine Procedural Mode. Using the Situational Leadership model, which emphasizes Task Behavior and Relationship Behavior, they described how each mode is used to resolve organizational problems. When the Crisis Mode is used for problem solving it requires high task behavior and low relationship. When the Organizational Mode is applied, high task and high relationship behavior takes place. The Interpersonal Mode suggests a high relationship and low task behavior. The Routine Mode uses low task and low relationship behavior.

Parnes, Noller, and Biondi (1977) developed a five-step model for problem solving. Their model provided for (a) fact finding, (b) problem finding, (c) idea finding, (d) solution finding, and (e) acceptance finding. Fact Finding centers on gathering information related to a situation. The Problem Finding step identifies the problems and sub problems. Idea finding employs techniques to create ideas about the problem. The Solution finding step uses some criteria to evaluate the ideas. Acceptance Finding is the stage where a plan of action is developed to address the problem.

COMPETENCY D: Identifies basic concepts of the change process.

    Skill 1: Demonstrates understanding of the concepts of basic change process.

Change is always easier to talk about than it is to accomplish. Yet change must be a consistent element of organizational vitality. Determining when to change and what to change in the organizational milieu presents difficulties for a leader. People resist change for a variety of reasons. Perhaps the most prominent barrier to change is the threat it poses to individual roles and the perceived security individuals have in an organization. Human beings resist change almost instinctively. Regardless of the way a certain task is being performed, individuals engaged in performing it are familiar with the details and comfortable using the existing format. Change is viewed as disruptive because members of an organization have devoted energy and resources to accomplishing certain tasks in prescribed ways. To alter the methodology used to accomplish the tasks engenders threat to competency—given a new way of doing it, individuals are not sure they can accomplish the task. Change entails the prospect of discarding the old way of doing something for a new way of doing a task. So much has been invested in the old way, that it is very difficult to acknowledge another method. As well, there is a legitimacy of the old versus the unknown qualities of the new.

Change entertained for the organization should be well thought through. Several points are illustrative and serve as advice for a change agent. The change that is to be introduced should not be done abruptly, but rather mentioned and discussed over a period of time preceding its intended implementation. Considerable support for the change should be marshaled so that it has sufficient sustaining forces in the organization. Details regarding the specific goals that are to be addressed by the change are important.

Doll (1996) discusses the process of change from three different perspectives. First, change is viewed as technical; that is, an innovation can be designed carefully and implemented into an organization with needed technical assistance. Second, change is political, meaning that there are special interests of individuals at work in the planning of change. The third is cultural. Each planned change has potential for disturbing or altering the cultural context.

The Northwest Regional Educational Laboratory used a modified version of the five classic steps in the change process in a plan called Research Utilizing Problem Solving Process. Those steps are (a) identifying a need for change, (b) diagnosing the situation in which change is to take place, (c) considering alternative courses of action, (d) testing the feasibility of a plan for change, and (e) adoption, diffusion, and adaptation of successful change effort. This plan presents one approach to the change process that concentrates primarily on the initiation phase of a change process.

The change process is further complicated by the fact that there is no or very little existing support structure for the change or innovation to be introduced in the organization. Generally, a different kind of support system is necessary to maintain the change once it is introduced. It is important for a school leader to be aware and to begin to develop a support system for change in the school environment. Teachers are the ones expected to implement innovations and sustain change in the school. For change to be successful, attention must be given to them and their emotional and professional needs regarding change. If teachers' emotional and professional needs, particularly technical assistance are neglected, the change or innovation will quite likely create difficulty. Change occurs best in a non-punitive, pressureless, supportive environment. School leaders who foster change on this basis increase the likelihood of change becoming legitimized in the school.

COMPETENCY E: Recognizes the importance of external influences, which impact upon the school.

    Skill 1: Identifies methods for the study of community power structure.

    Skill 2: Identifies types of power structures in communities.

    Skill 3: Understands the process of educational policy development at the state level.

The Constitution of the United States is silent on education. Hence, education is an obligation exercised by the state. State legislatures are responsible for education. Under Florida's cabinet form of government, the Governor and cabinet members constitute the State Board of Education (Florida Education Handbook 1997). The State Board of Education is the policy making body for public education. By law, the State Board of Education has seventeen specific duties to perform (Florida Education Handbook 1997).

Schools do not exist in a vacuum. As such, they are characterized as open systems. Open systems are a way of conceptualizing organizations, such as schools, as being interrelated with the environments within which they exist. The external environment is complex and poses difficulty in analyzing (Hoy & Miskel, 1988). The external environment of schools includes parents, businesses, taxpayers, and many others. All of these are important to the school because their actions in one way or another affect the operations of a school. Legislatures, colleges, and other educational agencies increasingly influence schools. However, schools cannot be everything to all constituents. All organizations depend upon the environment of which they are a part for resources and other types of support. Hence, schools must maintain public relations campaigns regarding their effectiveness. As well, it is important for school leaders to know who has power and exercises power in a community.

Community aspirations and values have a significant role in the operations of a school. Schools, to an extent, serve the needs of the community where they are located. Schools must relate and react to the changing environmental conditions as they relate to the demographics of the community and the economic base. Changes in the types of jobs require an understanding on the part of the educational organization to provide education for students relevant to the demands of the local economy. Significant departure by the school from standards and norms expected in the community can cause difficulty for a school leader.

COMPETENCY F: Demonstrates knowledge of the components, stages, and appropriate applications of macro and micro planning systems.

> **Skill 1:** Specifies long-range, short-range planning techniques.

> **Skill 2:** Recognizes and applies the logical stages of planning techniques to school-site endeavors.

All leaders must have the capacity to plan. The ability to plan is an essential skill in today's high pressure and ever-changing school environment. It serves the very practical function of assisting administrators to organize their work and to project solutions to problems. Making a determination about what to plan for precedes the activity of planning.

In schools, there is a need to plan the curriculum, to plan for students, and to plan for teachers. The aspect of planning emerges from problems in the environment. Problems are identified and defined. Planning is attached to goals and objectives that are to be achieved. Who participates in the planning process is also crucial to receiving a quality and dynamic plan for implementation.

The essential foundation of planning is that it begins with the identification of needs. A need is identified as a measurable discrepancy between what currently exists and a desired outcome. Planning is an important tool for administrators to cope with changes in the environment. There is a way of decision making wherein the decision-maker acts before thinking. Planning, however, is a commitment to think before acting, which prevents administrators from potentially being embroiled in a set of negative consequences. Planning can be defined as a conceptualization of activities to reach an objective. Planning has anticipated and unanticipated consequences. Planning, like decision making, often occurs in the absence of all the necessary information. Yet, planning is much too important not to do because no planning is worse than poor planning.

Plans develop from the process of planning. The planning function entails an agreement on long term and short term goals that move the school from where it is to where stakeholders want it to be (Kaiser, 1996). Schools need to have a strategic plan that details what the school wants to accomplish over a period of time. Planning in schools is based on student enrollments, staffing projections, curriculum needs, and the vision established by stakeholders.

Administrators engage in the planning process as a means of accomplishing desired objectives and accommodating future events which can impact the school positively or negatively. Schools, being open systems, are dependent on their external environment and are subject to the uncertainties that exist in that environment. Planning by administrators can be to identify potential support to accomplish school goals and to identify those elements that can have a negative influence on the functioning of the school.

Directions: Read each item and select the best response.

1. The scientific management movement conceptualized ways to use people effectively in industrial organizations. Select the term that is used as a metaphor for the scientific management movement.

   A. Brain

   B. Machine

   C. Political

   D. Humanistic

2. The Human Relations approach to administration accentuated developing and maintaining dynamic and harmonious relationships. Select the individual whose writings undergird this approach.

   A. Follett

   B. Friedrick

   C. Donmoyer

   D. Zuckerman

3. Identify the person associated with time and motion studies.

   A. Blumberg

   B. Herzberg

   C. Hawthorne

   D. Taylor

4. Much of our knowledge of leadership developed from four historical movements: Classical Organization Theory, Human Relations Movement, Organizational Behavior Movement, and Human Resource Management/ Development. Which of the following is a characteristic of Organizational Behavior Movement?

   A. The formal organization is the key to understanding behavior.

   B. There is a bright side and a dark side to human behavior that emerges in the organizational context.

   C. Both the formal and informal organizations explain human actions.

   D. Contingency variables are the keys in explaining organizational behavior.

5. The basic postulate of this theory is that there are factors that contribute to job satisfaction (motivators) and other factors that contribute to job dissatisfaction (hygienes). Select the theorist associated with this theory.

A. Abraham Maslow

B. Victor Vroom

C. Edwin A. Locke

D. Frederick Herzberg

6. A theorist conceived the ideal organization as having five important elements. Those elements are Hierarchical Structure, Division of Labor, Control by Rules, Impersonal Relations, and Career Orientation. Select the theory that best describes the above characterization.

A. Weber's Ideal Organizational Structure

B. Fayol's Management Concepts

C. A version of Gulick's POSDCoRB

D. Barnard's concepts of effectiveness and efficiency

7. Select the statement that best describes the table below.

High Supportive Low Directive Behavior (Supporting) S3	High Directive High Supporting Behavior (Coaching) S2
Low Supportive Low Directive Behavior (Delegating) S4	High Directive Low Supportive Behavior (Directing) S1

A. This is the criterion for developing individual goals.

B. This table describes the Four Basic Leadership Styles in Situational Leadership.

C. This table is a replication of Fiedler's Contingency Theory.

D. This table depicts the major steps in developing an MBO program.

8. **This model of leadership consists of two basic dimensions. The first is concern for production and the second is concern for people. Five possible leadership styles result from analysis.**

   A. This model is the Managerial Grid.

   B. This is the Least Preferred Co-worker model.

   C. This model is the Zone of Acceptance.

   D. This model depicts the Trait-Situation Dilemma.

9. **Which of the following definitions correctly identifies McClelland's Theory of Achievement?**

   A. It is a value-based approach to motivation, which stipulates that achievement satisfaction motivates the successful individual.

   B. Achievement is related to organization expectations.

   C. Achievement is inherently extrinsic and external rewards are sufficient for personal performance.

   D. Motivation is a result of internal states and needs that must be satisfied in order for an individual to self-actualize.

10. **Which of the following definitions correctly identifies Self-Efficacy Theory?**

    A. Success is the result of applying causal explanations regarding achievement efforts and influence on the effects of expectancies.

    B. A person's judgment about his or her ability to perform an activity at a specific level of performance.

    C. The causes of success or failure are due to uncontrollable factors.

    D. Attaching logic to emotional reactions engenders pride and responsibility.

11. **This theory of motivation is categorized as a cognitive process model of motivation. It is based on the concepts of Valence (perceived positive or negative returns for working in a organization), Instrumentality (perceived probability of return after performing at a given level of achievement), and Expectancy (belief of an individual that a given level of activity will result in the identified level of goal achievement. Which of the following titles matches the theory?**

    A. Goal Theory.

    B. Three Factor Theory.

    C. Expectancy Theory.

    D. Need Hierarchy Theory.

12. **The basic postulate of this theory of motivation is that intentions to achieve a goal form the primary motivating force behind work behavior. Select the theory that best conforms to this postulate.**

    A. Goal Theory

    B. Feedback Theory

    C. Attribution Theory

    D. Controllability Theory

13. **Which of the following statements about work groups is correct?**

    A. $[B = f(R \times T)]$.

    B. The work group is the mechanism by which bureaucratic expectations and individual needs interact and modify each other.

    C. When two people have the same motivational system, the work group can accomplish its goals to a significantly greater degree.

    D. Work groups tend to develop at least one individual to take advantage of ascendancy opportunities.

14. **Which of the following statements is an accurate characterization of groups in organizations?**

    A. Empirical studies indicate that perceived environmental uncertainties affect the goal accomplishment of groups.

    B. In-group disagreement compromise is recognized as the preferred style for conflict resolution.

    C. When concerns are important, only an integrative solution is acceptable and can bind groups members together.

    D. Groups in organizations develop their own practices, values, norms, and social relations as members interact with each other.

15. **Entropy is best defined as**

    A. Things outside the boundaries of a system that either influence the attributes of the internal elements or are changed by the social system.

    B. The process by which a group of governors act to maintain a steady state between system components.

    C. The tendency for any system to become depleted and cease to function or exist.

    D. Formal and informal communication within a system that allows the system to modify and correct itself.

16. Organizational culture is best defined as

    A. A shared set of characteristics, goals, and resources which help to form community.

    B. Shared orientations that hold the unit together and give it a distinctive identity.

    C. A general pattern of actions found in the rational administration that provides leadership and direction.

    D. A means of assessing the attractions and repulsion's of group members to one another.

17. Select the statement that best describes an important function of the informal organization.

    A. The informal organization serves as a means of cohesiveness.

    B. The informal organization tends to cause the centralization of power at the apex of the bureaucracy.

    C. The informal organization provides a rigid and highly controlled setting to maintain order.

    D. Informal organizations help to conceptualize the social climate in terms of subordinate control patterns.

18. The informal organization is an important source of authority but is under utilized by school principals. Which of the following is an effort to expand a principal's authority in the informal organization?

    A. Publication of an official teacher handbook

    B. An evaluative supervisory conference

    C. Participation in the school's social activities

    D. Distributing a memorandum specifying organizational rules

19. Consideration refers to a principal's behavior that is friendly, supportive, and open. Initiating structure refers to a principal's behavior that is task and achievement oriented. Select the statement that best describes Initiating Structure behavior.

    A. The principal uses suggestions made by the faculty.

    B. The principal informs the faculty of administrative expectations.

    C. The principal shows concern for the welfare of faculty members.

    D. The principal regularly compliments faculty members.

20. The drop-out rate at your school is above the district average. Your task is to reduce the number of students dropping out of school by five percentage points by the next reporting date. A statistical analysis reveals that the majority of students leaving school without a diploma are students entering the eleventh grade. Which of the following problem-solving sequences will you employ to reduce the dropout rate at your school?

A. 1) Discuss the problem with the 11th grade teachers, 2) suggest a strategy for them to follow, and 3) allow them to be creative in solving this problem.

B. 1) Recognize and define the problem, 2) analyze the difficulties in the present situation, 3) establish criteria for problem resolution, 4) develop a plan for action, and 5) initiate the plan of action.

C. 1) Identify the zone of acceptance, 2) develop a table of risks, 3) decide upon alternatives, 4) organize the resources for appropriate action, and 5) make a decision.

D. 1) Identify the time dimension, 2) contact multiple constituencies, 3) research the problem, 4) provide incentives to the target group, and 5) reward compliance.

21. Which of the following is an example of the informal organization in operation?

A. Assignment of a mentor teacher to a beginning teacher

B. The faculty Christmas party

C. A faculty meeting called by the principal

D. A district-sponsored staff development workshop

22. You were recently appointed as the new principal of a school. Upon arrival, the advisory council informed you that parent involvement in school activities is minimal. The council has this situation high on its list of priorities and has indicated that they expect leadership from you in addressing the problem. The council set a goal to increase parent participation in school activities by 20% for this year. Select from the following the appropriate problem-solving strategy to address this issue.

A. Put the monkey back on the back of the advisory council.

B. Exclude teachers because they do not possess the expertise to generate possible solutions.

C. Invite teachers, advisory council members, and others to propose solutions to the problem.

D. Review school strategies that have been used before to increase parent involvement and choose the one that has been most successful.

23. Which of the following statements best illustrates the administrative model of decision-making?

A. This strategy considers only alternatives that are similar to the existing situation, analyzes only differences between the current and proposed outcomes, and ignores outcomes beyond the decision makers narrow interests.

B. This strategy is completely rational and is characterized by a series of sequential steps.

C. This strategy's basic approach is satisfying, which emphasizes finding a satisfactory solution rather than the best solution.

D. This strategy is found in organizations where ambiguity accompanies steps of the decision-making process, cause-effect relationships are impossible to determine, and there is rapid turnover of participants.

24. Research on teacher participation in decision-making reveals that teachers' involvement in formulating policies is an important factor in morale and teachers prefer principals who involve them in decision making. The question that arises is under what conditions should subordinates be involved in decision-making. Which of the following statements best demonstrates an acceptable approach to resolving the question?

A. An acceptable approach is to apply the tests of relevance, which asks if subordinates have a personal stake in decision outcomes, and the test of expertise, which asks if subordinates have the expertise to contribute to a decision.

B. When it appears that the decision-making process will be victimized by the group-think syndrome, then inviting subordinates to participate in the decision making process is an acceptable approach.

C. After preliminary consensus is reached, then inviting subordinates to participate in the decision-making process is an acceptable approach.

D. Once the decision-making cycle has been completed and the possible outcomes predicted, then involving subordinates in the decision-making process is an acceptable approach.

25. School administrators respond to conflict in many ways. One way to handle conflict is to negotiate, seek middle ground, trade-off, and search for solutions acceptable to all parties. Which of the following terms characterize this type of conflict management?

A. Accommodating

B. Collaborating

C. Compromising

D. Avoiding

26. Pondy identified five stages to a conflict episode. They are
1) latent, the conditions underlying a conflict, 2) perceived, parties are aware of conflict conditions,
3) felt, the conflict is translated into feelings (hatred, jealousy),
4) manifest, there is a display of conflict behavior and 5) aftermath, episodes of conflict can occur again if parties are not satisfied. During lunch, Mr. Jones and Mr. Bock got into a heated argument. What stage of conflict is represented in this dispute?

A. Aftermath

B. Manifest

C. Felt

D. Latent

27. A school received a grant to cover the cost of putting computers and peripherals in every classroom. The district's technology coordinator and some teachers want the money to be spent to equip two computer labs. The school's principal listens to teachers and has acceded to their wishes in the past. In this situation, however, the administrator is adamant that the money will be used to put computers and peripherals in classrooms. Select the conflict management style of the administrator in this scenario.

   A. Accommodating

   B. Collaborating

   C. Competing

   D. Compromising

28. At a recent meeting of the school advisory council, two members disagreed on the amount of money another school spent in securing tickets for that school's annual carnival. Identify the conflict management style the principal should use to resolve this issue.

   A. Avoiding

   B. Accommodating

   C. Competing

   D. Compromising

29. Social scientists mostly agree that change occurs in three stages. The first stage is initiation, in which ideas are formulated and decisions are made regarding the nature and scope of change. The second stage is called implementation, in which the change is applied in the environment. The third stage, integration involves stabilizing the change in the environment. A school is interested in a new math series for students. A committee has been charged with responsibility for making a decision and doing what is necessary regarding this matter. Several meetings have taken place to consider the advantages and disadvantages of adopting the math series. A decision has been reached to adopt the math series. Select the statement that best determines the stage of change the committee is in.

   A. The committee is in the integration stage because a decision to adopt the math series has been made.

   B. The committee has gone through all three stages so its work is now complete.

   C. The committee is now in the second stage of change.

   D. The committee is poised between the second and third stages of change.

30. Jenkins proposed methodology for creating change based on the classic steps in social engineering: analyzing the situation, determining required changes, making these changes, and stabilizing the new situation. He also recognized the existence of "driving forces" that push in the direction of change and "restraining forces" that oppose that change. Changes will occur only as the forces are modified so that the level where the forces are equal is changed. Forces are modified when one (1) reduces of removes restraining forces, (2) strengthens the driving forces or adds to their number, and (3) change the direction of certain forces. Select the statement that best describes strengthening of driving forces or adding to their number.

A. The vote was deadlocked at six in favor and six opposing the nomination. No further action was taken.

B. The majority of the teachers expressed a willingness to implement the innovation. There was, however, some reluctance on their part.

C. The superintendent dismissed a committee member because of her refusal to support the initiative.

D. One of the reasons Mr. Locke was appointed to the committee is that he had a longstanding record of support for the principal's ideas.

31. Which of the following statements best describes the position method for studying community power structure?

A. Persons who hold the highest position in formal organizations are the community leaders.

B. Individuals who patronize the local population by distributing rewards and jobs are the community leaders.

C. Determination of community leaders is based entirely on money and who has the most.

D. Community leadership is based entirely on interlocking organizations and the relative power individuals can acquire as a member of numerous organizations.

32. One method used in studying a community's power structure is comprised of the following steps. One, select several decision areas. Two, conduct in-depth interviews. Three, analyze documentary evidence. Identify this technique.

A. Critical Inquiry Method

B. Decision Analysis Technique

C. Reputational Technique

D. Comparative Analysis Technique

33. Mrs. Jones has just been appointed the new principal at the local high school. New to the area, she decides to conduct a community power structure study. First, she asks people knowledgeable of civic affairs to provide a list of individuals prominent in business, government, and civic affairs. Next, she asks a panel of persons knowledgeable about community affairs to select the most prominent of the leaders selected. Third, she interviews each of the individuals identified by the panel. Then she analyzes the data to provide a view of the community power structure. Identify the technique used in studying the community power structure.

A. Comparative Analysis Technique

B. Critical Inquiry Method

C. Structured Analysis Model

D. Reputational Technique

34. A type of community power structure is termed amorphous. Which of the following statements is an accurate description of this type structure?

A. This power structure is characterized by a single group of individuals who make major decisions.

B. Multiple groups positioning for decision-making power characterize this power structure.

C. This power structure is characterized by various groups from at least two communities having a common goal to achieve.

D. This power structure is characterized by an absence of a pattern of individuals or groups making decisions.

35. Carver and Crowe summarized four basic community power structures as pyramidal or monolithic, caucus or factional, coalitional or polylithic, and amorphous. Which of the following statements best describes a factional or caucus power structure?

A. There exists a relatively stable and predictable power structure.

B. Multiple groups and organizations elicit and impart power to the community based upon their interests.

C. At least two or more groups vie for decision-making power.

D. Citizen input dominates decision-making.

36. The State Board of Education is the chief policymaking and coordinating body of public education. It has powers to adopt, and prescribe policies, rules, regulations, or standards that may be required by law or, as it deems necessary for the improvement of public education. Which of the following is not a specific duty of the State Board of Education (SBE)?

A. Adopt comprehensive educational objectives for public education.

B. Set the maximum discretionary operation mileage.

C. Create subordinate advisory bodies as it may find necessary for the improvement of education.

D. Administer the state school funds.

37. Florida's public schools are funded through the State General Appropriations Act. The process begins with the Commissioner of Education preparing a

A. LBR (Legislative Budget Request).

B. FEFP calculations.

C. CYA (Current Year Allocation)

D. FEFR (Funding of Educational Facilities Report)

38. Which of the following definitions correctly identifies the planning technique known as Planning-Programming- Budgeting Systems (PPBS)?

  A. A developmental system that specifies that every program or line item must be justified during each budgeting period

  B. A decentralized approach to budgeting that emphasizes a certain portion of the district's revenues be allocated according to formula to each school

  C. A focus on planning according to aims and objectives and consideration of the relative costs and anticipated benefits of alternative procedures, and basing future decisions on concrete findings

  D. A focus on the questions "what do we give" and "what do we get"

39. Which of the following definitions correctly identifies the planning technique known as Planning Evaluation and Review Technique (PERT)?

  A. A process which facilitates an organized assault on a project by dividing up and charting the activities that are to be completed so that the project can be completed

  B. An integrated approach to planning that emphasizes costs and expenditures as major determinants

  C. An approach that links decision making, accountability, and human resources

  D. A planning concept which advocates the evaluation of resources and expenditures prior to decision-making

40. A school administrator has determined a number of tasks that must be completed during the course of the school year. The tasks have been divided between two assistant principals. The assistant principals are instructed to organize the tasks using a Gantt Chart. A Gantt Chart graphically displays the activities and the time frame in which the activities are to be completed. Which of the following statements best describes the advantage to using a Gantt Chart for planning process mentioned above?

A. Using the Gantt Chart allows the administrator to identify the cause and effect associated with project completion or non-completion.

B. At any given point in time, the administrator can check on the progress of activities.

C. The chart will identify the resources needed in order to complete a specific activity on time.

D. The Gantt Chart projects who and what potential program needs to be altered or changed as project completion gets nearer.

41. After reviewing the reading scores of students on the state mandated reading test, the school principal has decided upon a new intervention to support the school's reading program. A memo to teachers contained the following specifications. Beginning January 1st and continuing to the end of the year, all classroom teachers will implement the new reading program changes which will be made available immediately. All classroom teachers will incorporate the strategies and techniques outlined in the new reading program. Which of the following statements best describe the above planning process?

A. The planning process follows the Impact Analysis model of planning.

B. The planning process adheres to Management by Objectives criteria.

C. This process conforms to the PDSA cycle.

D. The nominal technique is being implemented in the above planning process.

42. Public Education Capital Outlay funds are appropriated annually by the legislature and commonly called "gross receipts." Which of the following taxes support this appropriation?

A. Taxes on utility bills

B. Property taxes

C. Gasoline taxes

D. Tourism tax

43. From the statements that follow, identify the one about state politics in Florida that is correct?

A. The State Board of Education is appointed by the governor.

B. The Commissioner of Education is an elected position.

C. The Commissioner of Education is appointed by the State Board of Education.

D. The governor appoints the Commissioner of Education.

44. Which of the following statements is an assumption about human nature that underlies McGregor's Theory Y?

A. People have little capacity to solve organizational problems.

B. People must be closely controlled and supervised for optimal results.

C. People in general are not ambitious and do not want responsibility.

D. People are self-directed and creative at work if properly motivated.

45. Because schools are open systems and operate within a community environment, a school with an effective community relations program and a positive image may be more effective in

A. Obtaining federal grants to support school programs.

B. Securing support from the community to carry out projects.

C. Being selected to appear on television programs.

D. Sending more of its graduates off to college.

Answer Key (Subtest 1 – School Management, Leadership)

1. B	24. A
2. A	25. C
3. D	
4. C	26. B
5. D	27. C
	28. A
6. A	29. C
7. B	30. D
8. A	
9. A	31. A
10. B	32. B
	33. D
11. C	34. D
12. A	35. C
13. B	
14. D	36. B
15. C	37. A
	38. C
16. B	39. A
17. A	40. B
18. C	
19. B	41. B
20. B	42. A
	43. B
21. B	44. D
22. C	45. B
23. C	

Bibliography

Bonstingl, J. (1992). *Schools of Quality. An Introduction to Total Quality Management in Education.* Alexandria, VA: Association for Supervision and Curriculum Development.

Covey, S. (1990). *The 7 Habits of Highly Effective People: Powerful Lessons in Personal Change.* New York: Simon & Shuster.

Doll, R. (1995). *Curriculum Improvement. Decision Making and Process. Ninth Edition.* Boston: Allyn and Bacon.

Eggen, P. & Kauchak, D. (1997). *Educational Psychology: Windows on Classrooms* 3rd ed. Columbus, OH: Prentice-Hall, Inc.

Hersey, P. & Blanchard, K. (1988). *Management of Organizational Behavior. Utilizing Human Resources.* 5th ed. Englewood Cliffs, NJ: Prentice-Hall.

Hoy, W. & Miskel, C. (1987). *Educational Administration: Theory, Research, and Practice* 3rd ed. New York: Random House.

Hoy, W. & Miskel, C. (1996). *Educational Administration: Theory, Research, and Practice* 5th ed. New York. McGraw-Hill, Inc.

Kaiser, J. (1996). *The 21st Century Principal* 2nd ed. Mequon, WI: Stylex Publishing Company.

Kimbrough, R. & M. Nunnery (1988). *Educational Administration: An Introduction* 3rd ed. New York. Macmillan Publishing Company.

Lambert, L, Walker, D., Zimmerman, D., Cooper, J., Lambert, M., Gardner, M., & Slack, P. (1995). *The Constructivist Leader.* New York: Teachers College Press.

Lewis, A. (1993). *Leadership Styles.* Arlington, VA: American Association of School Administrators.

Peters, T. & Waterman, R. (1982). *In Search of Excellence: Lessons from America's Best-Run Companies.* New York: Warner Books.

Rebore, R. (1998). *Personnel Administration in Education: A Management Approach.* 5th ed. Boston: Allyn and Bacon.

Sergiovanni, T. & Carver, F. (1980). *The New School Executive: A Theory of Administration.* 2nd ed. New York: Harper and Row Publishers.

Sergiovanni, T. (1987). *The Principalship: A Reflective Practice Perspective.* Newton, MA.: Allyn and Bacon, Inc.

Short, P. & Greer, J. (1997). *Leadership in Empowered Schools: Themes from Innovative Efforts.* Upper Saddle River, NJ: Prentice-Hall, Inc.

Snowden, P. & Gorton, R. (1998). *School Leadership and Administration: Important Concepts, Case Studies, and Simulations.* New York: McGraw- Hill .

Webb, L., Montello, P. & Norton, M. (1994). *Human Resources Administration. Personnel Issues and Needs in Education.* 2nd ed. New York: Macmillan College Publishing Company.

Subtest 1 – School Management

1. Management

The school principal has traditionally managed the school through the use of democratic, autocratic or laissez-faire procedures. The advent of teachers' unions and other societal forces has resulted in a decrease in autocratic forms of managing schools. Increasingly, schools are employing site-based management techniques to operate schools. School advisory committees, comprised of a cross-section of the school's internal and external personnel and citizens, are an important part of the decision making process in schools of today. Schools must be well managed if they are to exist as organizations that meet the mission of educating children for the twenty-first century.

COMPETENCY A: Demonstrates the ability to recognize relationships among various sources of information and generates hypotheses based upon this information.

> **Skill 1:** Finds meaning in themes or patterns.

The principal of a school must have the ability to determine relationships between a variety of information sources and to determine possible hypotheses using this information. Patterns of information are critical to understanding the conclusions generated therefrom and the subsequent action needed by the principal and staff. Every school should have and should use demographic information and changes about the community, families and students whom it serves. This data provide such information as the transient rate, sources of volunteers, ages of residents, racial and ethnic compositions, businesses, job opportunities, occupations, new homes, and health factors. This information can be used to design school programs and to better meet student and family needs.

The achievement level of students constitutes another major data source that schools must use in long and short range planning, program implementation and evaluation, and redesign of school programs. Achievement levels of students have been at the core of education for decades. Most states, including Florida, have established benchmarks for student achievement. The *Florida Comprehensive Assessment Test (FCAT) is* the latest test required of Florida students. Teachers will also be judged on student performance. In Florida, test measures are used to determine the designation of schools as critically low or the next level above the critically low school. Schools so designated receive special attention and create many problems for management.

The earlier work of Binet is well recognized as a measure of student ability levels. Other individual tests of intelligence as well as group tests of intelligence are measures used to determine levels of ability of children. The advent of PL142 and other measures called particular attention to the ability levels of children who were being considered for placement in exceptional students programs. A number of other measures are used to determine the ability level of children.

The data from all sources must be combined and analyzed on individual, subgroup and group bases. The school staff, under the leadership of the principal, through this process, can determine needed changes in instances where current practices are failing to produce good results and areas to maintain because favorable results are taking place. Patterns within the data, not just a single incidence, are used in developing hypotheses that determine future directions in the educational enterprise.

COMPETENCY B: Demonstrates concern for the image of the school via impressions created by the students and staff, and manages these impressions and public information about the school.

> **Skill 1:** Demonstrates awareness of the need and the process to advertise successes.

> **Skill 2:** Demonstrates awareness of the need to control the flow of negative information.

Confidence in public education has eroded over the past several decades. Numerous private, parochial, charter and other types of schools have emerged during this period. Concomitant with this movement and resulting from public dissatisfaction with public schools is an increased attention to providing vouchers to parents for use in selecting schools of choice for their children. The perceptions of the public relative to students, faculty, staff, administration, and the total school are significant in the community's attitude about a school. Management of a school requires a clear understanding of knowledge about the importance of this public perception as well as techniques to handle successes and problems.

Schools handle accomplishment in a variety of ways. Brochures, speaking engagements, and student presentations are successful avenues. Cultivating a friendly relationship with all local media benefits a school since the good news is reported and the bad news is often given in a positive manner. A school committee is considered one outstanding way to handle public relations and to work with the media under the leadership of the principal. The public relations committee could also prepare press releases to share the "good news" about the school.

Perceptions are reality. The importance of perceptions by a school's community can never be overlooked. If the school is to be perceived by its publics in a positive light, it must control negative information about the students, staff, faculty, administration, and total school. The best control strategy is to remove those situations that create negativism. These may include such factors as a school that is not cohesive, students who do not achieve well, a few individuals who work at the school and talk negatively about it, undesirable student behavior, a few teachers who use unorthodox discipline measures, and leadership inadequacies. The removal of all such negative factors may not end the negative perceptions of the school unless the flow of information becomes a part of the school's public relations plan. The physical appearance of the school's building and grounds as well as the behavior and achievements of all segments of the learning community contribute to the school's image. The principal is required to manage this aspect of the school.

COMPETENCY C: Demonstrates an awareness of the importance of receiving adequate and timely feedback for monitoring the progress and work of others.

> **Skill 1:** Demonstrates an awareness of the need to plan and schedule follow-up activities on all delegated and assigned tasks.
>
> **Skill 2:** Demonstrates knowledge of a variety of evaluation techniques to assess productivity.

The principal must achieve work through and with others. The significance of clearly defining work and outcomes is important. In this process, the principal establishes procedures to obtain feedback in a timely manner on progress toward the intended outcome(s) of work in progress. Written and oral daily or weekly progress reports serve as avenues to monitor the progress of work and to provide assistance when needed to meet established deadlines.

The progress of work should be monitored through a variety of means. Department chairpersons and grade level chairpersons are important partners in providing feedback to the principal. In instances in which the work is assigned across grade and curriculum levels, the chairperson of the tasks should provide the timely feedback to the principal. In determining how well progress is being made, the principal can use a variety of techniques. Norm-referenced and criterion-referenced tests, observations, report reviews, checklists, team reviews, and external evaluations are proven means to determine how the work of others is being performed and if it is being done in a timely manner.

COMPETENCY D: Demonstrates an awareness of the need to establish plans to accomplish goals.

> **Skill 1:** Recognizes the importance of organizing group activities in order to develop a logical plan.
>
> **Skill 2:** Demonstrates knowledge that school leaders need to focus on time, deadlines, the flow of activities, and resources in order to get the job done.
>
> **Skill 3:** Identifies a procedure to review a task and construct a plan for redirection and/or enhancement.
>
> **Skill 4:** Demonstrates an awareness of a structure, which assures appropriate sequencing of communication and activities.

Planning has long been recognized as a key factor in getting the work of a school done. Mandates from superiors, desires of subordinates and others in the learning community, and a vision are but a few of the reasons that a school principal realizes the importance of planning. To develop a plan, the principal must organize all who are to be involved in the planning process.

In designing a plan, the school leader must adhere to meeting established deadlines, developing a flow of activities, identifying resource allocations, and ascertaining evaluation strategies. The deadlines must be for today or for a longer period time. Tasks to be accomplished must be prioritized with identification of persons who are to accomplish each. The principal plans for such tasks as student achievement, accreditation, co-curricular activities, master schedule, parent organizations, student trips, and school special events. Managerial competencies are required to get each of these tasks accomplished.

Prior to developing a plan, the principal has to identify what needs to be done and procedures to accomplish the task. Consultation with others in determining assigned and unassigned tasks is best accomplished through early involvement of others who are involved or will be involved with the tasks. The tasks may involve changing an existing situation or creating a new one to benefit the students.

Planning includes the flexibility to reorder plans as unexpected activities occur to enable the school to reach its goals. The principal is also able to see when and from whom help is needed to achieve the goals in a timely manner. Effective communication competencies are required to act in proactive ways to accomplish tasks identified in plans.

COMPETENCY E: Demonstrates an awareness of the need to delegate authority and responsibility clearly and appropriately to accomplish organizational goals.

> **Skill 1:** Demonstrates an awareness that clear directions about routine tasks are necessary when delegating assignments.

> **Skill 2:** Recognizes the appropriateness of delegating an activity outside of routine assignments with clear explanations of expected phases.

> **Skill 3:** Demonstrates an awareness of the need to define activities essential to carrying out an assigned task.

Organizational goals are accomplished in school through and with others. The principal's ability to delegate is crucial to meeting goals in the organization. Routine and non-routine assignments must be delegated with clearly stated tasks, expected outcomes and timelines for accomplishment. The kind of work that is delegated includes such areas as developing the basketball schedule, establishing the orientation program and agenda for kindergarten parents, preparing for an accreditation visit, and developing an assembly.

In delegating responsibility, it is important to ascertain the steps needed to achieve the tasks with persons designated to accomplish the tasks. In site-based management, the principal and staff involved act in a collegial manner and determine what is needed and how best to achieve it. Increasingly schools are using this model of management.

COMPETENCY F: Demonstrates an awareness of the effects of one's behavior and decisions on other people and groups in and out of the organization.

> **Skill 1:** Demonstrates knowledge that the principal's behavior effects the behavior of others.

> **Skill 2:** Demonstrates knowledge that the principal's decision effects the decision-making process of others.

Principals are leaders. Their behavior, stated communication and implied communication have a tremendous impact on those with whom they work. Others often follow the lead of the principal. If a principal is calm in difficult situations, the students, parents, staff, and faculty will usually assume this position; the reverse is also true. A principal who resolves conflict in a systematic, fair manner promotes this kind of behavior within the school. The means by which a principal shares information and reaches decisions are closely observed and followed.

The principal who shows partiality or insists that his or her position is the only one will not obtain meaningful input from those with whom he or she is working.

A result of this kind of management behavior is that people will say what they expect the principal to say, say nothing or agree with the principal's views. The result is that the best results are not achieved since the best collective thinking of the learning community are not a part of the planning, implementation and evaluation of the work of the school. If the principal appears to close or open up n discussion, others in the environment will respond accordingly. A strong principal realizes that there are times when decisions must be made and makes them in a timely fashion. For example, if a person enters the campus with a gun, the principal must take action to provide safety for everyone. If teachers have conflict, the principal must find means to resolve the problem before it becomes a major deterrent to achievement of organizational goals.

COMPETENCY G: Demonstrates the ability to make policies and decisions which appropriately govern the use of technological resources of a school.

> **Skill 1:** Assembles the elements of a resource use plan that governs access to and use of the physical resources of the school.

Schools never have enough resources to meet all the demands placed upon them. Technology is expensive and places tremendous demands on the budget. The proactive principal understands this and makes a plan to maximize available resources. These resources include relocation, renovation, new construction, and allocation of such resources as computer quantity and location, audio-visual equipment quantity and quality, media resources and space, meeting rooms, teacher and staff offices, multi-purpose rooms, classrooms, laboratories, cafeterias, playgrounds, physical education indoor and outdoor space, and auxiliary spaces.

COMPETENCY H: Demonstrates knowledge of the need to be "in charge," responsible for what happens.

> **Skill 1:** Demonstrates an awareness that being "in charge" includes being responsible for all that happens in a school.
>
> **Skill 2:** Recognizes the importance of accepting responsibility for failures and learns from experience to overcome potential or existing barriers.
>
>> **Subskill 2:** Recognizes the importance of taking overall responsibility for progress of mandated tasks.
>
> **Skill 3:** Recognizes the importance of learning from experience and assuming responsibility for correcting errors.

A leader must be in charge. The community of learners expects an ultimate source of authority. They insist that equity exists and that decisions will be reached in an effective and timely manner. The "buck stops" with the principal who is responsible for what happens and what does not happen in the school. Examples of being "in charge" include determining who does what when in clearly stated written or oral communication, designating persons responsible for given duties, handling security measures, safeguarding the internal account, and ensuring administrative personnel at all school events.

The principal accepts responsibility for what goes wrong and shares what goes right with those who made it happen. The principal understands his or her role in assuming responsibility for all required tasks and ensures that they are accomplished in a timely manner. To achieve this end of being "in charge", the principal must determine the barriers and ways to overcome them, avenues to achieve the goals, and how to best use available human and material resources to best advantage or how to secure additional resources to achieve the goals.

The bottom line is the principal must accept the responsibility for what happens. In this process, the principal must change behavior based upon prior experiences and successes or errors. The process requires continuous evaluations and reflections on what worked and why, as well as what did not work and why not. Through this process, the principal corrects past behavior and continues to grow and develop within a collegial environment. Although someone else on the faculty and staff may have created the problem, the principal is still responsible and must handle the bad situation. For example, if a child were illegally paddled and the parent is very angry, the principal must apologize. State school policy indicates she or he will investigate, take appropriate action, and inform the parent of what the investigation revealed and what was done by the principal to close the case in an equitable manner.

COMPETENCY I: Recognizes situations that require forcefulness and self-confidence in making decisions.

> **Skill 1:** Recognizes the importance of being capable of expressing forcefulness and self-confidence when a decision is made.

> **Skill 2:** Recognizes the importance of forcefulness and self-confidence in making decisions.

>> **Subskill 2:** Recognizes the importance of collecting relevant data to facilitate decision-making.

School leaders must often be forceful and feel confident about decisions made. Such leaders do not require confirmation from others although they may discuss the situation(s) with fellow administrators or supervisors as a means of sharing and acquiring other approaches for future use. Good leaders get all the facts possible on all sides of an issue prior to making a decision unless it is a life and death situation that requires immediate action for the safety and life of people. After getting all possible facts, the principal can use best principles of management to make the correct decision and to stick with the decision unless new evidence becomes available to change the original decision. An example of this decision-making activity is for the principal to deny a dance after an important football game because the students failed without just cause to live up to their attendance agreement the six weeks prior to the game. The forceful principal maintains this decision despite parental and student discontent.

COMPETENCY J: Demonstrates knowledge of the need for a set of values about the school, i.e., welfare of students and fairness to staff.

> **Skill 1:** Recognizes the importance of making difficult decisions followed by appropriate actions to protect the welfare of students, faculty, and staff.

The Florida Educator's Code of Ethics clearly spells out the values that a school leader must follow and must see that all in the learning community also use. These standards promote the welfare of students and adults in a fair manner. The *Code* delineates responsibilities of educators to students, society and the profession. Inherent in this *Code* is the requirement that principals must make difficult decisions to protect the interest of all under his or her supervision. Consistency in treatment and respect for others are of paramount importance as the school climate reflects the values essential to operation of the school.

COMPETENCY K: Demonstrates knowledge of the need to search for and gather different kinds of information before arriving at an understanding of an event or problem.

> **Skill 1:** Demonstrates an awareness of the importance of community involvement before arriving at certain decisions.
>
> **Skill 2:** Demonstrates an awareness of the need to gather sufficient information both inside and outside of the organization.
>
> **Skill 3:** Demonstrates an awareness of data sources and procedures for gathering data.

Some problems within a school are related to the larger community and require knowledge beyond the school. For example, if drugs are allegedly being sold a few blocks from a school and students are supposedly making purchases during the lunch hour, all information should be obtained and the community should be involved. Community involvement is critical in making a decision on how to handle this problem.

Prior to reaching a decision, the principal must gather as much information as possible from the community and the school. All potential data sources must be identified and information obtained therefrom. During the data gathering process analysis of the information and needs to explore other sources must be explored. This process must be systematic and include such information as the source(s) of the original information, potential data sources, ways to obtain the data, means to analyze the data, who to involve and when, and how to make the decision to create the fairest and best solution(s).

Directions: Read each item and select the best response.

1. The demographics have markedly changed over the past few years for the neighborhood from which the students at Jones High School come. The single-family homes are now occupied by multiple families. The first language of most adults has changed from English to Spanish. The businesses in the community are also changing and are requiring different types of skilled employees. You, as principal, have been asked to redesign your program to better meet the work force needed by the businesses. Your first step to meet this need is to

   A. Talk to the new residents at a town meeting you establish at the school

   B. Conduct a survey of the business owners to determine their needs

   C. Plan to enlarge the school to meet increased student enrollment

   D. Discuss the matter with your area supervisor

2. The students at Cornwell Elementary School have consistently surpassed district and state achievement test levels. During the current year, the scores are in the lower quartile. The MOST appropriate action for the principal to take at the school site would be to

   A. Meet with the parents to get their support

   B. Call an emergency faculty meeting to decide what to do

   C. Analyze test results to determine areas and patterns of poor performance by students

   D. Get assistance from your district supervisor on action that has worked elsewhere

3. Smithsonian School has been the site for undesirable publicity over the past years. Although the same and worse situations occur at a school attended by more affluent children, the information rarely hits the media. However, most of the bad news at Smithsonian School is headline news in the local media. As new principal of Smithsonian, what would be the LEAST appropriate measure to improve the image of Smithsonian School?

   A. Have an assembly and solicit student support for better grades and behavior

   B. Conduct a survey of parents and faculty on measures to take

   C. Develop a brochure and distribute it widely

   D. Meet with the assistant principals, department chairpersons and deans of students to discuss the problem and determine preliminary action steps

4. The local media has written a story about the decline of school morale among students and teachers at Inman Elementary School. As principal, you were not aware of this alleged pervasive problem. Action you would take now is to

   A. Determine the nature of the alleged problem and meet with the news media

   B. Determine the status of morale and send the news media a press release

   C. Gather data on the situation, prepare a news release and meet with the press to share the news release and answer questions

   D. Gather data on the situation and meet with the press to share the data and answer questions

5. The students in Callaway Prekindergarten School have been exposed to a curriculum that emphasizes the latest brain research information. As they graduate to kindergarten, each of the children is demonstrating abilities not previously seen by students as they leave Callaway. As principal, you would

   A. Call your liaisons at the local television station and newspaper to inform them of the changes and to share a press release with them

   B. Fax a press release to the local television station and newspaper

   C. Send a press release to your superintendent

   D. Inform the press through a telephone call

6. A teacher, transferred from School A to School B, had a reputation of failing students. Parental concerns at School A contributed to the transfer. Parents in School B have requested that the principal place their children in other classrooms. As principal, you should

   A. Put students in classes requested by the parents

   B. Ask the district office to place the teacher elsewhere

   C. Do nothing until the problem occurs, if it does

   D. Work with the transferred teacher and parents, monitor the teacher and provide support to remove the stigma from School A performance by the teacher

7. The superintendent has requested a report on the science program at Middlebrook Middle School for use in submitting a proposal to the legislature via the Department of Education. She needs the material in a week. As principal, you have given the assignment to the chairperson of the science department and asked him to involve all appropriate staff and faculty members. You will monitor the progress of this activity by having the chairperson report to you at least daily and as deemed necessary by the chairperson. This monitoring system is

A. Unnecessary meddling by the principal

B. An excellent delegation strategy

C. Time-consuming, but necessary to meet the superintendent's deadline

D. Important as an element in the management process

8. Smith Elementary School is on the critically low list for the second year. About 90 % of the students are on free and reduced lunches. Most live in the public housing project in single parent homes. Strategies used last year did not significantly improve student achievement. To change this school, you would

A. Have an initial session with a consultant and the teachers to determine how to proceed before developing a plan

B. Seek to involve more parents in the education of their children

C. Meet with the teachers and develop new strategies

D. Have a small committee to establish what should be done

9. The rating checklist used to evaluate teachers does not coincide with the job description for the teachers. As a consequence, the morale has reached an all time low for teachers who have committed to the change process that has improved student achievement. The best approach to take as principal is to

A. Inform the teachers that the checklist was created by the district with input from teachers and had to be used

B. Listen to the concerns of the teachers and make a commitment to take their concern to the district staff immediately in an effort to get the checklist revised

C. Get a written list of concerns from the teachers and send it to the district office

D. Revise the checklist at once and use the revised checklist

10. The school board recently ruled that the school day for high school students would begin at 10 a.m., the time when this age student learns best. Parents and students are really upset since many hold jobs in the afternoon and others care for younger siblings who get out of school prior to the parents' coming home. As principal you would resolve this situation by

A. Checking with the district office on what to do with these complaints

B. Developing with the faculty a plan to put the new requirement into operation

C. Determining how children, families and businesses would be impacted

D. Revising your student schedule immediately to reflect the new requirement

11. The superintendent has directed all school principals in the district to hire a security guard. As principal of a high crime area your most appropriate action would be to

A. Develop a statement to the superintendent on reasons not to employ a guard

B. Check with other principals on what they are doing

C. Hire a guard immediately

D. Develop a plan in cooperation with the staff to implement the requirement

12. The in-basket has 25 items for today. The most important item will take several hours, many items can be delegated, a few items are a lower priority. The principal needs to accomplish the tasks over the next few days by:

A. Prioritizing the list

B. Getting help to do the tasks

C. Reviewing the tasks with the secretary

D. All the above

13. The <u>deadline</u> for a number of critical reports is today. Many reports will require considerable time to complete. As the principal, you are the only person with the knowledge and authority to complete these reports. Unexpected situations require the principal to use time needed to complete the work. The principal would complete the work by

A. Giving some to the secretary to complete

B. Getting the teachers to do it while they sit in their classes

C. Organizing the work and securing substitutes for a few teachers who can work with the tasks

D. Letting the assistant principal handle the emergencies so you can complete the tasks

14. **Prior to leaving school on the previous day, the principal listed those tasks for completion the next day. At the beginning of today, the principal's first responsibility is to**

   A. Start a list for the day at the beginning of the day to include any new unexpected items or emergencies

   B. Prioritize the list made the previous day

   C. Determine who will do what using the previous day's list

   D. Begin a new list and discard the old one

15. **At the end of the school year, a number of reports must be sent to the district office by principals. The majority of reports are recurring although five are new. The principals knew about all the reports at least a month in advance of the due dates. Two days before the teachers leave, the principal is asked to do two additional reports. To meet this timeline, the principal should**

   A. Begin work immediately on the new tasks

   B. Inform the district that more time is needed to complete the new tasks

   C. Complete the new tasks and not attend the end-of-year luncheon

   D. Call a meeting of the staff, inform them of what has to be done, obtain suggestions on how to do the tasks, select the best approaches, and meet the deadline

16. After lunch, the principal receives a directive from the area superintendent to submit new information within two hours. The request requires compilation of data and writing a narrative. The principal reviews the schedule planned for the afternoon and gets the office manager attendance clerk to compile the data for the request. The principal then writes the narrative which later got applause regarding the attention to details. The managerial competency displayed by the principal's behavior is

    A. Proactive orientation

    B. Routine day to day

    C. Over confident

    D. Disorganized and reactionary

17. Middlebrook High School is scheduled to participate in the state level basketball tournament. The parent's plan to secure transportation by securing buses through a transportation service falls through the day before the trip. The principal should

    A. Meet with the administrative team, parent association executive committee and the basketball coaches to make changes in the previous plans

    B. Secure buses and make them available

    C. Use the buses available for transporting students on a daily bases

    D. Withdraw from the tournament

18. The students at Kain Middle School have performed poorly on the standardized test for a number of years. As new principal, you would

    A. Continue past practices for the first year

    B. Put in place new strategies to improve the scores

    C. Meet with the mathematics department and develop changes in strategies

    D. Get the teachers to put new strategies into the curriculum

19. The parent teacher organization has an executive board that has begun to negatively criticize the school's administration. These public statements have caused unfavorable publicity about the school. The principal should

A. Meet with the PTA executive board and work out a plan to handle the situation

B. Discontinue the PTA operations

C. Call a press conference to inform the media of the truth

D. Ignore the behavior of the PTA Executive Board

20. The after school program is not working well since the lead teacher became ill. The teacher is expected to return to work in eight weeks. The temporary leader has been unable to get the staff to report to work. Teachers and parents have expressed the tremendous value of this program and want it continued. As principal, you would savage the program by

A. Meeting with the staff

B. Determining the causes for the problem and addressing them

C. Reviewing the problem and replacing those individuals who created the problem

D. Meeting with the leader and letting her correct the problem

21. The debate team was recently selected to participate in a national tournament. To participate in this activity, a plan is needed to raise funds and to achieve a number of goals within a month. Prior to becoming principal last year, you served as debate coach. The new coach has been with the team for three weeks. You find that your time is being encroached upon and you must make some decisions at once. You find it necessary to

    A. Reassign some tasks to other administrators and take over the debate team

    B. Let the debate coach handle the situation

    C. Borrow a coach from a another school

    D. Decline the national offer

22. The school's cafeteria caught on fire at the beginning of the workday. As a consequence, breakfast is not available for the arrival of the children . Since 80% of the students eat breakfast, what action should you take as principal?

    A. Inform the parents

    B. Buy food from the local supermarket

    C. Call your district supervisor and follow the plan you developed to provide lunch

    D. Call the district supervisor and secure approval to purchase food from the local supermarket

23. The tasks for principals have increased markedly over the past few as a result of new state legislation. To accomplish the new and existing assignments, the principal should

   A. Work until all tasks are completed

   B. Get done what he can within the time allotted

   C. Develop a timeline for completing the tasks over the next two months

   D. Reassign some of his tasks to other administrators at the school

24. Trinity School will initiate its International Baccalaureate Program this fall. The principal has designated an assistant principal as coordinator for this program. At the initial meeting for the program, all the staff participated in the discussion and provided meaningful input. The principal told the assistant principal to do the initial plan and check with him before implementation. This principal's behavior demonstrated

   A. Organizing the activity of a group to develop a plan

   B. Delegating authority and responsibility

   C. Failing to trust the assistant principal

   D. Showing a developmental orientation toward the assistant principal

25. Faculty are scheduled to report for the new school year in three weeks. The first week is designated for faculty development and setting up activities in classrooms and throughout the school. In developing the agenda for the initial staff meeting, the principal should

   A. Develop the agenda

   B. Ask the teachers what they want on the agenda

   C. Use the agenda from last year

   D. Work with the administrative team and develop the agenda

26. The lunchroom behavior of children is always important in a school. Student behavior has deteriorated recently. The principal decides to change the situation by

   A. Having teachers and their aides monitor the behavior more closely

   B. Putting security guards in the cafeteria

   C. Denying lunch to students who misbehave

   D. Being in the cafeteria each day

27. The Honors Banquet is held the same night as an important town meeting. The main issue at the meeting involves use of the school as a community service center. The most appropriate action for you to take as principal is

   A. Attend the Honors Banquet

   B. Prepare a video for the Honors Banquet and attend the town meeting

   C. Assign the task to the guidance counselor and ask for a plan for the Honors Banquet including costs, speaker and location

   D. Attend the town meeting and represent the school's best interest

28. Johns School will have a ten-year visit from the Southern Association of Colleges and Schools. The visit is scheduled in two years. The chairperson of the committee recently resigned to move to another school district. To continue the work already begun, the principal might

    A. Designate a new chairperson

    B. Ask for a volunteer to chair the accreditation process

    C. Get a committee to do the work

    D. Review the current team and select a new chairperson from among those persons who have worked on the team

29. Black History month is in two months. Over a period of time, the committee has worked on an all-school assembly. The committee has recommended a very controversial speaker for the assembly. This speaker usually causes discord and creates negative images. His presence would create major problems since his appearance at another school two years ago almost created a riot. As principal, you would

    A. Cancel the assembly

    B. Meet with the planning team, deny their recommendation and request another speaker

    C. Approve the speaker

    D. Do nothing and see what happens

30. A special legislative committee to which you have been asked to speak conflicts with the parent orientation meeting at Semour Elementary School. The parent meeting was scheduled sometimes ago and cannot be changed to avoid your recent assignment. The MOST appropriate action to take as principal is to

    A. Have someone else represent you at the legislative committee hearing

    B. Explain your situation to the legislative contact person and go to the parent meeting

    C. Meet with the planning team for the parent meeting and leave the assistant principal in charge of the responsibilities you had for the meeting

    D. Come to the parent meeting late although you can only attend for about 15 minutes

31. During your fifth year as principal of Ermine Middle School, you have noticed that students need more information on life management skills. Some of these sensitive issues are beyond the knowledge of the current staff. After establishing the way to handle these sensitive topics with students and parents, the MOST appropriate action to meet this identified need is to

    A. Secure the services of community groups qualified to discuss the topics

    B. Send some teachers to training on the topics to enable them to present the materials

    C. Make parents aware of the needs and let the parents handle the topics at home

    D. Do not include the topics in the curriculum

32. **FCAT training is essential at Harris School, a new magnet program. In planning for staff development, the principal might**

    A. Appoint a committee to design the staff development program at the school site

    B. Send one teacher to a training session provided by the state

    C. Ask volunteers to handle the staff development

    D. Refer the matter to the school's assistant principal

33. **The original district calendar was distributed and has been revised to reflect new information that includes all schools in a year-round program. The best way to handle this situation with parents is to**

    A. Reschedule the parent orientation meeting to an earlier date and explain the new program and schedule

    B. Send the new schedule to parents with a letter explaining the new program and date changes

    C. Provide a news release to the media

    D. Discuss the changes at the parent meeting schedules for the week before school begins

34. The student handbook has remained unchanged for ten years. Faculty, parents and students have raised questions about the appropriateness of some parts of the handbook. Which of the following would be MOST appropriate?

    A. Keep the current handbook

    B. Appoint a representative task force to review the current handbook and make recommendations for changes within an established timeline

    C. Plan a workshop to discuss the handbook

    D. Send out a questionnaire to obtain information on concerns

35. An irate parent came to an appointment with the teacher of her child, the guidance counselor and the principal. The parent was very angry and accusatory . She smelled of alcohol and used profanity. She stated that the teacher was ignorant and did not know how to teach. She also stated that the teacher had caused other children to talk about her child's hygiene and had shared the concern with a friend of the parent. The BEST approach for the principal to use is to

    A. Discontinue the conference until the mother calms down

    B. Ask the teacher and guidance counselor to leave

    C. Admonish the teacher for what the parent said took place

    D. Listen to the parent, talk calmly, take charge of the meeting, and get the parties to talk about the best interest of the child

36. Two children got in an altercation. No major injuries resulted from this untoward behavior. The Dean of Students followed the school policies and placed both students in an in-school suspension program. One of the parents was a prominent citizen and came to school to return his child to the regularly scheduled classes. The other child was in the in-school suspension class. As principal, you should

   A. Let the parent remove his child

   B. Remove the in-school suspension requirement from both children

   C. Adhere to school policies

   D. Have the Dean of Students change his decision

37. A teacher became very irate in your office. An assistant principal, another teacher and you were in attendance at the conference. You remained calm, listened patiently at the irate teacher, accepted the emotions as understandable due to the information the irate teacher had received, and presented the complete information on the subject. The teacher became calm and apologized for her behavior. The example set by the principal was

   A. Meeting with a teacher who had a problem due to lack of information

   B. Being too easy on the irate teacher

   C. Organizing material for the conference with the irate teacher

   D. Supportive of teachers behaving in inappropriate ways

38. The Student Government Association could not reach consensus on homecoming activities after deliberating for a month. They asked the principal to attend their next meeting. The principal listened and informed the students that he would make a decision if the group could not give him a recommendation by the next day. The principal demonstrated to the advisor of the Student Government Association that

A. The Student Government Association could not make decisions

B. If decisions were not made by the next day by the students that the adults would decide

C. Students who failed to make decisions should be scolded

D. Students are in the learning process and should be given more time to make a major decision

39. Teachers could not reach a conclusion on how to organize the high school using a thematic approach. Committees of teachers had met over a period of time to determine a course of action. To put the plan in action for the next school year, a decision had to be reached within the next two weeks. The principal met with the faculty and discussed the history of this activity and the importance of presenting her with a plan within seven days. She also received approval from the faculty to make the decision if the faculty did not present the plan within seven days. The principal demonstrated

A. Control of faculty behavior

B. Irrational behavior

C. Leadership skills for a trying situation

D. A management decision to reach closure

40. Technological resources are limited in the school. The teacher in the Technology Lab does not want anyone else to use the equipment without her permission and supervision. Several teachers could operate the laboratory in an efficient manner. The best policy statement for the principal to make is to

    A. Require the technology teacher to permit others to use the lab as long as they adhere to lab policies and meet the mission of the school

    B. Enforce the procedures established by the technology teacher

    C. Reassign another teacher to the technology lab

    D. Get the teachers to reach an agreement

41. Although the principal had submitted a request and followed up on the request to correct a serious safety hazard at the school, the district had not corrected the problem. A student was injured and the parents were very angry since the problem had existed for some time. The principal took responsibility for the problem, offered to pay medical expenses and to get the situation rectified at once. The principal's behavior is an example of

    A. Being committed to the safety of the students

    B. Having a proactive sensitivity

    C. Having a proactive orientation

    D. Making plans to achieve school goals

42. **At Ellington Elementary School, the achievement scores in reading were not met this past year. As principal, you selected a committee several months ago to come up with a plan to meet the reading goals. The time to present the plan to the faculty for implementation next year is six weeks away. There is still time to get the plan formed. You find out that the committee has done nothing to develop the plan. Your immediate action should be to**

   A. Hire substitutes to allow the teachers to develop the plan

   B. Reevaluate the current committee members and select a motivated and revised committee of interested teachers, parents, students, and community members to develop the plan

   C. Give the responsibility to the assistant principal

   D. Develop the plan yourself

43. **In making a report to the superintendent involving the police at your school, you mistakenly named a teacher as a witness. The teacher was unable to provide the superintendent with details of the incident and you were called by the superintendent. The BEST action for you to take is to**

   A. Send the superintendent a corrected report

   B. Meet with the two teachers, apologize and send a corrected report to the superintendent

   C. Meet with the superintendent to correct the situation

   D. Get the information from the correct teacher and send it to the superintendent

44. The planning committee for the second semester opening activities has worked hard and come up with creative ways to launch a new semester to get maximum student performance and parental participation. You feel the plan is excellent although you have a few concerns. To preserve the relationship with this hard-working group and to be decisive, you as the principal should

A. Inform the team of your concerns, but show strong commitment and forcefulness in announcing the plan to the faculty

B. Inform the team of your concern and have them revise it before presentation to the faculty

C. Inform the team of your concern and leave it as is to see what the faculty will think

D. Disapprove the plan after informing the team of your concerns

45. Teachers, students and parents have become increasingly unhappy with the quality of mathematics knowledge students had upon entering college after graduation form Mary High School. As principal you have decided to

A. Redesign the mathematics program

B. Get an outside consultant team to recommend next steps

C. Select a committee of parents, teachers, students, college mathematics professors, and other interested citizens to review the mathematics program and to present their ideas to you including information on research done to reach the conclusions

D. Select a committee of parents, teachers, students, college mathematics professors, and other interested citizens to review the mathematics program and to present you a plan for improving the situation

Answer Key (Subtest 1 – School Management, Organizational Management)

1. B		26. A	
2. D		27. B	
3. C		28. D	
4. A		29. B	
5. D		30. C	
6. D		31. A	
7. A		32. A	
8. B		33. A	
9. B		34. B	
10. D		35. D	
11. C		36. C	
12. C		37. C	
13. B		38. B	
14. A		39. D	
15. D		40. A	
16. A		41. C	
17. C		42. B	
18. A		43. B	
19. A		44. C	
20. A		45. A	
21. C			
22. C			
23. C			
24. B			
25. D			

Subtest 1 - School Management

3. Human Resource Management and Development (Personnel)

The educational leader in schools must possess a number of competencies. The most time-consuming competency involves human resource management and development. Educational leaders must know and understand human relations as a primary area of emphasis since schools are labor intensive and use 80% to 90% of a school's budget. Personnel management roles for school administrators have expanded over the years. An understanding of the many aspects and importance of personnel management in achieving the vision and mission of schools is absolutely essential in creating and maintaining a successful and efficient school organization.

COMPETENCY A: Understands the role of the principal in selecting instructional and non-instructional personnel.

> **Skill 1:** Identifies appropriate responsibilities of principals in selecting instructional personnel.

> **Skill 2:** Uses job-related criteria in the selection process.

> **Skill 3:** Identifies the components of an effective interview.

> **Skill 4:** Identifies strategies which involve staff members in the process.

> **Skill 5:** Identifies sources of information about prospective candidates.

The role of the principal in selecting instructional and non-instructional personnel is often considered as the most important aspect of the many tasks that a principal performs as leader of a school, a business enterprise of greatest importance. An understanding of the significance of this function of the principal is crucial to successful schools. It is through people that the principal leads the staff in a collegial environment to achieve the mission of the school and to provide satisfying, useful work for the instructional and non-instructional personnel. The principal must possess an attitude that people are of greatest importance in organizations, particularly in schools. The personnel in a school constitute one of the set of customers that the principal must do all within her or his power to provide the best working conditions because the personnel will be empowered subsequently to do what is best for the students.

In selecting instructional personnel, the principal has many appropriate responsibilities. Planning, recruitment and selection are essential aspects of securing personnel. Planning requires the principal to look at the current staff and plan for future short-term and long-term personnel needs. The planning should occur within the context of site-based management. The principal involves the school personnel in developing and revising the personnel plan for the school. All other aspects of the school's program have to be considered in this process. Thus, personnel are looked at in terms of the current strengths and needs of the staff, students, parents, community, school district, state laws and rules, and federal rules and regulations. Facilities, equipment and other factors must be reviewed at this time also. Planning must be comprehensive and must take place well in advance of the need. The plan must allow sufficient time for the principal to prepare papers and get approval through the district system. The principal must know the process used in the school district to select personnel including how assignments are determined and the impact of the collective negotiation contract if there is one in the district. The plan must also provide for emergencies such as unexpected promotions, illnesses, resignations, and terminations that may occur with personnel.

Once the plan is completed, recruitment becomes the next step in obtaining personnel. Recruitment is critical to successful human resource functions of the principal. Only persons in the applicant pool may be considered for employment. Thus, it is important to recruit sufficient numbers of qualified persons for each vacancy or anticipated vacancy. The major factor should be the quality of the applicants. Each district has its own procedure for recruiting personnel. If the district does the recruiting, the principal has to inform the district early and get approval to fill the positions. The principal who has to recruit the staff must make contacts early. College and university career offices, as well as schools of education that promise the greatest possibility of supplying the kinds of personnel needed, must be contacted. Career fairs on college and university campuses, at the state level and on the local level provide other means to secure personnel. Dialogue with colleagues and current school staff also offer other opportunities to recruit new employees. Recruitment activities must use special effort if the desire is to diversify staff members. The process of obtaining staff is best handled through a selection committee.

The selection process involves screening the paper work, interviewing candidates and checking references. Using the job-related criteria for each position, the selection process requires that each applicant's papers are evaluated against the criteria. Those applicants whose qualifications do not meet these criteria are removed from the pool of applicants. The quality of the application is also judged for such factors as neatness, comprehensiveness, job stability, competencies, English errors, and training.

Certification in field is also a crucial factor to consider in selecting staff members. These files are confidential and should only be used by trained teachers, parents, students, and others who serve on the selection committee.

Those applicants who are selected as meeting the training and experience qualifications for the position are reviewed and a determination is made to interview. The interview takes the most amount of time in the process of selecting personnel. The selection committee determines and notifies each applicant who is being interviewed of the time and location for the interview. Prior to the interview, the committee must determine questions to be asked and criteria to judge responses to the questions. Each candidate for the same position must be asked the same questions and the same criteria must apply in judging the responses. The selection committee submits the names of the most qualified applicants, usually three to five persons listed alphabetically, to the principal.

The principal reviews the work of the committee, interviews the potential employees and does a reference check. Persons on and not on the reference list should be contacted. Visitation to the person's place of employment is another good strategy to use. Principals often contact persons at the institutions that trained the potential employee to get professional judgements about the candidate. Fingerprint records should receive attention to ensure that known criminals are not employed. The principal recommends to the superintendent the person who should be employed.

COMPETENCY B: Demonstrates knowledge about activities that make the induction process more meaningful to the new teacher.

   Skill I: Identifies orientation and socialization activities.

   Skill 2: Identifies orientation activities conducted by the school district and those conducted by the individual schools.

Newly hired employees receive assistance through the induction process. Beginning teachers need more assistance than experienced individuals. The first part of the induction process is orientation. Teachers new to a school must be oriented to the procedures, paper requirements, teaching and learning expectations, rules, and all aspects of the school culture. In some districts, the district does the orientation with the school providing additional orientation for those factors unique to that school. The socialization process is critical since it can determine how well new personnel become or fail to become contributing members of the teaching/learning community.

The induction process ranges from 90 days to a full school year. The best induction approach is one in which the teachers are assisted throughout the year by a mentor teacher who teaches the same grade level and subjects. The induction process should be based upon the orientation and should extend the orientation to cover every aspect of the work for the position.

COMPETENCY C: Identifies sources that can provide meaningful information to the new teacher about teaching practices in Florida.

> **Skill 1:** Selects Florida sources that will provide the new teacher information about teaching practices expectations in Florida.

The principal must know the sources to obtain the Florida Statutes, State Board of Education Rules, school board rules, and the school's teacher handbook. It is within these documents and others produced by the state and district that information is provided about teaching practices in Florida. The school district and Florida Department of Education can provide these materials developed outside the school. The principal should have copies of the latest student, parent, and teacher handbooks for the school.

COMPENTENCY D: Demonstrates knowledge of a staff development program.

> **Skill 1:** Identifies the advantages derived from a staff development program.

> **Skill 2:** Identifies in-service approaches and techniques that are likely to place participants in an active role.

> **Skill 3:** Identifies characteristics of effective staff development programs.

Personnel in schools must continuously maintain and upgrade their competencies if a school is to provide the maximum educational benefits to students. The principal must ensure that the staff development activities begin with orientation and continue throughout each person's employment at the school. It is only through this process that the staff can remain dynamic and current. Curriculum development—strategies, implementation, and evaluation; climatic conditions; recent research; benefits; supervision; and incentives are among the topics for inclusion in a staff development program. Staff development best achieves its purposes when provided at the school site during the regular school day.

COMPETENCY E: Demonstrates a knowledge of appraisal procedures for school district personnel.

Skill 1: Identifies objective performance criteria for evaluating the performance of instructional personnel.

Skill 2: Distinguishes between reliable and unreliable performance appraisal methods and techniques.

Skill 3: Distinguishes between performance appraisal responsibilities that belong at the building level and those that belong at the district level.

Skill 4: Identifies resources available outside the school district, which may assist in the development and implementation of the appraisal process.

Skill 5: Understands the requirements for successful completion of the Florida Professional Orientation Program.

Appraisal of personnel is a significant responsibility of the principal. Most districts use a district-wide criteria developed through a diverse committee, representative of the school community. The criteria establishes objective measures that can provide the principal with reliable methods of appraising staff. The most reliable methods provide the teacher with the criteria and understanding of how the criteria are used in evaluating the staff. Gossip, unsigned notes and other such techniques are deemed unreliable and should not be used.

The principal must know those responsibilities at the building level and those at the district level. The principal evaluates building level staff and must know the criteria and how to apply each. With the advent of performance-based appraisal in Florida , principals need training to tie performance to student learning. The principal knows that the district, state, university teachers, professional organizations, and consultants afford the best opportunities to acquire information on the development and implementation of the appraisal process.

The Florida Professional Orientation Program provides assistance to new and experienced teachers new to teaching in Florida. The assistance of a peer teacher and a variety of induction activities enabled the teachers to receive assistance without the implied threat of evaluation. This open system enables these teachers to seek help when or before it was needed.

COMPETENCY F: Demonstrates a knowledge of the organization and non-confidential information found in school personnel files.

Skill 1: Distinguishes between confidential and non-confidential information found in school personnel files.

Skill 2: Identifies the correct procedure for accessing information in school personnel files.

Skill 3: Identifies the correct procedure for placement of derogatory materials in personnel files.

Skill 4: Identifies the legal authority governing Florida school personnel files and records.

Principals must respect confidential materials, even though Florida is an open records state. This provision of state law does not permit sharing information from confidential records, identified in law. Each staff member should have two files: one handles confidential material and the other holds non-confidential information. The principal maintains a log of person who sees files and follows the correct procedure in providing access to files. The principal also knows when and if negative information may be placed in a personnel file and in which personnel file it may be placed. The principal informs the staff and uses the Florida statutes and rules that govern personnel matters (Chapter 231, Florida Statutes and State Board of Education Rules 6, as well as school district provisions that do not conflict with either the state or district provisions).

COMPETENCY G: Understands the procedures for termination of school employees.

Skill 1: Identifies the principal's responsibility in termination proceedings.

Skill 2: Identifies conditions of "due process" for school employees in Florida.

Skill 3: Identifies definitions of "just cause" as stipulated in Florida Statutes.

Termination is one of the most difficult tasks that a school principal must perform. The guiding principle should and must be—is this teacher permanently harming children because of incompetence or marginal teaching and learning results? There are only a few of these teachers. However, they should be counseled into other positions if they cannot be helped to become high quality teachers. The principal must identify these few teachers and notify them in a timely manner.

The principal must follow Due Process provisions and offer assistance to the teacher. A careful record must be kept on these teachers. These few individuals can consume almost all of a principal's time. The Employee's Assistance Program may be one source of help for this teacher. The principal must notify the teacher of charges. There should be adequate rebuttal preparation time. You should permit counsel of the person's choice. Next, have an impartial hearing. Then permit examination of evidence. When a decision is made based on the evidence, provide a transcript of the hearing and allow an appeal if there is a decision to terminate the employee or there is a severe loss to the teacher.

COMPETENCY H: Understands the objectives and administration of the collective bargaining process.

> **Skill 1:** Understands the state legislation, which governs the collective bargaining process.

> **Skill 2:** Identifies the procedures for resolving an impasse.

> **Skill 3:** Identifies the appropriate grievance procedure stipulated in the Public Employee's Collective Bargaining Act.

> **Skill 4:** Understands the responsibilities of the management negotiating team.

Collective bargaining is recognized in Florida. Employees in each school district determine if they wish to be represented by a bargaining agent. The principal must use the agreement on a daily basis and be thoroughly familiar with the document. The Public Employees Relations Commission is an important aspect of this program. Conditions for collective negotiating rest with laws promulgated by the Florida Legislature. When management and employees cannot reach an agreement, an impasse occurs. Procedures for impasse, established by law, include mediation, fact-finding and advisory arbitration, voluntary binding arbitration, last-best offer arbitration, and strikes. Florida laws forbid strikes by school personnel.

Florida Statutes also provide procedures for employees who desire to grieve. The principal must understand this right and have a good knowledge of the law that outlines the procedure to follow as a part of an employee's due process rights.

A principal may serve on a collective negotiation team for a district. In this case, the principal is on the management team. The negotiation process is lengthy and usually involved multi-year contracts. The process involves team determination, unit recognition, planning and preparation, agreement and implementation, and strategies to reach agreement, counterproposals, and others needed to get a contract.

COMPETENCY I: Understands that the purpose of a compensation and reward system is to attract and retain qualified employees.

Skill 1: Identifies the kind of benefits found in a school employee, wage compensation program.

Skill 2: Identifies the guidelines that are considered when developing a wage compensation program.

Skill 3: Identifies the relationship between reward and motivation.

A compensation and reward system is required in any organization, particularly schools. The compensation program is directed at attracting and maintaining quality employees, motivating employees, creating incentives for continual growth, and maintaining budgetary control in school districts (Webb, Greer, Montello, Norton, 1996). The district must have a compensation policy. Merit pay, paid leave, child care, cost of living increase, salary schedules, extracurricular stipends, early retirement plans, tax-sheltered annuity, and medical plans are types of compensation and rewards. Social Security, retirement plans, severance pay, sick leave, annual leave, sabbatical leave, religious leave, military leave, professional leave, and transportation allowance are among the many types of compensations and rewards available to school personnel. Supply and demand often determine the extent of the package available to employees.

"For God's Sake, think! Why is he being so nice to you?"

Directions: Read each item and select the best answer.

1. In selecting instructional personnel, the principal is responsible for

   A. Establishing a committee

   B. Initiating the process

   C. Determining the recommendations for employment

   D. All of the above

2. In selecting non-instructional personnel, the principal does not have to check for

   A. Past job performance

   B. Fingerprints

   C. Statements from references given by applicant

   D. Educational attainment

3. During the interview process, the principal may ask about the applicant's

   A. Reasons for applying for this job

   B. Mother's maiden name

   C. Ages of children

   D. Handicapping conditions

4. If the applicant pool is small, the principal should

   A. Select the best person

   B. Advertise the position again.

   C. Select the best person due to limited supply and high demand

   D. Get some other applicants although the application deadline has passed

5. Which of the following is the most appropriate to ask during a teacher selection interview?

   A. Past performance evaluation

   B. Union membership status

   C. Husband's reason for moving

   D. Reference letter item

6. **Which of the following would be most useful in gaining information about a candidate for an instructional position?**

   A. Ways in which undesirable administrators were handled by the applicant

   B. Techniques used to discipline students

   C. Knowledge of child growth

   D. Queries about a student's neighborhood

7. **The least appropriate questions to ask during an interview of a non-instructional applicant are**

   A. Questions about past performance

   B. Leading questions

   C. Open-ended questions

   D. Slanted questions

8. **A principal should involve a diverse population on the screening committee for instructional personnel because**

   A. Law requires it

   B. It avoids conflict when the choice is made

   C. The superintendent requires it

   D. Site-based management gets better results

9. **The most reliable source of information about an applicant for an instructional position is**

   A. The application packet

   B. Reference letters supplied by the applicant

   C. Past performance evaluations

   D. Observation on-the-job

10. **An inappropriate source of information about an instructional candidate is**

    A. The resume

    B. The reference letter

    C. A photograph

    D. A transcript.

11. **During the induction process, the principal should ensure that the new teacher receives information about**

    A. The school mission

    B. Students who misbehave

    C. Outdated policy handbook

    D. Parent attitudes

12. The principal should introduce new faculty members

    A. Whenever anyone comes around

    B. At established meetings of faculty, students, and parents

    C. Over the intercom

    D. When the teacher requests it

13. The induction process should provide new teachers with information required by the state for

    A. Disciplining students

    B. Meeting curriculum objectives

    C. Confirming employment

    D. All of the above

14. An appropriate district level orientation activity for the new teacher is

    A. A review of school philosophy

    B. An introduction to faculty

    C. Getting information about school board policies

    D. A statement of the school's vision

15. Usually, the orientation process includes a school level meeting that provides information on

    A. Retirement benefits

    B. Insurance benefits

    C. Certification requirements

    D. The school's faculty handbook

16. If you were principal of a school and had a staff of 40 teachers of whom 15 were new, which strategy would you use to induct the new teachers?

    A. Assign mentor teachers

    B. Give written materials

    C. Supervise each class each day

    D. Get district help

17. The principal wants to make new teachers aware of requirements in Florida. The principal would refer the new teachers to which of the following documents?

    A. Florida School Laws

    B. Florida School Laws and State Board of Education Rules

    C. Laws of Florida and the Florida Employee Handbook

    D. The Beginning Teacher Research Manual and Florida School Laws

18. Your school was put on the critically low school list by the state. No measurable gains were recorded the second year and you are on the list two consecutive years. How would you get your school off the list?

   A. Involve the community

   B. Have a meeting with teachers and establish a strategic plan that involved the parents and community

   C. Secure advice from the state and district and work on the problem

   D. Conduct a series of meetings with teachers, students, parents, and community members to obtain information in developing a plan of action with the faculty

19. The method to use to assist participants in staff development activities to retain information and apply it in the classroom is

   A. Role-play

   B. Case study

   C. Lecture

   D. Active learning that uses all senses

20. The best way to improve a school through staff development activities is to

   A. Obtain a nationally recognized authority on the topic determined by teachers

   B. Involve teachers in initiating, planning, implementing, and evaluating the program

   C. Have a few teachers set up the program

   D. Have the principal plan and let a few teachers review the plan

21. In your district, impasse was reached during the negotiation process. The teachers are very upset and have started slowing down on their job performance. As a member of the district management negotiation team, what would you recommend to the management team?

   A. Continue binding arbitration

   B. Continue negotiation

   C. Discontinue negotiation

   D. Hire new teachers

22. Criteria to evaluate personnel in Florida should include which of the following?

    A. How well the parents like the teacher

    B. How well the children like the teacher

    C. How well the other teachers relate to the teacher

    D. Test score gains by students

23. In redesigning your performance appraisal system at your school, which of the following methods would you use?

    A. Checklist

    B. Ranking

    C. Peer review

    D. A paper written by the teacher

24. The building level principal should perform which of the following performance appraisal tasks?

    A. Develop appraisal criteria

    B. Design the appraisal process

    C. Conduct post-appraisal conferences

    D. Assess the appraisal system

25. An employee has been incompetent all year although you have followed all steps to help her. She has instituted a grievance against you of allegedly harassing her and claims that she is an excellent teacher as demonstrated by her work at other schools. You have documented her work and realized she was under personal stress and did not perform well. What will be your recommendation for her employment next year?

    A. Terminate her

    B. Conduct a hearing before an impartial tribunal before a final decision

    C. Rehire her because she had problems

    D. Request her to take a leave of absence for the next year

Answer Key (Subtest 1 – School Management, Human Resource Management)

1. D
2. C
3. A
4. C
5. A
6. B
7. B
8. D
9. D
10. C
11. A
12. B
13. D
14. C
15. D
16. A
17. D
18. D
19. D
20. B
21. A
22. D
23. C
24. C
25. B

Subtest 2 - Communication

1. Communication

In any organization or business, more than half of any administrator or supervisor's time is spent in communicating. Good communication is essential to any education organization—classroom, school, district, or state department of education. The more effective the communication process, the more successful the education process. The roles of the administrator as goal setter, task organizer, employee motivator, decision-maker, and public relations agent are facilitated by her ability to manage the communication process effectively.

Communication is the exchange of information (message) between a sender and a receiver. The process involves six steps:

1. **Ideating** - development of the idea or message to be communicated

2. **Encoding** - organization of the idea into a sequence of symbols (written or

   spoken words, nonverbal cues, or medium) to convey the message

3. **Transmitting** - delivery of the encoded message through a medium (face-to-face, telephone, written statements, video or computer products)

4. **Receiving** - claiming of the message by the receiver, who must be a good reader/listener, attentive to the message's meaning

5. **Decoding** - the receiver's translation of the message

6. **Acting** - action taken by the receiver in response to the message (ignore, store, react). Feedback to the sender that the message has been received and understood is what makes communication reciprocal.

Educational leadership training programs often explain the communication process in terms of sources and channels. The main source elements are expertise, credibility, composure, and dynamism. The ability to incorporate these elements into idea presentation results in the most persuasive communication.

The means of message transmission are referred to as channels. The characteristics of channels are such elements as the need to use different media for different audiences, the need to use recognizably respected channels, the need to select mass media that serve different purposes, and the recognition of personal channels as more effective than mass media in changing opinions.

Direction of Communication (Formal)

1. **Downward** - the transmission of information from people at higher levels to people at lower levels (superintendents to principals, principals to faculty and staff)

2. **Upward** - the transmission of information (usually feedback) from people who are at lower levels to people who are at lower levels (principals to directors of instruction, department heads/team leaders to principals)

3. **Lateral (horizontal)** - transmission of information between people on the same level in the organizational structure (assistant superintendent of instruction to assistant superintendent of facilities)

4. **Diagonal** - direct transmission of information between people at different levels in the hierarchy (usually reserved for instances when information cannot go through proper channels in a timely fashion—special reports from principals that go directly to the superintendent or assistant superintendents for transmission to the state)

A fifth form of communication exists apart from direction or formal practice—the grapevine. In actuality, the majority of information transmitted by employees laterally is carried through the grapevine. Its face-to-face informality transmits information rapidly.

Administrators should be aware of the operation of the school grapevine and incorporate its positive aspects into the communication structure. The negative aspect of unsubstantiated rumor-passing will be overridden if the administrator

- keeps employees informed about matters relevant to school or district and about issues that impact the employees' jobs.

- provides employees the opportunity to express attitudes and feelings about issues.

- tests employees' reactions to information before making decisions.

- builds morale by repeating positive reactions/comments made by employees to higher level administrators or the community and vice versa.

Teaching professionals do not like the feeling that they are being kept in the dark or are getting only partial or untimely information. Telling teachers in a faculty meeting that the district is going to reduce the faculty at their school before transfer provisions have been established will create distrust. It may seem an open gesture on the principal's part, but the timing is wrong.

Barriers to Communication

♦ The communication process requires that the sender and receiver have a common **frame of reference**. Because we all interpret information based on previous experience and cultural background, receivers may interpret the ideas in messages differently than the sender intended. For example, information, delivered during contract negotiations, is interpreted differently by union representatives than by district contract negotiators. These distorted perceptions arise because the participants are operating from different frames of reference. To make the communication effective, all parties must realize the specific goal of the talks is to spend funds in the most educationally sound manner, not to deprive either group of its just desserts.

♦ **Filtering** is a barrier that occurs during transmission of information from one level to another. It may be intentional or unintentional. In downward communication, it may be the omission of some of the message or improper encoding for the intended audience. Administrators frequently deliver information only on a need-to-know basis or deliver only positive information, fearing that negative information will damage the decoding process. This succeeds only in causing the receivers to be confused as to the message's intent or to feel patronized. In upward communication, employees may limit information to those facts that shed favorable light on their personal performance because of previous experience with inconsistent or arbitrary evaluations.

♦ Another barrier results from **improper listening skills**. The receiver must heed the entire message, decode it non-judgmentally, and seek clarification of any unclear points. This happens best when the sender creates a non-threatening environment in which the listener can practice non-evaluative listening.

♦ **Biases** against race, gender, or status can prejudice receivers against a message. Senders can suggest bias by words, nonverbal clues, and attitudes. A male principal with chauvinist attitudes may alienate female teachers; a male teacher who resents a female principal may tune her out.

Overcoming these barriers becomes an administrative responsibility. To establish effective communication, the supervisor should

- establish trust by sincerely correlating her message and behavior. Never being available after stating the existence of an open-door policy will not create trust.
- listen carefully and provide open channels for feedback. Avoid giving non-verbal cues that contradict the message.
- understand and respect employees' needs, interests, and attitudes. Allow discussion, even disagreement. The important thing is that employees know they are being heard.

- time information delivery properly. Timing affects the manner in which employees perceive the message. Avoid leaking partial information. Transmit accurate information in time for employees to provide feedback.

- use appropriate media for transmitting the message. Written or face-to-face communication is necessary when the message is of concern to a single receiver or when the message is of immediate concern to a group with common interests. Oral or video presentations are appropriate for delivery of information that affects a department or faculty, such as safety measures or reporting abuse.

The educational leader must be adept in the many skills of communication.

The **communication competencies for principals**, formulated by the Florida Council on Educational Management (established by the Florida legislature) and adopted by the Florida Board of Education for use in certification, appraisal, and training of new principals as well as the evaluation of practicing principals, include **self-presentation, written communication, and organizational sensitivity.** These points will be discussed in detail in the text.

COMPETENCY A: Know public information management.

Public information management is a **systematic** communication process between an educational organization and its public, both within and outside the schools. It is the exchange of two-way information, designed to encourage public interest in and understanding of education. The Principal competency "concern for image" in the consensus management area specifies that a principal shows concern for the school's image through impressions created by students and staff and manages both these impressions and public information about the school by (1) advertising successes and (2) controlling the flow of negative information.

To be effective, communication between school leaders and the public must be **open, honest, and unbiased.** The attitudes of parents and members of the community at large have been adversely affected by reports in the decline of American education and the media coverage which appears to focus on negative perceptions. Despite the general perception of poor public education, the majority of parents surveyed nationally expressed satisfaction with their children's schools and teachers. The most positive feedback resulted when parents felt that their concerns were being heard and addressed and that they were involved in the decision-making process.

Public relations must be carefully **organized.** Information deliverers must have accurate information, understand their roles in the disseminating of the information, and provide appropriate channels for feedback. The public must perceive that they are being given complete, timely information by officials who respect their feelings and sincerely want feedback. They must have an established frame of reference, i.e. know the schools' vision/mission statements, goals and objectives, and legislative issues that affect local education.

Public Relations Process

1. Public information management requires **analyzing** the community attitude toward educational issues. In Florida, the required School Improvement surveys conducted each spring provide not only feedback on the issues but priorities for addressing them. Public workshops and meetings allow community members to become involved in learning about budget, discipline, and academic issues. Information gathering should be structured to obtain the most scientific results, i.e. ensuring a representative sampling by mailing surveys rather than entrusting their delivery and return to students.

2. The **planning** phase requires setting specific goals and designing the campaign to achieve the goals. During this phase, educational leaders should determine the audiences, forums, and time frames in which their message(s) will be delivered to the public. Presentations to senior citizens concerning a tax increase may require a different slant than a presentation to people who have children in the schools. Issues that require voter decisions should be presented with ample time for study and cooperative decision-making or at least discussion.

3. **Following the communication process** is equally important whether information is delivered internally or externally. Student groups are a segment of the internal public and should be treated with the same open respect as elements of the community at large. The information campaign must be encoded with specific audiences in mind. Especially important is selection of the media (transmission methods) to convey the message. [Specific strategies are outlined in 2.0.] First-approach media are usually in the form of newsletters to parents, press releases, annual reports—any written document that can be distributed to the intended audiences. Follow-up transmissions include open houses, school committee or school board meetings, education fairs—any face-to-face communication that brings the public and school representatives together for a two-way exchange.

4. Finally, school/district officials must **evaluate** the results of the public relations effort. Some evaluation is immediate, as in the defeat of a candidate or the passage of a bond issue. Periodic evaluations in the form of brief questionnaires in school newsletters, telephone surveys, or written assessments at the end of public meetings can help test the public's understanding and the level of community support.

Other Considerations

1. Schools must establish good relationships with the media. When there are more complaints in the "Letters to the Editor" section of the newspaper that there are news articles about school events, there is obviously a poor interaction between media and the schools.

Of course, there are several reasons for the amount of educational coverage provided by various media.

- Small, hometown newspapers give broader coverage to local issues/events. They may devote a whole page or section to school/classroom events.
- Newspapers have to evaluate the "newsworthiness" of stories. Local spelling bees get better coverage than Mrs. Clarke's debate class's mock trial because one spelling bee winner in each district will compete nationally. Most newspapers consider a story of vandalism or fire at a school or a union walkout to be more newsworthy than a piece about students working at an animal shelter. Large city newspapers and television stations focus more on national and state news and regrettably often focus on educational issues that have negative or sensational impact.
- Local radio and television stations may be a better venue for school news; interviews with school officials, teachers, or students; or debates on education issues that have local impact.

2. School/district publications—newsletters, information brochures, handbooks, annual reports—may be more useful in providing a positive link with the community.

3. Displays of student work in public places—malls, building lobbies, and business waiting rooms—provide visual evidence of student achievement.

Establishing a Good Relationship with the Media

Educational leaders need to apply the communication process to public information management.

1. **Ideating** - Create messages that reflect understanding of the audience (the general public) and the nature of different media (newspapers, radio, television). Ask editors and producers to provide information concerning the types of material they consider newsworthy. Be available when asked to meet with reporters. Make sure press releases meet the space and time constraints of news copy.

2. **Encoding** - Speak in plain English, avoiding educational jargon. If you must use terms such as "block scheduling" or "outcome-based education," be sure you can define, explain, or give examples that can be easily understood. Remember the receiver for whom you are encoding the message.

3. **Transmitting** - Be open and honest with reporters. Assume a cooperative, rather than an adversarial, posture. Be prepared to provide specific, accurate information or to direct the reporter to the person(s) who can give solid answers to his questions. Refusing to answer may only lead to the reporter getting information from an unreliable source.

Having followed these steps, the receiver should be able to decode your message and feel free to give feedback.

COMPETENCY B: Know effective communication strategies.

Effective communication strategies can include the practices of good communication as well as the specific transmission methods.

Practices

- **Think first.** This applies to both preparation before a formal written or oral presentation and to pausing to gather your thoughts before impromptu speaking.

- **Keep informed.** Never speak or write off-the-cuff or attempt to discuss matters beyond your scope of knowledge. Stay abreast of education issues, especially in leadership and supervision. Read journals and participate in professional organizations. Keep a notebook of newsletters, clippings, and resource lists that can be highlighted and used to add credibility to your communication.

- **Assess your audience.** Know the addressed person or group's interests and attitudes. Show respect for their points of view by your tone and pace as well as your volume and posture when speaking. Demonstrate a genuine liking for people by a willingness to share your ideas and solicit their responses.

- **Focus attention on your message, not on yourself.** A little nervousness about communicating well is normal even for practiced writers/speakers. Familiarity with your topic, the ability to develop clear, complete sentences, and the use of concrete examples will enhance delivery.

- **Speak/write correctly.** Use of proper grammar, usage, and sentence structure will allow listeners/readers to concentrate on what you say, rather than on distracting language errors.
- **Be concise.** Get to the point and then quit. Use words and sentences economically. Being unnecessarily long-winded is a sure way to lose your audience.

- **Use delivery techniques to your advantage.** In written communication, be sure to state the main idea, give examples or explanations, and link the ideas in a logical manner. In oral communication, use eye contact to establish sincerity and hold listener attention. Use body language to add enthusiasm and conviction to your words, but avoid expansive or repetitive movements that can distract. Modulate the pitch and volume of your voice foe emphasis.

- **Listen thoughtfully to feedback.** In face-to-face communication, be aware of nonverbal cues that suggest either active listening or boredom.

Transmission methods

- **Written (for internal audience)**
⇒ Daily announcements for students and faculty
⇒ Student newspapers
⇒ Superintendent's monthly newsletter to faculties
⇒ Reports of school board meetings
⇒ Memorandums from all levels, downward or laterally

- **Written (for external audience)**
⇒ Principal's newsletter to parents
⇒ Annual reports
⇒ News releases

- **Oral (for internal audiences)**
⇒ Daily announcements or other student broadcasts over intercom or closed circuit television
⇒ Meetings of committees of students, parents, teachers, and administrators
⇒ Faculty meetings
⇒ Student government or club meetings
⇒ Pep rallies

- **Oral (for external audience)**
⇒ Video-taped promotions of schools or school-related events
⇒ Direct telephone contacts with parents
⇒ Student presentations—concerts, plays, content area fairs, awards ceremonies
⇒ Radio and television programs to promote school events or discuss education issues

COMPETENCY C: Know the effect one's behavior and decision-making have on others.

Because communication is a process in which a person or group learns another's ideas, attitudes, and beliefs, the process becomes a prime focus of supervisory behavior. If a positive interaction is to occur, the educational leader must understand the cause/effect relationship between her actions and the reactions of others. Behavioral characteristics relate to leadership styles—absentee, laissez faire, democratic, authoritarian. The democratic leader creates an atmosphere of cooperation by exhibiting positive behaviors.

Positive Behaviors

Show an interest in the work of others.
- Cause:

    Assistant principals and principals should take note of student and teacher performance and offer assistance as indicated. Superintendents should exhibit knowledge of work of teachers, administrators, and students by first-hand observation.
⇒ Effect:

    Workers at all levels will recognize the consideration given to their achievements and will feel more comfortable in seeking help to solve problems.

Be knowledgeable of job requirements for all personnel and give praise.
- Cause: Supervisors must evaluate performance on job descriptors. Focus on good performance; avoid being overly critical. Pass on compliments to higher level management.
⇒ Effect: Employees respond with better performance when supervisors show the ability to note specific facets of the employee's work.

Exhibit pleasing personality traits.
- Cause: Being courteous, fair, and honest and having high integrity are desirable because supervisors serve as role models for the type of behavior expected of everyone in the system.
⇒ Effect: Workers in the system will strive to emulate desirable personality traits. Members of the community form an opinion of the system based on the personalities of educational leaders that they meet at school functions or in other community organizations.

Stand by convictions.

- Cause: Supervisors should formulate strong beliefs, state them unequivocally, and support them despite opposition.
- ⇒ Effect: Students, teachers, and other leaders do not respect fence-sitters. They may not always agree with the stated beliefs, but they will defend the right to express them.

Show confidence in employees' abilities and allow self-direction.

- Cause: Supervisors at all levels must recognize the professional qualities of other professionals. Allow subordinates to work flexibly within prescribed guidelines.
- ⇒ Effect: Employees will become confident decision makers, capable of completing their jobs without constant supervision.

Be firm in following school and district guidelines for student discipline.

- Cause: School administrators should consistently adhere to discipline policy. Show no favoritism, but be fair. Principals should receive support from superintendent and school board.
- ⇒ Effect: Students will know that their misdeeds will be dealt with efficiently. Teachers will see more effectiveness in classroom management.

Exhibit a sense of humor.

- Cause: A sincere sense of humor—not sarcasm or facetiousness—encourages an amiable environment for communication. It can be used to release tension and to foster the relaxed climate in which comfortable exchange can occur.
- ⇒ Effect: Employees recognize a supervisor's ability to establish rapport by not taking herself or the demands of her position too seriously. An occasional shared laugh at some absurdity puts the situation in proportion and creates a climate in which all parties can view the issue in proper perspective.

The Florida principal competency "organizational sensitivity" relates to the principal's awareness of the effect of behavior and decisions on others. The objectives for evaluation include that the principal should

- use tactful oral and written responses to persons within and outside the school.
- inform members of the school community of information that is or could be relevant to them.
- consider the position, emotions, and attitudes of others when organizing, planning, and making decisions.

COMPETENCY D: Know the relationship between interpersonal influence and effective communication.

Traditionally, interpersonal influence related to the managerial motivation elements— need for power and need for achievement. The successful traditional educational leader was recognized as an effective communicator if he possessed the skills of persuading subordinates of the validity of striving toward challenging goals. Measuring leadership success in these terms resulted in some assumptions that current research has shown to inhibit effective communication.

- The leader's ideas/goals are viewed as best for the institution. This assumption fosters an authoritative style which communicates downward and discounts the value of ideas generated by employees. Honest feedback is discouraged.

- The setting of goals is the responsibility of an individual or administrative group not the result of collegial collaboration. This assumption reflects the leadership attitude that employees lack the professional knowledge to participate in the decision making process.

Post World War II studies of the social organization of work environments revealed that greater communication restraints existed in businesses with rigid social structures that encouraged stereotypical role perceptions. The emphasis on hierarchical status creates low-quality or non-existent communication between persons who feel inferior to those in power and authority figures who perceive themselves as superior.

The development of instructional leadership models in the 1970s were based on traditional assumptions that effective school leaders were firm disciplinarians who set high expectations of employee performance. They set the goals that staff and faculty were expected to meet; task orientation was tantamount regardless of anxiety levels.

Studies of human dynamics in the 1980s and 90s led to total quality management in business and industry, a concept that has many names in education. **Facilitative leadership** seems to most accurately apply. This leadership model stresses that productive work environments depend on interpersonal relationships that are high in collaboration and empowerment of all persons involved in the education process.

The needs for power and achievement become shared criteria. The leadership role focuses on involving employees in the solving of problems that lead to improved performance and higher levels of achievement. Similar to cooperative learning models of classroom management, facilitative leadership requires improved communication based on the perceptions of senders and receivers. It also recognizes behavior and emotions as communication tools.

Sender Perceptions

1. Open communication is sharing, not persuading. Although favorable presentation of an idea necessitates the persuasive technique of analyzing the audience's biases, interests, and emotions, the object is not to refute any conflicting ideas based on these receiver elements but to use them as a means to better understand the issues that evolve from the idea as it is decoded. Encouraging the discussion of issues from all perspectives results in better decoding and appropriate action. The outcome will be the arrival at truth, i.e. a mutually acceptable position, not the imposition of convincing.

2. Open communication results from relating to, not controlling, others. Exhibiting the positive behaviors outlined in 3.0 reflects a leader's ability to constantly assess the consequences of his words and behaviors against the ideas and actions of others. Behavior is recognized as communication as much as language is.

The non-verbal messages inherent in behavior must be as conscientiously encoded as language if the message is to be properly decoded. Because the receiver decodes emotionally as well as cognitively, the sender must recognize that the listener may not react appropriately if he does not understand the expected type of response or if he feels anxiety which blocks an appropriate response. Misinterpretation of the message may result from the lack of experience with the sequential nature of behavior communication—antecedent, behavior, consequence.

For example, if in their experience with a former principal, a faculty has become accustomed to being patronized, they may not recognize sincere praise. They may view praise, especially general praise, as condescension. They may respond with signals of disbelief because that reaction was acceptable in the old pattern of behavior. The principal's sensitivity to this barrier to communication (filtering) may need to develop another means of transmission (another medium or sender) until the teachers learn the skill of accepting praise based on trust of the sender and his delivery method.

3. Open communication relies on reciprocal trust. Supervisors must deliver consistent verbal and non-verbal messages; exhibit empathy for the values and ideas of others; demonstrate sincere commitment to the school's vision and the work of the staff and students; be honest in information sharing; and be accessible to all members of the school community.

4. Use vocabulary and complete sentence structures that leads to appropriate interpretation of the message. Select words and symbols that are understood by all or can be explained with alternate word choice. Avoid making incomplete statements to which listeners are expected to fill in the blank. Encourage questioning for clarification.

5. Use feedback as a means to evaluate the effectiveness of communication.
    -Concentrate on listening non-judgmentally to listener reactions.
    -View disagreement as a tool for analyzing the clarity of presentation.
    -Ask focused questions that give the listener the opportunity to ask for additional information.
    -Use perception checking and behavior description as a means of eliciting understanding from listeners' perceived feelings or observable behavior.

Receiver Perceptions
1. Seek understanding, not judgment. Do not argue points of disagreement. Try to understand what the sender is saying. Identify specific points of agreement and disagreement. Paraphrase areas of agreement to determine if interpretation is correct. Point out areas of disagreement for further examination and discussion.

2. Practice active listening skills. Recognize that receiver decoding skills are affected by feelings and perception about the sender that hinder receipt of the message. As receivers ask questions or paraphrase your message, focus on their ideas, ask specific questions to reveal their level of attentiveness, and avoid drawing heated emotional responses. Avoid defensive or attacking responses. Remember that open communication is based on reciprocal trust.

The Florida principal competency of self-presentation relates to the ability to convey a message effectively and to share ideas in a non-evaluative manner.
The principal should

- communicate ideas (his own and others') in clear, informative way in both one-on-one and group situations.
- stimulate others to ask questions about their own issues.
- present himself in a way that is not viewed as controlling or demanding or conformity.

Included in the realm of self-presentation are the qualities of good grooming, a pleasant speaking voice, and a likable personality. The more things employees can find to commend, the better the working relationship.

COMPETENCY E: Know the relationship between self-concept and effective communication.

Effective communication relies on the ability of the supervisor, especially the school principal, to project a positive self-image and to instill in others the feelings that foster self-esteem.

Self-concept (a person's concept of what he is within the organization or social structure) results from his perceptions of what he would like to be, what he wants others to think he is, and what he thinks others already think he is. A mature employee must have an awareness of and control of self to satisfy the psychological need for acknowledgment of worth. The supervisor contributes to this satisfaction by modeling positive behaviors (3.0) that create respect and trust. He enhances his staff's individual and group self-concept through encouragement, constructive criticism, and non-threatening discipline.

Encouragement

Use the techniques of successful coaches.

- Demonstrate patience and caring. When you are introducing new ideas or information, give the staff members on the school team the sense that you are constantly taking into consideration what is best for the school, the teachers, the support staff, and the students. Referring often to the school's vision and the objectives to achieve that mission will keep team efforts focused and give members the sense of the role each of them plays in the organization.

- Take time to explain and demonstrate and give learners ample time to practice. Even professionals cannot be expected to grasp new concepts and perform with improvement until they have had plenty of time to implement the new skills. Suggest that they observe experienced teachers who exhibit mastery of the expected skills.

- Offer praise and advise. Be cautious that praise is sincere and advise is warranted and wanted.

- Provide support and positive reinforcement. During the improvement process, make sure to note specific elements of success. Focus on those successes, not on mistakes.

- Challenge people to do their best. We humans often settle for less than we are truly capable of. Help team members see an ultimate goal and the steps to its achievement; then, cheerlead them toward the goal.

- Encourage enjoyment and appreciation of work. Work is drudgery when the workers do not believe in the product and in their own ability to turn out the best product. The coach has to help the team members realize that the reward of the work is doing it. This means that everyone on the team must have the goal clearly in mind, have the ability to strive for the objectives that lead to the goal, and participate in activities that are relevant to the goal's accomplishment.

Constructive Criticism

- Lace criticism with deserved, specific, positive praise. To achieve this goal, the supervisor must be prepared to recognize individual differences shaped by societal values and professional attitudes. Planning for constructive criticism requires personal knowledge of performance in the work setting and understanding of each person's interests and emotions. Then, channeling staff members creative energies into productive participation reinforces their sense of worth. Make a point to note the value of their contributions orally or in writing. The collective self-concepts of the individuals in the school community then contribute to the image of the school.

- Encourage improved performance in a relaxed atmosphere. Severe criticism is threatening and non-productive. It forces the criticized individual or group into a defensive posture. Supervisors should therefore provide opportunities for employees to critique their own performance and offer strategies for improvement.

Non-threatening Discipline

Use effective communication strategies when the need for disciplining employees arises.

- Improving performance requires putting interventions in place in a timely manner, that is, as soon as the problem is diagnosed.

- Criticize performance, not the person. Be sure that your personal judgments do not influence your opinions and actions.

- Maintain emotional stability by offering caring support in a courteous manner and voice.

- Address specifics, not generalities. Have your facts straight and adhere to the prescribed method for handling each situation.

- Protect the confidentiality of the diagnosis and interventions.

COMPETENCY F: Write in a logical, clear style using appropriate grammar and structure.

The principal competency "written communication" concerns writing in a clear, accurate style. The writer should

- express meaning clearly.
- use adequate vocabulary (effective word choice).
- use correct and appropriate sentence and paragraph structures.
- use correct spelling and punctuation.

These objectives are applicable in all forms of written communication. Below are a few helps toward these objectives.

CLEAR EXPRESSION

Clear expression of meaning relies on the appropriate use of vocabulary, syntax, and mechanics. It also relates to considering the audience (age, social status, interests, opinions); maintaining a consistent point of view (personal, impersonal); and adopting an appropriate tone (sincere, satirical). These will be discussed in more detail in the presentation on writing a composition.

VOCABULARY

Choosing effective words to convey meaning includes using words properly in context. Because words have both denotative (explicit) meanings and connotative (implied) meanings, the writer must select words that, when combined with other words in a given sentence or paragraph, allow the reader to properly decode his meaning with reading something that was not intended.

Proper word choice also requires the writer to avoid slang or jargon. In any profession there are those catch-words which have current meaning to those in the profession. However, when writing for a lay public, it is always preferable to use generally understood words or be prepared to give clearly understandable definitions to educational terms that cannot be avoided.

Finally, effective word choice also implies the avoidance of wordiness. Say what you mean in as few words as possible; this forces you to choose words carefully. The exact syntactical error of redundancy is addressed in the next section.

SYNTAX

Sentence completeness

Avoid fragments and run-on sentences. Recognition of sentence elements necessary to make a complete thought, proper use of independent and dependent clauses (see *Use correct coordination and subordination*), and proper punctuation will correct such errors.

Sentence structure. Recognize simple, compound, complex, and compound-complex sentences. Use dependent (subordinate) and independent clauses correctly to create these sentence structures.

Simple	Joyce wrote a letter.
Compound	Joyce wrote a letter, and Dot drew a picture.
Complex	While Joyce wrote a letter, Dot drew a picture.
Compound/complex	When Mother asked the girls to demonstrate their new-found skills, Joyce wrote a letter, and Dot drew a picture.

Note: Do **not** confuse compound sentence elements with compound sentences.

-Simple sentence with compound subject

<u>Bill</u> and <u>Fred</u> wrote letters.

The <u>girl</u> in row three and the <u>boy</u> next to her were passing notes across the aisle.

-Simple sentence with compound predicate

Joe <u>wrote letters</u> and <u>drew pictures</u>.

The captain of the high school debate team <u>graduated with honors</u> and <u>studied broadcast journalism in college</u>.

-Simple sentence with compound object of preposition

Nancy graded the students' essays for <u>style</u> and <u>mechanical accuracy</u>.

Parallelism. Recognize parallel structures using phrases (prepositional, gerund, participial, and infinitive) and omissions from sentences that create the lack of parallelism.

-Prepositional phrase/single modifier

Incorrect: Coleen ate the ice cream with enthusiasm and hurriedly.

Correct: Coleen ate the ice cream with enthusiasm and in a hurry.

Correct: Coleen ate the ice cream enthusiastically and hurriedly.

-Participial phrase/infinitive phrase

Incorrect: After hiking for hours and to sweat profusely, Joe sat down to rest and drinking water.

Correct: After hiking for hours and sweating profusely, Joe sat down to rest and drink water.

-Recognition of dangling modifiers

Dangling phrases are attached to sentence parts in such a way they create ambiguity and incorrectness of meaning.

-Participial phrase

Incorrect: Hanging from her skirt, Dot tugged at a loose thread.

Correct: Dot tugged at a loose thread hanging from her skirt.

Incorrect: Relaxing in the bathtub, the telephone rang.

Correct: While I was relaxing in the bathtub, the telephone rang.

-Infinitive phrase

Incorrect: To improve his behavior, the dean warned Fred.

Correct: The dean warned Fred to improve his behavior.

-Prepositional phrase

Incorrect: On the floor, Father saw the dog eating table scraps.

Correct: Father saw the dog eating table scraps on the floor.

Recognition of syntactical redundancy or omission

These errors occur when superfluous words have been added to a sentence or key words have been omitted from a sentence.

-Redundancy

Incorrect: Joyce made sure that when her plane arrived that she retrieved all of her luggage.

Correct: Joyce made sure that when her plane arrived she retrieved all of her luggage.

Incorrect: He was a mere skeleton of his former self.

Correct: He was a skeleton of his former self.

-Omission

Incorrect: Dot opened her book, recited her textbook, and answered the teacher's subsequent question.

Correct: Dot opened her book, recited from the textbook, and answered the teacher's subsequent question.

Avoidance of double negatives

This error occurs from positioning two negatives that, in fact, cancel each other in meaning.

Incorrect: Harold couldn't care less whether he passes this class.

Correct: Harold could care less whether he passes this class.

Incorrect: Dot didn't have no double negatives in her paper.

Correct: Dot didn't have any double negatives in her paper.

Correct use of coordination and subordination

Connect independent clauses with the coordinating conjunctions - *and, but, or, for,* or *nor* - when their content is of equal importance. Use subordinating conjunctions - although, because, before, if, since, though, until, when, whenever, where - and relative pronouns - that, who, whom, which - to introduce clauses that express ideas that are subordinate to main ideas expressed in independent clauses. (See *Sentence Structure* above.)

Be sure to place the conjunctions so that they express the proper relationship between ideas (cause/effect, condition, time, space).

Incorrect: Because Mother scolded me, I was late.

Correct: Mother scolded me because I was late.

Incorrect: The sun rose after the fog lifted.

Correct: The fog lifted after the sun rose.

Notice that placement of the conjunction can completely change the meaning of the sentence. Main emphasis is shifted by the change.

Although Jenny was pleased, the teacher was disappointed.

Although the teacher was disappointed, Jenny was pleased.

The boys who wrote the essay won the contest.

The boys who won the contest wrote the essay. (While not syntactically incorrect, the second sentence makes it appear that the boys won the contest for something else before they wrote the essay.)

GRAMMAR
Subject-verb agreement

A verb agrees in number with its subject. Making them agree relies on the ability to properly identify the subject.

> <u>One</u> of the boys *was playing* too rough.
> <u>No one</u> in the class, not the teacher nor the students, <u>was listening</u> to the message from the intercom.
> The <u>candidates,</u> including a grandmother and a teenager, <u>are debating</u> some controversial issues.

If two singular subjects are connected by *and* the verb must be plural.

A *man* and his *dog* were jogging on the beach.

If two singular subjects are connected by *or* or *nor*, a singular verb is required.

> Neither <u>Dot</u> nor <u>Joyce</u> <u>has</u> missed a day of school this year.

> Either <u>Fran</u> or <u>Paul</u> <u>is</u> missing.

If one singular subject and one plural subject are connected by *or* or *nor*, the verb agrees with the subject nearest to the verb.

> Neither the <u>coach</u> nor the <u>players</u> <u>were</u> able to sleep on the bus.

If the subject is a collective noun, its sense of number is the sentence determines the verb: singular if the noun represents a group or unit and plural if the noun represents individuals.

> The <u>House of Representatives</u> <u>has adjourned</u> for the holidays.

> The House of Representatives have failed to reach agreement on the subject of adjournment.

MECHANICS

The candidate should be cognizant of proper rules and conventions of punctuation, capitalization, and spelling. Competency exams will generally test the ability to apply the more advanced skills; thus, a limited number of more frustrating rules are presented here. Rules should be applied according to the American style of English, i.e. spelling *theater* instead of *theatre* and placing terminal marks of punctuation almost exclusively within other marks of punctuation.

Punctuation

Using terminal punctuation in relation to quotation marks

- In a quoted statement that is either declarative or imperative, place the period inside the closing quotation marks.

  "The airplane crashed on the runway during takeoff."

- If the quotation is followed by other words in the sentence, place a comma inside the closing quotations marks and a period at the end of the sentence.

  "The airplane crashed on the runway during takeoff," said the announcer.

- In most instances in which a quoted title or expression occur at the end of a sentence, the period is placed before either the single or double quotation marks.

  "The middle school readers were prepared to understand the theme of Jesse Stuart's "Split Cherry Tree."

  Early book length adventure stories like *Don Quixote* and *The Three Musketeers* were known as "picaresque novels."

In sentences that are interrogatory or exclamatory, the question mark or exclamation point should be positioned outside the closing quotation marks if the quote itself is a statement or command or cited title. Who decided to lead us in the recitation of the "Pledge of Allegiance"?

  Why was Tillie shaking as she began her recitation, "Once upon a midnight dreary..."?

I could have died when Mrs. White said, "Your slip is showing "!

Cory shrieked, "Is there a mouse in the room?" (In this instance, the question supersedes the exclamation.)

Using periods with parentheses or brackets

- Place the period inside the parentheses or brackets if they enclose a complete sentence, independent of the other sentences around it.

   Stephen Crane was a confirmed alcohol and drug addict. (He admitted as much to other journalists with in Cuba.)

- If the parenthetical expression is a statement inserted within another statement, the period in the enclosure is omitted.

   Mark Twain used the character Indian Joe (He also appeared in *The Adventures of Tom Sawyer*) as a foil for Jim in *The Adventures of Huckleberry Finn*.

- When enclosed matter comes at the end of a sentence requiring quotation marks, place the period outside the parentheses or brackets.

   "The secretary of state consulted with the ambassador [Albright]."

Using commas

- Separate two or more coordinate adjectives, modifying the same word and three or more nouns, phrases, or clauses in a list.

   Maggie's hair was dull, dirty, and lice-ridden.

   Dickens portrayed the Artful Dodger as skillful pickpocket, loyal follower of Fagin, and defendant of Oliver Twist.

   Ellen daydreamed about getting out of the rain, taking a shower, and eating a hot dinner.

   In Elizabethan England, Ben Johnson wrote comedy, Christopher Marlowe wrote tragedies, and William Shakespeare composed both.

- Use commas to separate antithetical or complimentary expressions from the rest of the sentence.

> The veterinarian, not his assistant, would perform the delicate surgery.

> The more he knew about her, the less he wished her knew.

> Randy hopes to, and probably will, get an appointment to the Naval Academy.

> His thorough, though esoteric, scientific research could not easily be understood by high school students.

- Use quotation marks to enclose the titles of shorter works: songs, short poems, short stories, essays, magazine articles, and chapters of books. (See "Using Italics" for punctuating longer titles.)

"The Tell-Tale Heart"   "Casey at the Bat"   "America the Beautiful"

Using semicolons

- Use semicolons to separate independent clauses when the second clause is introduced by an transitional adverb. (These clauses may also be written as separate sentences, preferably by placing the adverb within the second sentence.)

> The Elizabethans modified the rhyme scheme of the sonnet; thus, it was called the English sonnet.
> > *or*
> The Elizabethans modified the rhyme scheme of the sonnet. It, thus, was called the English sonnet.

- Use semicolons to separate items in a series that are long and complex or have internal punctuation.

> The Italian Renaissance produced masters in the fine arts: Dante Alighieri, author of the *Divine Comedy;* Leonardo da Vinci, painter of *The Last Supper;* and Donatello, sculptor of the *Quattro Coronati,* the four saints.

The leading scorers in the WNBA were Haizhaw Zheng, averaging 23.9 points per game; Lisa Leslie, 22; and Cynthia Cooper, 19.5.

Using colons

- Place a colon at the beginning of a list of items. (Note its use in the sentence about Renaissance Italians on the previous page.)

> The teacher directed us to compare Faulkner's three symbolic novels: *Absalom, Absalom; As I Lay Dying,* and *Light in August.*

Do **not** use a comma if the list is preceded by a verb.

> Three of Faulkner's symbolic novels are *Absalom, Absalom; As I Lay Dying,* and *Light in August.*

Using dashes

- Place dashes to denote sudden breaks in thought.

> Some periods in literature - the Romantic Age, for example - spanned different time periods in different countries.

- Use dashes instead of commas if commas are already used elsewhere in the sentence for amplification or explanation.

> The Fireside Poets included three Brahmans - James Russell Lowell, Henry David Wadsworth, and Oliver Wendell Holmes - and John Greenleaf Whittier.

- Use italics to punctuate the titles of long works of literature, names of periodical publications, musical scores, works of art, and motion picture television, and radio programs. (Unable to write in italics, students should be instructed to underline in their own writing where italics would be appropriate.)

The Idylls of the King	*Hiawatha*	*The Sound and the Fury*
Mary Poppins	*Newsweek*	*The Nutcracker Suite*

Capitalization

- Capitalize all proper names of persons (including specific organizations or agencies of government); places (countries, states, cities, parks, and specific geographical areas); and things (political parties, structures, historical and cultural terms, and calendar and time designations); and religious terms (any deity, revered person or group, sacred writings).

Percy Bysshe Shelley, Argentina, Mount Rainier National Park, Grand Canyon, League of Nations, the Sears Towers, Birmingham, Lyric Theater, Americans, Midwesterners, Democrats, Renaissance, Boy Scouts of America, Easter, God, Bible, Dead Sea Scrolls, Koran

- Capitalize proper adjectives and titles used with proper names.

California gold rush, President John Adams, French fries, Homeric epic, Romanesque architecture, Senator John Glenn

Note: Some words that represent titles and offices are not capitalized unless used with a proper name.

Capitalized	Not Capitalized
Congressman McKay	the congressman from Florida
Commander Alger	commander of the Pacific Fleet
Queen Elizabeth	the queen of England

- Capitalize all main words in titles of works of literature, art, and music. (See "Using Italics" in the Punctuation section above.)

Spelling

Concentration in this section will be on spelling plurals and possessives. The multiplicity and complexity of spellings rules based on phonics, letter doubling, and exceptions to rules - not mastered by adulthood - should be replaced by a good dictionary. As spelling mastery is also difficult for adolescents, our recommendation is the same. Learning the use of a dictionary and thesaurus will be a more rewarding use of time.

- Most plurals of nouns that end in hard consonants or hard consonant sounds followed by a silent *e* are made by adding *s*. Some words ending in vowels only add *s*.

  fingers, numerals, banks, bugs, riots, homes, gates, radios, bananas

- Nouns that end in soft consonant sounds *s, j, x, z, ch,* and *sh,* add *es*. Some nouns ending in *o* add *es*.

  dresses, waxes, churches, brushes, tomatoes

- Nouns ending in *y* preceded by a vowel just add *s*.

  boys, alleys

- Nouns ending in *y* preceded by a consonant change the *y* to *I* and add *es*.

  babies, corollaries, frugality, poppies

- Some nouns plurals are formed irregularly or remain the same.

  sheep, deer, children, leaves, oxen
- Some nouns derived from foreign words, especially Latin, may make their plurals in two different ways - one of them Anglicized. Sometimes, the meanings are the same; other times, the two plurals are used in slightly different contexts. It is always wise to consult the dictionary.

  appendices, appendixes   criterion, criteria
  indexes, indices   crisis, crises

- Make the plurals of closed (solid) compound words in the usual way except for words ending in *ful* which make their plurals on the root word.
  timelines, hairpins, cupsful

- Make the plurals of open or hypenated compounds by adding the change in inflection to the word that changes in number.
  fathers-in-law, courts-martial, masters of art, doctors of medicine

- Make the plurals of letters, numbers, and abbreviations by adding *s*.

  fives and tens, IBMs, 1990s, *p*s and *q*s (Note that letters are italicized.)

Possessives

- Make the possessives of singular nouns by adding 's.

  baby's bottle, father's job, elephant's eye, teacher's desk, sympathizer's protests, week's postponement

- Make the possessive of singular nouns ending in s by adding either an apostrophe or an 's depending upon common usage or sound. When making the possessive causes difficulty, use a prepositional phrase instead. Even with the sibilant ending, with a few exceptions, it is advisable to use the 's construction.

  dress's color, species' characteristics or characteristics of the species, James' hat or James's hat, Delores's shirt

- Make the possessive of plural nouns ending in s by adding the apostrophe after the s.

  horses' coats, jockeys' times, four days' time

- Make possessives of plural nouns that do not end in s the same as singular nouns by adding 's.

  children's shoes, deer's antlers, cattle's horns

- Make possessives of compound nouns by adding the inflection at the end of the word or phrase.

  the mayor of Los Angeles' campaign, the mailman's new truck, the mailmen's new trucks, my father-in-law's first wife, the keepsakes' values, several daughters-in-law's husbands

Note: Because a gerund functions as a noun, any noun preceding it and operating as a possessive adjective must reflect the necessary inflection. However, if the gerundive following the noun is a participle, no inflection is added.

The general was perturbed by the private's sleeping on duty. (The word
sleeping is a gerund (the object of the preposition *by*.)
> *but*

The general was perturbed to see the private sleeping on duty. (The word
sleeping is a participle modifying *private*.)

The strategies provided here apply to dealing with the writing of a specific essay for testing purposes as well as for all written communication in general.

GENERAL STRATEGIES FOR WRITING THE ESSAY

* Budget your time. You will not have time to revise your essay. It is important that you write a good first draft.
* Read the question carefully. Make sure you understand what the question is asking you to do.
* Take time to pre-write.
* Write a thesis statement by restating the question.
* Keep your purpose in mind as you write your essay.
* Connect the ideas of your essay in a brief conclusion.
* Leave enough time to quickly proofread and edit your essay.

The essay that you are to write must demonstrate the ability to write on a specific topic. As you practice the steps provided to prepare for this test, please keep in mind that this review will not teach you how to address content. It is expected that the fundamentals of educational leadership have been a focus of your course of study. The following steps in writing an essay in a timed situation will aid you in preparing to write the essay in the most time efficient manner possible. It is important to keep in mind that a good essay has focus, organization, support and correct usage.

Part I - Understanding the question

When you receive your question, the first thing you need to do is decide what the question is asking you to do. Look for key words that will establish the purpose of your essay. Examine the chart on the next page and review the key words and purpose each word establishes.

PRACTICE - Examine the chart on this page. The chart identifies some of the key words you might find on an essay test. Please note that for each key word the purpose and an example are illustrated.

KEY WORD	PURPOSE	EXAMPLE
Analyze	to examine the parts of a news release	Read a passage and analyze how the author achieves effective communication using good communication practices
Compare	to identify the similarities	Read two memoranda concerning the handling of a safety issue and compare the similarities in each writer's methods for explaining the procedures for handling safety concerns
Contrast	to identify differences	Read two newsletters to parents and contrast how each writer uses communication techniques to elicit feedback
Discuss	examine in detail	Read a personnel evaluation and discuss how the writer conveys constructive criticism by addressing appropriate and specific job descriptors .
Explain	provide reasons/ examples or clarify the meaning	Read the opening passage of a school annual report and explain how the author provides specific directions to the contents.

When writing an essay, consider the following things before you begin to pre-write.

** **Identifying the elements for analysis**. If you are asked to examine the effect of the message, you might need to look at the impact of word choice and usage or if you are asked to examine listener feedback and explain how a writer interprets this feedback, you might need to examine appropriate listening skills.

** **Deciding on your main idea**. Use the question as a guideline. However, do not merely restate the question. Make sure that in restating the topic you have taken a position on how you will answer the prompt. For example, you might be asked to read a superintendent's letter on facing a budget crisis and discuss not only the tone of the letter, but also the way the writer created the tone. It is important, if you wish to receive a high score on the essay, that your main idea clearly states what you think is the tone and how it is created.

** **Considering Audience, Purpose, and Tone**. Keep in mind that as you write an essay for a test, your purpose is to demonstrate knowledge of leadership skills by addressing an issue or solving a problem. Remember to match the style of writing to the audience for which the message is intended. In on-the-job writing, you must use good encoding skills to create your own messages.

Part 2 - Prewriting for ideas and planning your essay

Prior to writing, you will need to pre-write for ideas and details as well as decide how the essay will be organized. In the time you have to write, you should spend no more than a tenth of the time (5-10 minutes for an hour's writing) for prewriting and organizing your ideas. As you pre-write, it might be helpful to remember you should have at least three main points and at least two to three details to support your main ideas. There are several types of graphic organizers that you should practice using as you prepare for the essay portion of the test.

PRACTICE - Choose one topic from the chart and complete the cluster.

PREWRITE TO EXPLAIN HOW OR WHY

Reread a question from the chart on the previous page that asks you to explain how a writer communicates effectively using good practices. Locate an appropriate news release(s) in a local newspaper. Then, fill out the organizer on the following page that identifies how the writer effectively applied those practices. Support with examples from the news release.

VISUAL ORGANIZER: GIVING REASONS

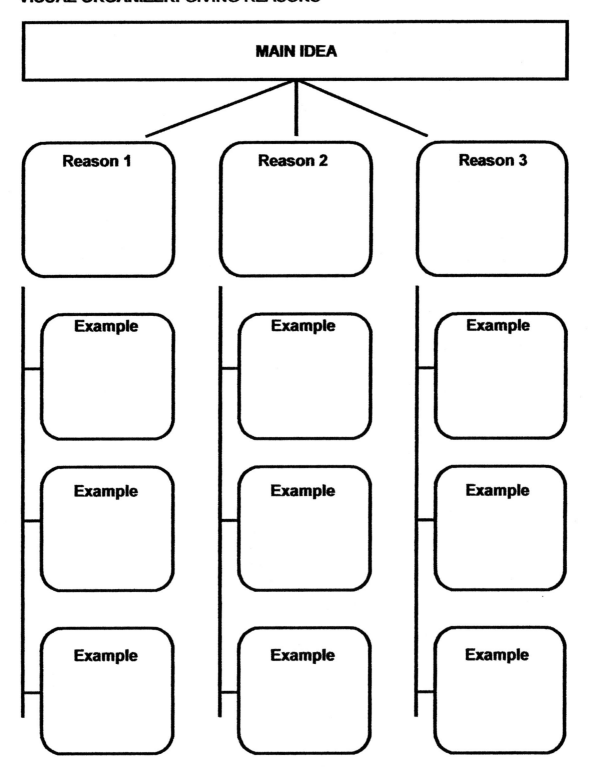

STEP 3: PREWRITE TO ORGANIZE IDEAS

After you have completed a graphic organizer, you need to decide how you will organize your essay. To organize your essay, you might consider one of the following patterns to structure your essay.

Examine individual elements such as knowledge of audience, conciseness and specificity of information, timeliness of content, etc.

SINGLE ELEMENT OUTLINE
Intro - main idea statement
Main point 1 with at least two supporting details
Main point 2 with at least two supporting details
Main point 3 with at least two supporting details
Conclusion (restates main ideas and summary of main pts)

2. **Compare and contrast two elements.**

POINT BY POINT	BLOCK
Introduction Statement of main idea about A and B	Introduction Statement of main idea about A and B
Main Point 1 Discussion of A Discussion of B	Discussion of A Main Point 1 Main Point 2 Main point 3
Main Point 2 Discussion of A Discussion of B	Discussion of B Main Point 1 Main Point 2 Main Point 3
Main Point 3 Discussion of A Discussion of B	Conclusion Restate main idea
Conclusion Restatement or summary of main idea	

PRACTICE:
Using the cluster, choose an organizing chart and complete for your topic.

VISUAL ORGANIZER: GIVING INFORMATION

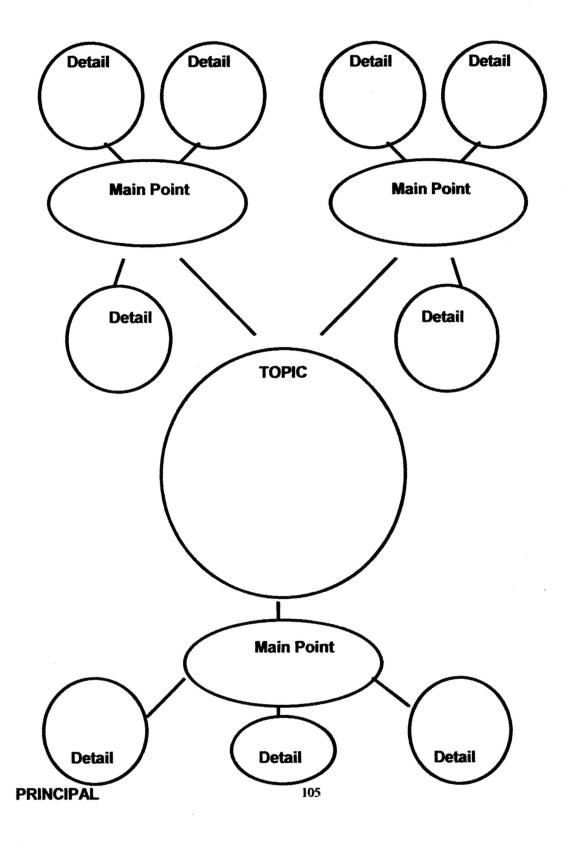

Part 4 - Write The Thesis Statement

First: **Identify the topic.**

I am going to write about the use of good communication practices in the news release concerning the need to raise the standards for athletic eligibility.

Second: **State your point of view about the topic.**

The positive and optimistic tone of the superintendent's release is created by his word choice, structure, and tone.

Third: **Summarize the main points you will make in your essay.**

The superintendent creates an optimistic tone by examining specific benefits to be gained with a clear, concise word choice and a positive tone.

PRACTICE:
Using the topic and prewriting you completed on the previous page, write the Thesis Statement for your essay. Follow the steps outlined above.

"You will have to excuse my wife.
She's a bit of a control freak."

Part 5: State the main point of each body paragraph and organize support.

PARAGRAPH	PURPOSE	SUPPORT
1-INTRO	MAIN IDEA STATEMENT	
2-1ST BODY PARA- GRAPH	MAIN POINT 1	QUOTES OR SPECIFICS FROM THE TEXT WITH ANALYSIS OR EXPLANATION OF HOW EACH DETAIL SUPPORTS YOUR MAIN POINT.
3-2ND BODY PARA- GRAPH	MAIN POINT 2	QUOTES OR SPECIFICS FROM THE TEXT WITH ANALYSIS OR EXPLANATION OF HOW EACH DETAIL SUPPORTS YOUR MAIN POINT.
4-3RD BODY PARA- GRAPH	MAIN POINT 3	QUOTES OR SPECIFICS FROM THE TEXT WITH ANALYSIS OR EXPLANATION OF HOW EACH DETAIL SUPPORTS YOUR MAIN POINT.
5-CLOSING	SUMMARIZE IDEAS	

PRACTICE:
Using the given information cluster, complete your own organizing chart like the one above.

Part 6 - Write the introduction of your essay.

Remember that your introduction should accomplish the following things:
1. It should introduce the topic.
2. It should capture your reader's interest.
3. It should state your thesis.
4. It should prepare the reader for the main points of your essay.

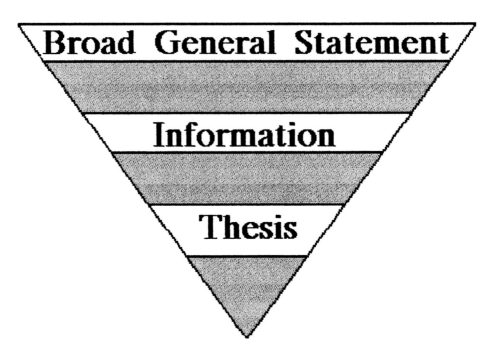

INVERTED TRIANGLE INTRODUCTION

Try to imagine the introduction as an inverted triangle. To write the introduction, follow the steps below.

1. On your prewriting sheet, write down your thesis. Check to see you have made it specific, prepared the reader for what will follow, and clearly addressed the topic.

2. Open your introduction with a broad general statement.

3. Follow the broad general statement with one or more sentences that add interest and information about the topic.

4. Write your thesis at the end of the introduction.

PRACTICE:

Now, you are ready to write your introduction. Complete the steps for writing an introduction using the ideas from your prewriting and organizing chart.

Part 7 - Writing the body paragraphs

Once you have written your introduction, move on to the body paragraphs. Remember the following guidelines as you write your body paragraphs.

Suggestions for Writing Body Paragraphs

* Write at least **three** body paragraphs.
* For each paragraph, you should write a main idea sentence, supporting details, and a closing sentence.
* Use transitions between and within each paragraph.
* Vary your sentence structure by using participial phrases, gerunds, infinitives and adjective and noun clauses. Vary the length of sentences— simple sentences for main points, complex sentences for explanations.

PRACTICE:

Using your prewriting cluster and organizing chart, write the body paragraphs for your essay. Try to follow the suggestions listed above when writing your paragraphs.

Part 8 - Writing the conclusion

The closing paragraph of an essay summarizes the essay and reinforces the principal ideas of the essay. A good conclusion usually restates the thesis and main ideas from each body paragraph. It often ends with a clincher sentence,   an unforgettable sentence that ends the paper.

PRACTICE:

Now, take out the essay for which you have already written an introduction and the body paragraphs. Write a conclusion to your essay and be sure to include a clincher sentence.

Part 9 - Editing and proofreading

In a testing situation, you will be assessed on your ability to write an essay that demonstrates structural and grammatical skill in a limited amount of time; you will not have time to revise. However, correct usage will be a factor in your score. It is important to leave five minutes to reread, edit, and proofread your paper.

In on-the-job writing, you will usually have more time for pre-writing and editing, though we are all occasionally pressured by deadlines. The more accurate you can make the first draft, the more time saved from editing.

Editing occurs when you change words or phrases to clarify your ideas. If you make any changes, cross out the word or words once and write the new word or phrase directly above it. Make sure that any changes you make are clear.

Proofreading is checking your essay for any errors in mechanics or punctuation. Although you are writing in a timed situation, you are expected to follow the standards of correct usage. If you find an error, cross it out with a single line and write the correction directly above the error.

PRACTICE:

Take out the essay for which you have written an introduction, a body, and a conclusion. Take five minutes to edit and proofread your essay.

FINAL PREPARATIONS

Practice the steps outlined here on another topic. Keep in mind that often the essay question on the exam asks you to read an unfamiliar passage and write an essay that expresses a point of view, uses logical reasoning, and supports ideas with specifics.

*NOTE: Statistics compiled by the testing division of the Florida Department of Education reveal that communication is the competency most often failed on the Educational Leadership Exam.

Subtest 2 Communications

The candidate has two hours to complete this section.

The test consists of approximately 25 multiple choice questions and one essay, a response to one of two prompts. The response is scored holistically on the quality of these factors:
- unity, organization, and focus
- sufficiency and development
- usage and syntax
- clarity and paragraph and sentence structure
- spelling, capitalization, and punctuation

PART I   Directions: Read each item and select the best response.

1. **Which of the following represents the proper sequential order in the communication process?**

   A. Ideating, decoding, transmitting, receiving, encoding, acting

   B. Ideating, encoding, transmitting, receiving, decoding, acting

   C. Ideating, transmitting, encoding, receiving, decoding, acting

   D. Ideating, encoding, transmitting, receiving, acting, decoding

2. **Communication in which a school principal receives feedback from the faculty/staff is**

   A. Downward

   B. Lateral

   C. Upward

   D. Diagonal

3. **Which of the following is _not_ true of the educational grapevine?**

   A. It is the least reliable source of transmitting information

   B. It is the means by which most information is passed laterally among employees

   C. Its most negative feature is the transmission of unsubstantiated rumor

   D. It can be used effectively by administrators to test employee reactions that facilitate the decision making process

4. **Which of the following is an example of the communication barrier *filtering*?**

   A. In an in-service planning meeting, the district director of student in instruction recommends that CPR training be deleted from the mid-year, full in-service day, citing the reason that PE teachers always fill the classes instead of registering for other educationally sound offerings

   B. Parents at an elementary school improvement committee meeting interpret the principal's reference to declining scores on the fourth grade writing assessment as a result of poor teaching. The principal fails to explain that scoring standards were increased and therefore all schools showed a slight lowering of rubric points

   C. A janitor has been asked not to clean the blackboards in a classroom shared by two social studies teachers, Mr. Anderson and Mrs. Clark. Mr. Anderson, who was never told of his colleague's request, complains to the head custodian that his room is not being cleaned properly

   D. In a middle school faculty meeting, language arts teachers become upset when the principal, having informed them that a number of language arts positions will be transferred due to population shifts within the district, cannot cite how many teachers and which schools will be affected

5. **An article appears in the local newspaper congratulating the winners of the district PRIDE contests. The small district has only two high schools, thus winners in the four content areas are selected from the combined senior classes. Because three of the winners attend the same school, the reporter makes a biased statement concerning the lack of qualified candidates from the second school. How should the principals of these schools react?**

   A. Ignore the comment, assuming that the readers in the community will realize the fallacy of the statement

   B. Call the reporter and ask for clarification and rectification of the printed comment

   C. Collaboratively pen a letter to the editor, which explains the selections in the correct light

   D. Use the comment as a positive device to fire school rivalry

6. Your district is considering implementing block scheduling in each of its high schools. As principal of one of these schools and a strong advocate of block scheduling, your best approach to involving the faculty in the decision making process is to

   A. Present only the advantage of block scheduling

   B. Present and invalidate all objections to block scheduling

   C. Present advantages and objections, relating each to the school's vision

   D. Present the school board position as inevitable and seek best methods of implementing block scheduling at your school site

7. The first step in using good group persuasive techniques is to

   A. Plan an in-depth report of facts and statistics to support your argument

   B. Analyze the biases, emotions, and interests of the group to be addressed

   C. Make an impassioned, emotional appeal

   D. Solicit listener opinion before stating your objective

8. A report in a regional television exposé cites your school as having a large percentage of students who engage in recreational drinking of alcoholic beverages. When parents call for action, the principal's best course of action is

   A. Refuting the statistics in a letter to the editor

   B. Scheduling an assembly to inform students of the dangers of alcohol

   C. Asking parents, students, and teachers to develop a plan of action and informing the press of the plan

   D. Making no response

9. The appropriate administrator completes the master plan of teaching assignments for the coming school year in time to notify teachers of their assignments before the end of the current school year. This step will increase teacher morale

   A. If the plan is published so they can make lesson planning adjustments during the summer

   B. If its purpose is to solicit feedback in order to make changes satisfactory to the majority of teachers

   C. Even if last minute changes have to be made before school opens

   D. Because they know that the administration is acting in good faith

10. The discipline dean of your middle school reports that a beginning teacher sends students daily for minor infractions, such as not having their pencils or notebooks. As principal your best approach to the dean's complaint should be

   A. To reiterate in a general faculty meeting the reasons for sending students to the dean

   B. To make impromptu visits to the teacher's classes to explain the importance of class preparedness to the students

   C. To ask the dean to inform the teacher that he will accept no more referrals from her for a specified period of time

   D. To ask a peer teacher to discuss effective classroom management procedures with the teacher

11. You are a new principal in a school where 95% of the faculty has been on staff during your previous five-year tenure as assistant principal at the same site. Grapevine says that during faculty meetings you speak in half sentences and frequently make reference to events and situations with which only long-time teachers are familiar. You should

    A. Bring a larger group into your inner circle

    B. Allow teachers to ask clarification questions

    C. Continue to seek grapevine feedback

    D. Speak to teachers about their problems decoding your presentations

12. Your high school's drama academy has just won first place honors at the State Thespian Festival. Which of these actions would best serve to promote the performing arts program's image to the community?

    A. Invite reporters from local newspaper, radio, and television to a news conference

    B. Write an article for a nationally recognized education journal

    C. Schedule an "open to the public" evening at which students present their winning vignettes

    D. Post the news on the activities sign board in front of the school

13. A third grade teacher approaches the principal in the hall with a complaint about student behavior at recess. The most appropriate response for the principal is

    A. Listening carefully and reacting only when the teacher has completed her complaint.

    B. Reacting to each point as it is made

    C. Asking the teacher to schedule a meeting where you can discuss the matter at length

    D. Immediately suggesting that the teacher pursue the matter with other members of her grade-level team

14. Which of the following would be the best means of analyzing community attitude toward the district's adopting a stricter grading scale than required by the state?

    A. The end-of-year school improvement survey

    B. Meetings with small groups of parent volunteers

    C. A presentation at a school board meeting

    D. An interview on a local radio station with responses to called-in questions

15. In the acting phase of the communication process, which of the following is not a proper receiver behavior?

    A. Storing the message for later processing

    B. Ignoring the message

    C. Reacting to the message

    D. Transmitting the message

16. You are principal of a rural high school with limited parking space. The previous principal allowed all students in the senior class to drive to school and to park on a first-come, first-served basis. Faculty members were given no priority parking privileges. During the first semester, teachers complained of finding no spaces available in the morning. In addition, several accidents have been caused by students hurrying to school in the morning. You decide to assign faculty spaces and to limit student drivers to seniors with at least a C average. Student government leaders accuse you of arbitrary decision making. You should

A. Be courteous in listening to their arguments and agree to reconsider if they can propose a better solution

B. Allow them to voice their objections but stand by your decision, citing the reasons for the decision

C. Ask them to submit their arguments in writing for review

D. Tell them that you will take the matter under advisement for the subsequent school year

17. At a district principals' meeting, two elementary school principals are overheard denigrating a teacher who had not received continuing contract at the end of his first three years. These principals are exhibiting a lack of

A. A sense of humor

B. Organizational sensitivity

C. Clinical supervision skills

D. Facilitative leadership

18. Which of the following receiver behaviors is least likely to block accurate decoding of a message?

A. A feeling of anxiety that the message will have negative implications for the receiver's work environment

B. Distrust of the sender's motives

C. Decoding from a judgmental point of view

D. The need to ask for frequent clarification

19. You are a high school assistant principal charged with the responsibility for dealing with personnel problems. Students in a physics class complain that the teacher employs teaching strategies and evaluation procedures that make it impossible for any student to earn an A in his class. After checking student records and consulting with the science department chair, you determine that the students have a legitimate concern. Your best approach in dealing with the teacher is to

A. Stress the negative effects that his grading policy will have on the grade point averages of the abler students in his class

B. Encourage the teacher to do a self-evaluation of his teaching methods and to propose solutions to help students achieve greater success

C. Recommend procedures for the teacher to adopt if he intends to remain on staff

D. Schedule a classroom evaluation and give a copy of the results to the teacher as well as filing it in his permanent record

20. The superintendent of schools has asked you, principal of a new middle school, to write an article for the monthly district newsletter to parents concerning the rationale for redistricting to balance middle school populations. Which of the following problems with clear written expression would contribute most to improper decoding of your explanation?

A. Use of undefined educational jargon

B. Excessive mechanical errors

C. An inconsistent point of view

D. A lack of balance between simple and complex sentences

21. Given an hour to write a response to a prompt, what is the maximum time that should be spent in prewriting?

A. Five minutes

B. Fifteen minutes

C. Ten minutes

D. Twenty minutes

22. **The inverted essay introduction requires placing the statement of the main idea (thesis)**

    A. At the beginning of the first paragraph

    B. At the middle of the first paragraph

    C. At the end of the first paragraph

    D. In the second paragraph

23. **A prewriting technique for using a visual organizer where main ideas with supporting details are arranged around the topic statement is**

    A. Brainstorming

    B. Comparing

    C. Analysis

    D. Clustering

24. **You are a curriculum coordinator who has been asked to write an article for the school newspaper identifying the relationship between the International Baccalaureate Program and the Advanced Placement program. As you evaluate the assignment, which of the following purposes of writing would be the most appropriate approach?**

    A. Comparison

    B. Discussion

    C. Analysis

    D. Explanation

25. **The most important factors in the effectiveness of a communication source include**

    A. Credibility, pleasing personality, use of statistics

    B. Credibility, composure, expertise

    C. Expertise, tenure, voice quality

    D. Pleasing personality, voice quality, composure

Part II

The following poses a possible test prompt for an essay, examines the prewriting process, provides an example of a mediocre response that might receive a low score, and provides another example of a response more likely to receive a higher score.

Prompt

You are the principal of an elementary school, which has just been redesigned as a magnet school in the performing arts. You have the responsibility of notifying parents of the criteria for student entrance, the time line for admission, and the alternatives for attendance at other schools in the district. This notification will appear in the form of a letter to be mailed to all parents of students currently attending your school.

Prewriting

1. Understanding the question. This prompt expects you to provide information through discussion, not to explain, compare, or analyze. You are not asked to explain why this action will be taken. That decision has already been made. You are expected to discuss its implementation. Because the audience is all parents and the message is a serious one, you need to use lay language and a formal tone. Neither are you expected to explain your credentials—they are a given since you are to remain principal of the school. Remember it is important in step 1 to rule out inappropriate methods of delivery in order to decide which method is preferable.

2. As you plan your essay, determine your main idea, then select an organizational pattern that will best present this idea. In this case, since you are giving information, a clustering approach would be best.

3. Complete the prewriting exercise. (See the cluster on the next page.)

4. Write the thesis statement. Actually, the prompt has provided you with the three main points that need to be covered in the letter. Thus, your thesis statement might read, "Parents are being given an opportunity to review the criteria for attendance at the Charles Griffin School of the Performing Arts in order to make a timely decision about placement of their children in the 1999-2000 school year." This sentence encompasses the main idea as well as establishing a tone that implies collaborative decision making based on predetermined standards.

5. Prepare an organizational chart in paragraph order of the main points and the supporting details. This may be done on the cluster page if time is a premium.

VISUAL ORGANIZER: GIVING INFORMATION

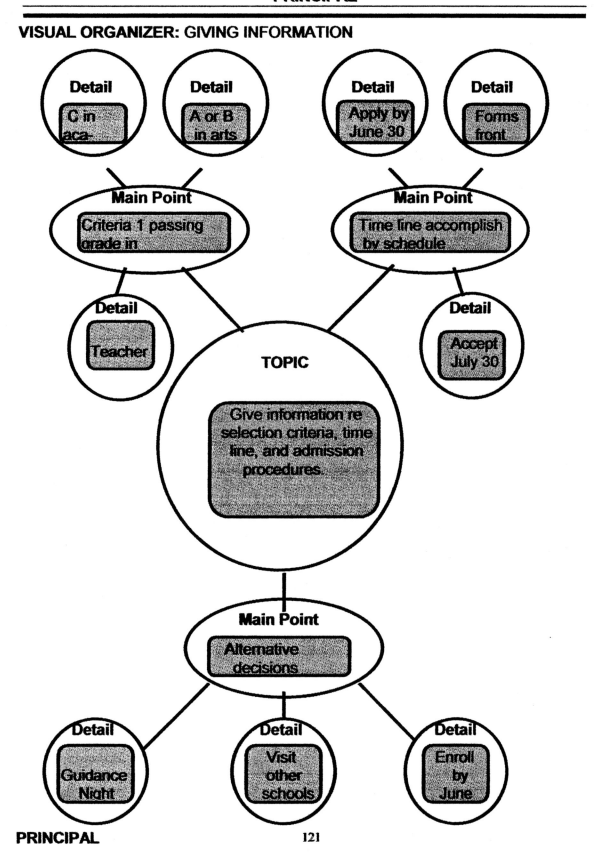

Writing

6. Write the introduction to the essay. Consider using the inverted triangle format, opening with a broad statement that introduces the topic in a general way and also captures the reader's interest. You might begin, "Current research indicates that students who learn by performing develop into creative, successful adults. The earlier these talents can be explored and expanded, the more likely the student will apply himself/herself to all areas of learning."

7. Write the body paragraphs. (Note the development in the second letter.)

8. Write the conclusion. Restate the thesis in different words if possible, summarize the main points, and close with a sentence that will stay with the parents as they make their decision.

Editing and proofreading

9. If your prewriting has been thorough and you have followed the organizational chart, little editing will be required. A final read through to correct mechanical errors should be all that is necessary. Remember if you decide to change words or phrases, cross out the deletions and write the corrections clearly above the cross out.

Essay 1

Charles Griffin School of the Performing Arts
300 Hazelton Road
Griffin AN 00000

Dear Parent:

On February 8, 1998, a group of parents, teachers, and administrators met to finalize plans for our new magnet school. Now, we are letting you know the results of these plans and how you can decide whether to have your son or daughter remain at Griffin or choose one of the other schools to attend in the fall.

We will have a Guidance Night on June 15 to give parents the chance to ask questions, review the programs at other schools, and meet the principles. Application forms for admission to Griffin or transfer to other schools are available in the front office and will be also passed out on Guidance Night.

Forms must be submitted by June 30 and student placements will be completed by July 30.

In order remain at Griffin, students must have a cumulative average of C in all academic subject and a B or better in related arts courses. Borderline students will be admitted with techer recommendation. If parents do not indicate prefrences by June 30, students will be assigned for the 1999-2000 school year and parents will be notified in a mailing on July 30.

We look forward to answering your questions. Please be prompt in making your decision. We are looking forward to seeing many of our current students back next year. We feel that there is a lot of talent at Griffin and except a positive response to the new format.

Sincerely

Walt Jumble, Principle

*Note the principal's name. I selected it because that is how this essay was written. It appears that the writer did all planning in his head and just hauled the details out in helter-skelter fashion. Also, the tone is condescending; it's almost as though parents' concerns are being given lip service. Word choice such as "borderline" is insulting; many sentences are run-on or simply too long; spelling is deplorable. (Do you know how hard it is to write a letter with so many errors?)

Essay 2

Charles Griffin School of the Performing Arts
300 Hazelton Road
Griffin AN 00000

Dear Parent:

Current research indicates that students who learn by performing develop into creative, successful adults. The earlier these talents can be explored and expanded, the more likely the student will apply himself/herself to all areas of learning. During this school year, a committee of administrators, teachers, and parents studied the research on elementary schools of the performing arts. After much debate and input from many other individuals in the school and community, it was decided to restructure Griffin as a magnet school. All parents are now being given an opportunity to review the criteria for attendance at the Charles Griffin School of the Performing Arts in order to make a timely decision about placement of their children in the 1999-2000 school year.

Though we welcome all students currently at Griffin to apply for the magnet school, certain criteria for attendance had to be established. First, the applicant must have a C average in his academic subjects and an A or B in one of the related arts—vocal music, instrumental music, or art. Drama will be included in the new program. A written teacher recommendation will be required to indicate the child's aptitude for dramatic performance.

Parents on the committee selected the following time line for applying and being accepted:

June 15-30   Exploration and Application
June 30   Application Deadline
July 30   Notification to Parents of Acceptance

On June 15, we will kick off our orientation by having a Guidance Night. Teachers, counselors and principals from all schools will be present to answer questions and help parents with application forms. Parents may schedule school visitations at this time. These visits will be offered for every day or evening in the last two weeks of June. We want you to have every opportunity to make the best decision for your child. You may decide to submit an application of admission to Griffin or transfer to one of the other schools. Completed applications may be brought to the school office or mailed to the school addresses provided on the application forms.

We know there are many students in our district who can benefit from attending a school that provides them with outlets for their artistic talents. We hope parents will carefully review the grade criteria and speak with teachers about recommendations. Please take the opportunity to attend our orientation or let us know if you cannot be there on the 15th. We will be happy to arrange another time to answer your questions. Help with admission forms is available every day in the school's front office. We hope to see many of Griffin students back in the fall and we look forward to seeing many new faces as well. Help us make the Griffin School of the Performing Arts a model for elementary schools in our district. Who knows where this may lead— a science and technology magnet, an agriculture magnet? The possibilities are many.

Sincerely,

Margaret Marvel, Principal

Answer Key (Subtest 2 – School Communications)
Part I

1. B
2. C
3. A
4. D
5. C

6. C
7. B
8. C
9. B
10. D

11. B
12. C
13. A
14. D
15. B

16. B
17. B
18. D
19. B
20. A

21. B
22. C
23. D
24. A
25. B

Bibliography

Armistead, Lew. (1984) "Communicating the Program." *Instructional Leadership Handbook*. Eds. James W. Keefe and John M. Jenkins. Reston, Virginia: National Association of Secondary School Principals, pp.80-81.

Chruden, Herbert J. and Arthur W. Sherman Jr. (1984) *Managing Human Resources* 7th ed. Cincinnati, Ohio: South-Western Publishing Company.

Guthrie, James W. and Rodney J. Reed. (1991) *Educational Administration and Policy: Effective Leadership for American Education*. 2nd ed. Boston: Allyn and Bacon, pp. 353-370.

Harrison, Bernard T. "Managing to Make Things Happen: Critical Issues in Team Management." *Vision and Values in Managing Education*. London: David Fulton Publishers, pp.44-59.

Hoyle, John R.; Fenwick English; and Betty Steffy (1985) *Skills for Successful School Leaders*. Arlington, Virginia: American Association of School Administrators, pp. 42-54.

Irnsher, Karen. "Communication Skills." ERIC Digest, January 1996.

Kimbrough, Ralph B. and Michael Y. Nunnery. (1988) *Educational Administration*. New York: Macmillan Publishing Company, pp.365-371.

Lashway, Larry. "Facilitative Leadership." ERIC Digest, April 1995.

Lovell, John T. and Kimball Wiles. (1983) *Supervision for Better Schools* 5th ed. Englewood Cliffs, New Jersey: Prentice-Hall, pp. 89-113.

Lunenburg, Fred C. and Allan C. Ornstein (1991) *Educational Administration*. Belmont, California: Wadsworth Publishing Company, pp.184-209.

Marks, James; Emery Stoops; and Joyce King-Stoops (1985) *Handbook of Educational Supervision* 3rd ed. Boston: Allyn and Bacon, pp.73-95.

Subtest 3 - School Operations

5. Curriculum

Curriculum provides you with foundations, principles,
issues in curriculum planning and design including
theory, structure, content implementation and evaluation.

COMPETENCY A: Demonstrates knowledge of the principles of curriculum
development.

Skill 1: Specifies data sources for selection of curriculum

Skill 2: Identifies school objectives based on data sources

Skill 3: Identifies screening criteria for curriculum selection.

Skill 4: Identifies functions and utilities served by school curriculum.

The school curriculum is an action plan to educate children. As such, it is influenced
by many different forces to affect change. The aims and goals that shape education
are generated from nationwide commissions and task forces comprised of educators,
and other influential citizens, including politicians. One example is the efforts to
affect change by the 1938 Nation-At-Risk Report in which the Commission on
Excellent in Education reported its findings on the quality of education in America and
made specific recommendations. Another example is the effort made between
President Bush and the governors of the states with the Goals 2000 effort, which
emerged in 1990.

At the local level, task forces of parents, educators, and community groups impact
school curriculum changes in similar ways as do nationwide groups. Data sources
to affect change at the local level sometimes include attitudinal surveys of the
students, parent groups, teachers, and other community groups. Other **data
sources for curriculum selection** include direct student information, such as
interviews and conferences which yield information related to disposition for learning,
likes and dislikes, as well as difficulties experienced by students, because of the
design of the curriculum or other related situations. Additionally, anecdotal records
held by teachers and the contents of the cumulative folder, such as testing results
and report cards, may contribute to the development of profiles of students to aide in
the decision-making process regarding curriculum selection.

Research findings about curriculum principles and design, as well as content organization are also valuable information for decision-making.

Sources curriculum selection reflect the expectations of society and they directly impact the objectives for learning. For example, Goal Four (4) of Goals 2000 states: " By the year 2000, U.S. students will be first in the world in science and mathematics achievement." The expectations of this societal goal affected the curriculum in every state, district, and school. Even if this goal is lofty and may not be fully attained, it has affected the selection and content of the local curriculum. The Commission for Goals 2000 uncovered the deplorable state of our students in math and science and by disclosing these conditions, parent, teachers, and community groups endorsed these goals as a way of improving education. As a result, they influenced a chain of reaction so that objectives would be identified at the lowest levels to change the outcomes in these subject areas. As a result, goals of the discipline were clearly written and became the driving force of curriculum change. Society is also concerned with producing citizens who are prepared to transmit the ideals of a democratic society. Therefore, the school as a societal institution must include in its teaching and learning process objectives that will produce desirable learner outcomes.

Curriculum selection must also take into account the contribution from the field of psychology, which is responsible for the major theories of learning. Learning theories serve as the foundation for methods of teaching, materials for learning, and activities that are age and developmentally appropriate for learning while providing the impetus for curriculum selection. Major theories of learning include the behaviorism, cognitive development and phenomenology or humanistic psychology.

Behaviorism represents traditional psychology that emphasizes conditioning the behavior of the learner and altering the environment to obtain specific responses. As the oldest theories of learning, behaviorism focuses specifically on stimulus response and reinforcement for learning. The work experiments of Thorndike led to the development of **connectionism theories** from which came the laws of learning.

Law of Readiness: when the conduction is ready to conduct, satisfaction is obtained and, if readiness is not present, it results in dissatisfaction.

Law of Exercise: a connection is strengthened based on the proportion to the number of times it occurs, its duration and intensity.

Law of Effect: responses accompanied by satisfaction strengthens the connection while responses accompanied by dissatisfaction weakens the connection.

These laws also influenced the curriculum contributions of Ralph Tyler, Hilda Taba, and Jerome Brunner who discarded the view of specific stimuli and responses to endorse broader views of learning. For example, Taba recognized that practice alone does not transfer learning; therefore, rote learning and memorization should not be emphasized.

Jerome Bruner, on the other hand, contributed the notion that learning the structure provides a better basis for transferring learning than rote memorization. **Classical conditioning theories** of learning emphasized the elicit response aspect of learning through adequate stimuli. The experiments of Pavlov and Watson (the dog learned to salivate at the sound of the bell at which time food was presented simultaneously as a stimulus) gave the notion that the learner could be conditioned for learning and thus be trained to become educated in any profession. **Operant conditioning theories or behavioral theories** promoted by B. Frederick Skinner which emphasizes positive and negative reinforcers to operant behaviors *(operant: no stimuli explains the response)* by either providing or withdrawing the stimuli or providing new operants. Behavioral theories gave birth to behavior modification approaches to discipline and learning. Albert Bandura's theory of **Observational Learning and Modeling** focuses on children learning through modeling the behaviors of others. This theory contributed the notion that children's behavior are shaped through observation of the behaviors of others which are interned modeled by the observer. **Hierarchical Learning Theories** represented by Robert Gagne organize types of learning in a classical model of hierarchy encompassing intellectual skills, information, cognitive strategies, motor skills, and attitudes learned through positive experiences.

Cognitive development theories focus on human growth and development in terms of cognitive, social, psychological, and physical development even though learning in school settings is cognitive in nature. The **Developmental Theories** of Jean Piaget is based on the supposition that growth and development take place in stages. Piaget identified four stages of development including the sensory stage (birth to age two) in which the child the child manipulates the physical surroundings; the pre-operational stage (ages 2-7) in which complex learning takes place through experiences; concrete operation stage (age 7-11) in which the child organizes information in logical forms using concrete objects; and the formal operation stage (age 11 and above) in which the child can perform formal and abstract operations.

Phenomenology or Humanistic psychology, while not widely recognized as a school of psychology, is recognized by many observers as a third grouping because it emphasizes the total organism of a person during the learning process rather than separating learning into the domains of behavior and cognition. Psychology rejects this school because of the belief that psychology in-and-of-itself is humanistic in nature. Therefore, there is no need for such school. The Gestalt psychology is representative of phenomenology and humanistic psychology. It represents wholeness as recognized in Maslow's Hierarchy of needs in which the end-product is a wholesome, happy and healthy child/person who has self-actualized and is fulfilled.

The school curriculum should satisfy societal needs and specific goals to produce an individual who has the social, intellectual, moral, emotional and civic development to function as an integral part of our democratic society. However, selecting the best curriculum to meet all of these needs is not an easy task. It should be a collaborative effort. A response to why program changes are necessary should be given through a clear rationale that examines the existing district and school goals. Clarification is needed pertaining to subject structure and content, and also the needs of the students regarding ability, performance, level of success and needed strategies. Consider the motivation of students and instructional staff, feasibility of time and resources, curriculum balance in terms of concepts, skills, and application.

COMPETENCY B: Demonstrates ability to identify and organize resources to achieve curricular and instructional goals.

> **Skill 1:** Identifies materials, facilities, and human resources available for structuring school programs.

> **Skill 2:** Identifies organizational patterns appropriate for horizontal and vertical planning.

> **Skill 3:** Identifies different patterns of content organizing.

The design of the curriculum accounts for the manner in which the elements of the curriculum are organized. The design must account for the nature and organization of the aims, goals, and objectives, as well as the subject matter, learning activities, and the evaluation. **Curriculum design** precedes instructional design. It is the phase concerned with the nature of the component parts, which is influenced by various philosophies, theories, and practical issues. The designer must specify the nature of each of the elements included in the design to develop a blueprint before initiating the process of implementation. The goals and objectives should be specific so that all those involved will clearly understand what will be done and what behaviors are expected of the learner. The next step is to identify the resources needed to attain the preset goals and objectives for the curriculum. All material and human resources deemed necessary must be identified and secured. Materials include textbooks, charts, maps, and other technology and equipment, such as projectors, computers, calculators, sport equipment, and microscopes. Human resources include administrators, teachers, volunteers, support staff, and others. Facilities are classrooms, gym, athletic fields, cafeteria, auditorium, and others. The subject matter, methods of organization, and activities, as well as the methods and instruments to evaluate the program, must be determined.

The **conceptual framework** or the **organization of the components of the curriculum** consists of two distinct organizational dimensions, which include horizontal and vertical organization. **Horizontal organization** is a typical side-by side course arrangement where the content of one subject is made relative to the concepts of another related subject. **Vertical organization** is concerned with longitudinal treatment of concepts within a subject across grade levels. The success of the horizontal organization depends heavily on the collaboration of teachers of various disciplines at the grade level, while the vertical organization depends heavily on collaboration and planning among teachers of various grade levels.

The **dimensions within the curriculum content** are also of important consideration in curriculum design.   Therefore, attention should be given to curriculum scope, sequence, integration, continuity, articulation and balance. **Curriculum scope** refers to the breadth and depth of the curriculum content at any grade level in terms of the content, learning activities and experiences, and topics. **Curriculum sequence** refers to the order of topics to be studied over time in a vertical dimension.   The sequencing of the curriculum is usually organized from simple to complex learning, but it can also emphasize chronological learning, whole to part learning, or prerequisite learning.   **Curriculum integration** refers to the linking of the concepts, skills, and experiences in the subjects taught. **Curriculum continuity** deals with the spiral or vertical smoothness of knowledge repetition from one grade level to another in specific subjects or areas of study.   **Curriculum articulation** refers to the interrelationship within and among subjects both vertically and horizontally. **Curriculum balance** refers to the opportunities offered for the learners to master knowledge and apply it in their personal, social, intellectual life pursuits.

Curriculum content can be based on subject centered designs which includes, subject design, discipline design, broad fields design, and process designs. The **subject design** corresponds with the specialists concept held by many teacher training programs.   It reflects the mental discipline approach to learning. The curriculum is organized according to essential knowledge that must be learned in the different subject matters.   The **discipline design** is based on the organization of content, which allows for in-depth understanding of the content and the application of meaning. It is used primarily in secondary schools to emphasize the organizational content inherent to the academic discipline such as science, math, English, etc. so that the students in science, for example, would approach science like a scientist would. Therefore, the emphasis becomes experiencing the discipline as learning takes place. In the **broad fields design,** unlike the subject field where a subject is studied separately from other subjects that are related, related subjects are broadened into categories, such as social studies encompassing history, geography, and civics or physical science encompassing physics and chemistry.   The intent of the broad field design is to integrate the traditional subjects so that the learner develops a broader understanding of the areas included.

The **process centered design** addresses how students learn and apply the process to the subject matter. This design focuses on the student thinking process and incorporates procedures and processes for children to advance knowledge.

COMPETENCY C: Demonstrates the ability to employ principles of implementing the curriculum by establishing goals and motivating staff.

> **Skill 1:** Demonstrates the knowledge of when and how to disseminate information about a curriculum component to appropriate audiences.

> **Skill 2:** Identifies appropriate strategies for curriculum planning based upon needs assessment data.

> **Skill 3:** States clear goals and establishes an agenda of specific actions for Implementation.

Successful curriculum implementation is highly dependent on careful planning. Yet communication during the implementation process is pivotal, especially when the new curriculum will upset the status quo. The channels of communication must always be open so that frequent discussions and exchange is ongoing at all levels and across groups. **Effective communication** requires high quality exchange through two-way channels within a defined network. While the formal network remains the official way of communicating in organizations, the informal network should not be ignored or discouraged because it can be shaped into a very healthy system of communication between members of the organization.

School restructuring calls for communication models other than the traditional top-down model. Curriculum implementation requires that administrators and support personnel not only understand the curriculum but provide support to the classroom so that needs can be met. Therefore, the communication model must be responsive to the needs of all involved. **Effective lateral communication** allows information flow among all participants at varying levels of involvement in the curriculum while valuing their contribution and promoting involvement through the process of **networking**. Lateral communication is usually formal within the organization, yet the informal channels tend to be lateral as well. Informal lateral communication might be a small group of teachers deciding amongst themselves to get together and share ideas from an article that could be useful with certain children in their classroom or it could be the development of a simulation project for the grade level. Formal lateral communication massages may be written and disseminated in a systematic mode through newsletters, bulletin, memos, reports, and the like. Formal lateral communication may also be verbal and communicated through speeches, lectures, oral reports where body language, tone of voice and other physical expressions can enhance the message being communicated.

The mode of communication should be adjusted to meet the needs of the audience. Workshops, bulletins, lectures, and other written and oral reports are all appropriate formats for disseminating program information, but while each approach serves a definite purpose they must be adjusted to meet the needs of their intended audiences. The approach used with teachers may generally be in-service training on procedures and methodology for curriculum implementation where well define educational terms are used and specific strategies are developed or practiced. Conversely, a presentation for parents, community groups and other lay individuals should be free of educational jargon and adjusted to their educational levels and school experiences. Whatever the mode or approaches to communication, a steady flow of information exchange at every stage of program implementation is necessary.

A needs assessment is always the initial step in program planning. It provides the opportunity to survey and identify the context in which the program will be developed. The needs assessment survey should focus primarily on the needs of the students so that the achievement problems can be identified and goals can be written for the initial planning stage and specific objectives instruction can be formulated.

Identifying the educational goals and setting priorities before developing the curriculum are essential aspects of planning. Additionally, setting and prioritizing the goals must be carefully inked to the performance of the learner. The design of the curriculum follows with the careful selection and recommendation of instructional materials and equipment, as well as methods to attain the pre-established goals and objectives. The steps following include the actual organization of the personnel involved, the implementation of a plan to supervise and give direction and focus to the project. Finally, the product planning and implementation at the classroom level are followed by the evaluation process, which determines the effectiveness and attainment of the goals and objectives of the curriculum.

Data gathering in any assessment process is pivotal to give meaning to what is being measured. Ornstein and Huskins (1993) identify five distinct phases for gathering data to assess program effectiveness. These include the curriculum phenomena to be evaluated, the stage of collecting information, the stage of organizing the information, which is followed by analyzing the information, and finally the state of reporting and recycling the information. **The curriculum phenomena to be evaluated** is the phase in which the evaluator determines the design of the evaluation which includes exactly what will be evaluated. The evaluators will determine if the entire school will be included or just selected grade levels or subject areas. Whatever is decided at this stage must include a clear delineation of the relationship between the variables. This includes establishing a clear relationship between the objectives, the constraints of the learning activities and the expected outcomes.

Collecting information is the phase where the evaluator must identify the sources of the information to be collected which is based on the designed established in the previous phase. At this juncture, the evaluator must develop a plan to actually collect hard data from various sources including parents, teachers, staff, students, and other members of the school community. **Organizing the information** leads the evaluator to arrange the data so that it is usable. This includes coding and storing the data into a system where it can be retrieved for analyzes. The phase of **analyzing the information** leads to the use of selected techniques based on the design of the evaluative process. From the onset of the process, beginning with the identification of the curriculum phenomena, the evaluator identifies the specific data analyzes or statistical approaches that are suitable for the information collected. **Reporting the information** leads the evaluator to a number of important decisions related to the level of formality of reporting to meet the needs of the various audiences. While it does not negate the use of statistical analysis, it does call for making a judgement on how to best convey appropriate meaning and make recommendations for use. Finally, **recycling the information** obtained gives meaning to the notion that evaluation is a continuous process. The implication is that the information received from this process will provide feedback for program modification and adjustment which will leads to continuous change in an organization that is continuously changing.

The implementation process must be strategically planned with benchmarks to determine specific levels of program goal attainment leading to the reexamination of the strategies being used for specific learning outcomes. When placed on a time line, the benchmarks may also serve as pointers for communicating with the various audiences. Feedback from the various audiences must be used to determine the extent to which the curriculum goals and expected outcomes, content and implementation strategies, as well as outcome measures, are clearly understood. The plan will supply the agenda items which will be acted upon in a timely manner and hence drive the implementation process as well as the dissemination process.

In the process of educational program evaluation or classroom instructional evaluation, outcomes are reflected in terms of aims, goals, and objectives. **Aims** are general statements that reflect value judgements that give overall direction of the curriculum. They guide the educational process to achieve future behavioral outcomes. Aims are the results of societal concerns, which usually are expressed through national commissions and task forces. **Goals** are more specific than aims. Even though goals may be written in a general manner similar to aims, aims become goals when the statement of purpose reflects specificity to particular areas of the curriculum. Objectives are the most specific statements of expected learner outcomes. Examples of goals are expressed in the 1990 national Goals 2000. Goal one states "By the year 2000 all children in America will start school ready to learn. Goal two states "By the year 2000 the high school graduation rate will increase."

As observed, these goal statements are very general and they do not include specific behaviors or terms for the behavior. Objectives are generally expressed in behavioral terms, which are measurable. Non-behavioral objectives, on the other hand, are generally used to express higher order learning suggesting non-quantifiable measurement, such as appreciation, understanding, and the like. In most schools, behavioral objectives are preferred to non-behavioral objectives. **Behavioral objectives** state what is expected of the student at the conclusion of the unit or lesson. They state the terms for the behavior and the minimum expectancy. An example of a well-written behavioral objective follows: after completing the unit on telling time, the students will be able to complete 25 problems with 80% accuracy within a thirty minute time span.

From the onset of the program, the goals and objectives are vital. It is through the goals and objectives that the identified problems are addressed. Goals and objectives should be clearly written and examined to make sure that they represent what is expected to be attained. This must be a process that involves not only faculty, but also parents, students, staff, and other members of the school community to provide buy-in and obtain ownership in the attainment of the goals and objectives set by the team. Objectives should be written in measurable terms. With objectives being more specific, special attention must be given to the behavior to be measured and the situation in which the performance will take place and the criterion for the performance. For example, students will be able to solve multiplication word problems (behavior) at the rate of one problem per minute (situation) with 80% accuracy (condition). Objectives can be written to give directions at various program levels including grade levels or subject levels. (See also section D for more information on goals and objectives).

COMPETENCY D: Demonstrates an understanding of the methods and principles of program evaluation.

> **Skill 1:** Demonstrates a basic understanding of common program evaluation and testing terminology.

> **Skill 2:** Identifies appropriate and measurable goals for a specific curriculum or program.

> **Skill 3:** Demonstrates a basic understanding of common methods used for data collection in program evaluation.

The evaluation of students is a very important aspect of the teaching and learning process. Periodic testing assesses learning outcomes based on the objectives established for learning and it provides information at various stages in the learning process to determine future learning needs such as periodic reviews, re-teaching, and enrichment. As the end process, the evaluation of students' performance measures the level of goal attainment, which is operationalized through the learning activities planned by the teacher. At varying stages of the teaching and learning process, the intended outcome must be measured and the level of goal attainment is established in order to proceed with this continuous cycle of student evaluation.

Evaluation and measurement are often used interchangeably to imply the same process. However, while closely related, they should be differentiated. **Evaluation** is identified as the process of making judgements regarding student performance and **measurement** is the actual data collection that is used to make judgements of student performance. Evaluation is related to student performance when the focus is on how well a student carries out a given task is measured or when a student work or product is the focus of the measurement.

The purpose of the student evaluation will determine the type of process to use. Diagnostic evaluation, formative, and summative evaluations are the three types of student evaluations most commonly used. **Diagnostic evaluation** is provided prior to instruction to identify problems, to place students in certain groups, and to make assignments that are appropriate to their needs. While it is important to address the specific needs of students, teachers must be cautious of the ramifications of grouping children in homogeneous groups versus heterogeneous groupings. It may appear time effective to group and work with children of like situations, yet often it fails to foster students' intellectual and social growth and development. In fact, it has been proven that children in mixed groups benefit from the diversity within the group. **Formative evaluation** is used to obtain feedback during the instructional process. It informs teachers of the extent to which students are really learning the concepts and skills being taught. The information obtained through the formative process should lead to modification in the teaching and learning process to address specific needs of the students before arriving at the end of the unit. Formative evaluation is designed to promote learning. Therefore, it must be done frequently using the specific objectives stated for learning outcomes. **Summative evaluation** is used to culminate a unit or series of lessons to arrive at a grade. It is the sum of all the accomplishments of the student over a specified period of learning. Knowing the content studied and having the specific skills required to score well on tests are two different endeavors which require not only learning content, but also following form. Therefore, It is also the responsibility of teachers to train the students in test taking skills with regard to following directions, managing time effectively, and giving special attention to the type of tests and the skills required.

Regardless of the type of assessment, educators must gather and analyze the information they yield to determine problem areas. The problem areas uncovered should be discussed with the students collectively and individually and also be presented as items for discussion at teacher conferences with parents. Whether diagnostic, formative or summative, the evaluation of student performance should be a continuous process.

The accuracy of student evaluation is essential. The accuracy is related to consistency of measurement, which is observed through reliability and validity of the instruments used to measure student performance as well as usability of the instrument.

Validity is the extent to which a test measures what it is intended to measure. For example, a test may lack validity if it was designed to measure the creative writing of students, but it is also used to measure handwriting even though it was not designed for the latter.

Reliability refers to the consistency of the test to measure what it should measure. For example, the items on a true or false quiz, given by a classroom teacher, are reliable if they convey the same meaning every time the quiz is administered to similar groups of students under similar situations. In other words, there is no ambiguity or confusion with the items on the quiz.

Usability is another factor in the evaluation process, which refers to practical considerations such as scoring procedures, level of difficulty, and time to administer the test. The usability of a test will be questionable if the scoring procedures had to be changed to accommodate local financial circumstances or if the allotted time for the test had to be reduced because of other circumstances.

With the purpose of assessment instruments being one of data gathering, it is important to use various forms of information gathering tools to assess the knowledge and progress of students. **Standardized Achievement Tests** have become popular in education and perhaps overused in the past few years. The reliance on standardized achievement tests to provide information for accountability to the public has driven many teachers to teach to the test and embrace more objective formats of teaching and learning. Although these tests are very limited in what they measure, too often they are used to make major decisions for which they are not designed. Standardized achievement measurements can be **norm-referenced or criterion-reference.** In norm-referenced measurements the performance of the student is compared with the performance of other students who also took the same test. The original group of students who took the test establishes the norm. Norms can be based on age, sex, grade level, geographical location, ethnicity, or other broad combination of classifications.

Standardized norm-referenced achievement tests are designed to measure what a student knows in a particular subject in relation to other students of similar characteristics. The test batteries provide a broad scope of content areas coverage so that it may be used on a larger scale in many different states and school districts. However, they do not measure the goals and content emphasized in a particular local curricula. Therefore, using standardized tests to assess the success of the curriculum or teachers' effectiveness should be avoided (McMillan 1997).

Norm-reference standardized achievement tests produce different types of scores that are useful in different ways. The most common types of scores are the percentile rank or **percentile score, grade equivalent score, stanine, and percentage of items answered correctly**. The **percentile score** indicates how the students' performance compares to the norming group. It tells us that the percentage of the norming group was outscored by a particular student taking the test. For example, a student scoring at the eightieth percentile did better than 80% of the students in the norming group. Likewise, 20% of the norming group scored above the particular student and 80% scored below. The scores are indicative of relative strengths and weaknesses. A student may show consistent strengths in language arts and consistent weakness in mathematics as indicated by the scores derived from the test. Yet one could not base remediation solely on these conclusions without a closer item analysis or a closer review of the objectives measured by the test. **The grade equivalent score** is expressed by year and month in school for each student. It is used to measure growth and progress. It indicates where a student stands in reference to the norming group. For example, a second grade student who obtained a grade equivalent score of 4.5 on the language arts section of the test is really not achieving at the fourth grade five month level as one think. The 4.5 grade equivalence means that the second grader has achieved at about the same level of the norming group who is in the fifth month of the fourth grade, if indeed such a student did take the test. However, when compared to other second graders in the norming group, the student is about average.

A point of consideration with grade equivalence is that one may never know how well the second grader might do if placed in the fourth grade or how poorly the second grader might do if given the fourth grade test as compared to other second graders in the norming group.

Another type of standard score for standardized testing is the **stanine**, which indicates where the score is located on the normal curve for the norming group. Stanines are statistically determined but are not as precise as percentile ranking because it only gives the area in which the score is located, but not the precise location. Using stanines to report standard scores is still found to be practical and easy to understand for many parents and school personnel. Stanines range from one to nine (1-9) with five being the middle of the distribution.

Finally, achievement test scores can be reported by **percentage of items answered correctly**. This form of reporting may not be very meaningful when the items in a particular area are few. This makes it difficult to determine if the student guessed well at the items, was just lucky at selecting the right answers, or indeed chose the correct responses.

Criterion-Referenced Standardized Achievement Tests are designed to indicate the student performance that is directly related to specific educational objectives, thus indicating what the student can or cannot do. For example, the test may measure how well a student can subtract by regrouping in the tens place or how well a student can identify the long vowel sound in specific words. Criterion reference tests are specific to a particular curriculum, which allows the determination of the effectiveness of the curriculum, as well as specific skills acquired by the students. They also provide information needed to plan for future student needs. Because of the recognized value of criterion-referenced standardized achievement tests, many publishers have developed tailor-made tests to correlate with state and districts' general goals and specific learning objectives by pulling from a test bank of field-tested items. The test scores are reported by percentage of items answered correctly to indicate mastery or non-mastery.

Aptitude tests are another standardized form of testing that measure the cognitive ability of students. They also measure potential and capacity for learning. While they do not test specific academic ability, the ability level is influenced by the child's experiences in and out of the academic setting. Whether broad in measurement of the child's ability or focused, aptitude tests are used to predict achievement and for advanced placements of students.

Teacher-made tests are also evaluative instruments designed by classroom teachers to measure the attainment of objectives. While they may lack validity, they serve the immediate purpose of measuring instructional outcomes. Teacher-made tests should be constructed to measure specific objectives, but they also take into account the nature of the behavior that is being measured. Among teacher-made tests are multiple choice, essay, quizzes, matching, alternative choices (yes/no, agree, disagree, and the like), and completion (fill in the blanks). Portfolio assessment is fast becoming a leading form of teacher assessment, in which the student and teacher collect sample work in a systematic and organized manner to provide evidence of accomplishments and progress toward attaining specific objectives.

Certainly, testing is very important in the assessment of students' progress, but there are other sources of information that can be used for assessment. For example, conferencing can provide factual information for affective assessment, while the cumulative records of a child may also provide factual information for cognitive and psychomotor assessments. Other information sources may include interviews, diaries, self-assessment, observation, simulations, and other creative forms.

Program effectiveness can only be measured through the process of evaluation. **Program evaluation** is the process of collecting and analyzing data to discover whether the design, development or implementation is producing the desired outcomes. The data gathering and analyses also carry the purpose of making informed decisions about the program. It may lead to changing or eliminating aspects of the program.

The **CIPP** (Content, Input Process Product) model developed by Daniel Sufflebeam is the most used model in program evaluation. In a three-step process, information is provided for decisions, including delineating the information to be collected, obtaining the information, and providing the information to others. These steps must then correspond with four distinct types of evaluation: content, input, process and product evaluations (Onstein and Hunskin 1993). **Content Evaluation** is concerned with the environment of the program in terms of needs and unmet needs. Context evaluation constitutes the diagnostic stage of the evaluative process. It provides baseline information related to the entire system of operation. **Input Evaluation** is concerned with providing information and determining how to utilize resources to attain the goals of the program. It focuses on whether the goals and objectives for the program are appropriate to the expected outcome or if the goals and objectives are stated appropriately. It also takes into account whether the resources to implement specific strategies are adequate, whether or not the strategies are appropriate to attain the goals, or if the time allotted is appropriate to meet the objectives set forth for the program. **Process Evaluation** focuses on decisions regarding curriculum implementation. It is concerned with whether the activities planned are being implemented and with the logistics of the total operation so that procedures are recorded as they occur and monitoring is continuous to identify potential problems.

The continuous process of identifying potential problems leads to decisions to make corrections before or during the implementation of the program. For example, it might be necessary to establish special planning sessions or teacher in-service at specific grade levels to work on modification of some of the strategies established for the program because of problems uncovered. Process evaluation is also known as the piloting process prior to the actual implementation of a school-wide or district-wide program (Ornstein and Hunskin, 1993). Finally, **Product Evaluation** takes into account whether the final product or curriculum is accomplishing the goals or objectives and to what degree.

At this point decisions must be made regarding the continuation, termination or modification of the program. Since the evaluation process is continuous, the evaluators may, at this point in the cycle, link specific actions back to other stages or make changes based on the data collected. The data obtained may very well indicate the need to delay full implementation of the program until such time that corrections are made, or it may lead to the decision that the program is ready for large scale implementation.

In summary, the main purpose of the evaluative process is to diagnose strengths and weaknesses, and to provide feedback to make appropriate decisions for programs and schools. The data collection for the evaluation process originates from a number of sources, including classroom observation, interviews and discussions with students, discussion with teachers and parents, testing and measurement data, information from pupil services or guidance services, and surveys of the school and school community.

COMPETENCY E: Demonstrates the ability to determine school needs and to use principles of implementing and evaluating curricular and instructional innovations.

>   **Skill 1:** Demonstrates knowledge of ability to conduct a systematic assessment of school needs.

>   **Skill 2:** Demonstrates the ability to determine discrepancies between existing And desired curriculum and instruction.

>   **Skill 3:** Identifies elements required to successfully promote change in the school's curriculum and instruction.

Systematic assessment of school needs may range from grade level surveys of needs to school-wide surveys. This practice is insignificant, unless careful attention is given to a cohesive set of goals that are developed jointly with administrators, teachers, parents, and members of the school community to address specific needs. It is important that the instrument gathers pertinent information related to students' needs and the program situation at the school. Once the instrument is administered and the results are quantified, analyzed, and interpreted, the direction to follow is then determined.

When the purpose of the **needs assessment** is for program development, goal statements are carefully stated and established, and goals are prioritized and linked to performance outcomes of the learner. High priority goals are placed into a plan of implementation with specific strategies delineated. However, if the purpose of the assessment is for a progress check then the assessment instrument should reflect statements concerning activities and functions of the students and the staff, as well communication between the various levels. The systematic assessment of school needs should go beyond surveys to include cumulative folder content, anectdotal records, test results, interviews, classroom sociograms, direct teacher observation, and other means deemed appropriate.

Change is, generally, desirable for growth and development, but not all reasons for change are plausible. In many instances, the acceptance of change is dependent on concrete measures of comparison between the existing and the desired programs. Such comparison might be done through the Purvus **Discrepancy Evaluation Model** in which program standards and performance must first be determined, then both performance and standards are compared to determine if indeed there are discrepancies. The discrepancy between standards and performance is established throughout every aspect of the program including the design, installation, processes, products and cost.

While change is necessary, it will not occur just because someone has the knowledge for a bright idea that may very well be beneficial and may work beautifully. Change will occur when the individuals at all levels in the organization recognize that there is a need for it. It takes effective leadership and open two-way communication to initiate the change process. Problem solving, support, and continuous assessment of the process are also important aspects of promoting change.

Understanding administrative theories of change can be very useful in the process of implementing new curriculum. Kirt Lewin's **Force Field Model** looks at how two groups of opposing forces when equalized acquire a balance or equilibrium. But once unfreezing occurs, the driving force reduces the power of the restraining force and increases actions to attain change. The restraining force is generally governed by fear of the unknown and strong identification with traditional values of the organization and obsolete knowledge, which helps to keep the status quo. The driving force is armed with knowledge and technology, new societal values, processes and institutional approval to initiate the change process.

Specific strategies for curriculum implementation depend greatly on the curriculum implementation model for change. Among these are the Organizational Resistance to Change model (OCR model), the Organizational Development model, the Organizational Parts, Units and Loops model, and the Educational Change model.

The **OCR Model** accepts that resistance to change is natural because individuals become very comfortable with what they know and afraid of the unknown. Therefore, they resist change in order to preserve the status quo. However, this model sees change and innovation as inevitable and essential to organizational and curriculum growth and development. This approach produces a high level of success especially because it levels the playing field for those involved by endorsing power equalization between administrators and teachers. Change must be planned. Planning must address strategies to involve all key players. The plan should address all levels of concerns whether personal or programmatic. Individuals may need to share their values and beliefs concerning the difference between the new program and the existing one. Such dialogue and exchange may be the starting point of building consensus and resolving critical issues. Participants may need to listen to the opinions and visions of other colleagues. Participants may have concerns regarding materials for program implementation, time lines or strategies to be used. Whatever the concerns may be, they must be dealt with. The plan of action should allow time for all individuals to buy-in to the concept and take ownership for the successes and failures.

The **Organizational Development Model** uses a top down, vertical approach where the key players are the administrators, directors, and supervisors. This model uses the rational planning approach to change, which emphasizes teamwork that is focused on specific issues as identified by the key players. The culture emphasized is the dominant organizational culture, which drives the program. The strategies used in this model are planned through careful deliberation and consideration of available alternatives to make sure the organization retains what is valued so that the new program fits within the organization.

The **Organization Parts, Units and Loops Model** asserts that units and departments of the organization comprise the whole organization. According to Rensis Likert, persons in these overlapping workgroups are the linking pins between the groups in the organization. The interaction of the linking pins between the groups has direct impact on the attitudes and behavior of both groups, which also implies that they can influence administrators by gaining support, respects, and trust. Therefore, it utilizes the change process they may provide the links needed for administration and teachers to work together. The concept promoted by this model is that the organization can create the situation and atmosphere for change by influencing perceptions and involving key individuals in the process.

The **Educational Change Model** calls for a clear understanding of the characteristics of the change being implemented. Individuals should have clarity of the goals and means to implement the program. The complexity or difficulty of the program implementation must be looked at in terms of the level of experiences of the participants. To buy-in and provide support to the change process, participants must perceive that there is worth in the efforts being made, that there is a sense of quality control, and the process and outcome is practical.

The process of educating students is accomplished through instruction that is designed to attain specific objectives that are reflected in the educational aims and goals. Change occurs because people such as principal, curriculum leaders, teachers, parents, staff, and students work together by accepting their roles as agents of change. The organizational pattern and climate must be transformed in order to accept change.

COMPETENCY F: Demonstrates knowledge of the most prevalent concepts of schooling.

   Skill 1: Identifies conceptions of schooling.

The school **curriculum** is in reality a plan of action to educate children. The plan includes goals and objectives, activities for learning and materials to support learning and the evaluation process to determine the attainment of the goals and objectives. This plan is placed into a design that is under-girded by the selected approach and philosophy of learning. There are many different approaches to curriculum. These approaches are a reflection of educational philosophies, psychological foundations and social and developmental theories. Approaches to curriculum also include viewpoints about curriculum design; the roles of the learner, teachers, specialists, goals and objectives; and other important content to be examined.

Curriculum approaches can be **technical scientific** or **non-technical/non-scientific**. Among the technical scientific are the behavioral approach, the managerial approach and the systems approach. Among the non-technical/nonscientific approaches to curriculum are the academic approach and the humanistic approaches.

The **Behavioral Approach** pioneered by Ralph Tyler, Franklin Babbit, Hilda Tabba and others is a very efficient model to run schools. It is a blueprint that is inclusive of goals and objectives, step-by-step sequencing of content, activities, and learning outcome. Their legacy is still observed in teacher lesson plans and units. This approach is rooted in the scientific management theory of Frederick Taylor, which emphasized efficiency and productivity.

The **managerial approach** considers the school as a social system in which students, teachers, administrators, and other members of the school community interact based on certain social norms. In this setting, space, schedules, and programs are important factors. While logical and sequential steps are expected, the focus is on the organizational aspect of curriculum rather than the implementation. This approach brought about innovations, such as non-graded schools, departmentalization, the homeroom concept, and others. Its main goal is to organize the curriculum into a system.

The **system approach** views units and sub-units of organization as integral parts of the whole. Diagrams and flow charts are important to view the curriculum as a whole system that can be monitored. It is viewed as curriculum engineering. With this approach, particular issues are related to the whole system in terms of the relationship of the entire program.

The **academic approach** is among the nonscientific/non-technical approaches to curriculum. It is philosophical and theoretical and especially concerned with broad aspects of schooling, background information, and overview of events and people which makes it rigid and non-practical for the classroom and schools. Nonetheless, it does reflect useful educational views for curriculum developers and theorists.

The **humanistic approach** is another non-scientific/non-technical approach rooted in the child-centered movement, which gained recognition with the growth of child psychology and humanistic psychology in the 1940s and 1950s. This approach is concerned with the social, artistic, physical, and cultural aspects of curriculum. Additionally, it is concerned with the need for self-reflection and self-actualization of the learner along with the social and psychological environmental dynamics of the classroom.

Educational philosophies provide the primary foundation on which educators build the curriculum. Philosophies reflect a particular school of thought, which also provide the impetus for the aims, goals, and content as well as the organization of the curriculum. Educational Philosophies provides educators with a basis for school and classroom organization. They provide information related to methodology to be used, materials for instruction, what content should be taught, what experiences to prefer, and other structural issues related to the teaching and learning process.

In the United States, four major philosophies influenced education: Idealism, Realism, Pragmatism, and Existentialism. Idealism and realism are considered traditional philosophies while pragmatism and realism are considered contemporary philosophies (Pulliam and Patten, 1995). **Idealism** places emphasis on moral and spiritual concepts to explain the reality of the world truth and other values as timeless, universal and permanent, and unalterable.

Idealism is the philosophy of early philosophers such as Plato and others. Based on this philosophy, learning involves conceptualization and recall. The curriculum is hierarchical and should include and prefer abstract thoughts such as philosophy and theology, which are at the highest level of the hierarchy. Next mathematics which is absolute, history and literature which provide moral and cultural values, and language which fosters communication to support the concepts and thoughts that are central to this philosophy.

Realism views the world in terms of objects and matter that are real and perceived through sensing and reasoning. This school of thought is represented by great philosophers such as Aristotle and Pestalozzy. The notion that all things are derived from nature and are governed by the laws of nature, including human behavior, is prevalent in this school of thought. The type of curriculum stressed is one that is organized and separated into subject matter consistent of specific knowledge. Therefore, content and subjects that can be classified should be included into the curriculum. Basic skills such as reading, writing and mathematics would have priority.

Pragmatism is mainly an American philosophy as opposed to the previous philosophies, which originated in Europe. Pragmatism is based on change and experimentation. It views knowledge as a process in which change is constant. In this school of thought, learning occurs through problem solving, which is transferable to a variety of situations. Scientific development of the turn of the century influenced the development of this school of thought as well as the work of John Dewey and the child study movement. Pragmatists see learning through the scientific process where learning takes place through discovery and problem solving in response to the stimulus from the world that surrounds the learner.

Existentialism emerged as a response to previous philosophies. It stresses individualism and personal self-fulfillment. It is subjective to values chosen on the basis on the individuals' own perceptions. In this school of thought, the teacher's role is to cultivate the student's personal choice and help the individual to self-define. The curriculum endorsed by this school of thought is one that is void of structured discipline where students select their learning situations. Also favored by this philosophy are literature, drama, art and other areas that foster choice making and self-expressive activities, dialogue between the teacher and students, and discussions for new choices.

COMPETENCY G: Demonstrates knowledge of research on instructional effectiveness.

   Skill 1: Identifies teacher planning practices which can increase the probability of effective classroom performance.

   Skill 2: Identifies teacher classroom management practices, which will decrease student disruptive behavior.

   Skill 3: Identifies teacher instructional organization practices, which enhance student learning and achievement.

   Skill 4: Identifies teacher presentation of subject matter practices, which serve to enhance student comprehension of the subject.

   Skill 5: Identifies teacher verbal skills, which generally result in increased student achievement.

Effective teachers plan for instructional delivery even if they have taught the same lessons before. They continue to improve upon the presentation by finding new or additional materials to bring new energy into the teaching and learning process. As part of teaching, planning is a deliberate act that can be long-range, short range, formal, and informal. Long-range planning, such as units or semester plans, takes into account milestones, standards, and major goals over a period of time. It takes into account the nature of the content to be covered, the process in which the content will be covered, the approaches to take at varying stages, the activities to be used as well as resources needed. Short-term planning consists of daily lesson plans, weekly or even monthly plans or units for instruction. Daily and weekly lesson plans are usually more detail and specific, while unit plans can be more general and serve as the source of the daily lesson plans. Daily, weekly or unit written plans, grouping of students, instructional materials selection, activities for specific experiences to attain specific goals, student assessment, and the like are all part of the planning process

The formal aspect of planning has greater breadth and scope, which include long-term and short-term written plans. The informal aspect of planning is continuous and includes teachers ideas that emerge as resourceful teachers gather materials they believe useful for learning, as teachers consider varying experiences that could be used for specific students, as they share ideas with other professionals and generally as they toy with ideas on how to do things better. Informal planning often is incorporated into the formal process of planning, yet many good ideas remain as good ideas that are never tried. Whether long-term or short-term, effective planning begins with goals and objectives specification for learning.

Once the goals and objectives are specified, instructional strategies and materials should be selected, followed by the appropriate evaluation technique to assess learning.

The dynamics of classroom management generally corresponds to the leadership style of the individual teacher. An autocratic leadership style yields a punitive, harsh, and critical classroom environment. A laissez-faire leadership style, on the other hand, yields a permissive classroom environment where disorder and anarchy dominate. The democratic leadership style is more characteristic of today's school reform in which a participatory classroom is expected. The democratic leadership style yields a classroom that is firm but friendly, encouraging and stimulating, caring and guiding, and most of all fairness prevails as a way of resolving conflicts (Moore, 1995).

Regardless of the discipline model endorsed by the school, the effectively managed classroom follows basic principles generated by research. Discipline models such as the Behavior Modification, Glasser Model, Lee Canter Assertive Discipline Model, and other models dealing with prevention and correction of misbehavior may produce good results based on the teacher's leadership/management style and philosophy. Yet, a general focus on procedures to manage and prevent behavioral problems may prove much more effective than many of the leading models. Current educational research supporting effective school concepts, such as beginning class on time, setting up classroom procedures and routines, and keeping desk and storage spaces clean and organized from the very beginning of the school year, seem to set the initial expectation of order.

Making smooth transitions from one activity to another or from one class to another in a quick and orderly manner cuts down on idle time that generally encourages misbehavior. Making eye contact with students, being polite to the students and reinforcing positive interaction with and among the students, provide a healthy learning atmosphere. Having a general sense of what is going on in the classroom at all times, giving verbal and nonverbal encouragement, and stopping misbehavior in a firm and consistent manner as soon as they occur, without the use of threats, conveys constancy of purpose and expectations. Careful instructional planning and pace of teaching may also reduce opportunities for problems in the classroom. Additionally, involving the parents as partners in the education of their children serves as a prevention to discipline problems and as a support to continuous involvement in the solutions of problems as they occur.

Instructional planning also involves organizing the students for learning. Whole group and small group instruction are beneficial in different ways. Whole group instruction is beneficial when the teacher is introducing new concepts and skills while small group instruction is recommended when teachers want to ensure that the student master the material or that thorough learning has taken place. Students may be placed in ability groups for short-term activities. Long-term ability grouping such as tracking should be avoided to allow children, who would have been place in regular track and higher college bound track, to benefit from each other by learning together.

Generally, teachers believe that ability groups save time and allow focusing on the specific collective needs of the students. However, it is recognized that approaches such as cooperative groups at all levels of schooling where students of mixed ability work together, result in higher academic achievement. Other added benefits are that time on task is improved, interpersonal skills are increased, and more positive attitudes toward learning are developed. Cooperative grouping as a dominant approach to instruction does not negate the need to use, on a short-term basis, homogeneous groupings to work with children within the classroom. The teacher must be careful that short-term ability groups remain as such and that the lower groups still receive high quality instruction.

Instruction should be clear and focused, beginning with an orientation to the lesson and instructional objectives presented to students in a language that they can easily understand. The relationship between the current lesson and previous lessons should be made. Key points should be emphasized, concepts defined with examples and non-examples, cause and effect relationships established, and careful attention given to learning styles through the use of appropriate materials and strategies for learning. Students are provided ample time for guided and independent practice in the form of class work and homework, and strategies to develop higher level thinking skills are used.

Effective teacher expressions are key in the verbal aspect of instructional delivery. Enthusiasm and challenges that are clearly articulated and modulated are as important as the planned delivery of instruction of itself. Instruction, demonstrated through body language that expresses interest and caring, may also contribute to verbal effectiveness. The teacher should use good verbal skills for effective questioning to monitor understanding, to keep student focus, and to give feedback to reinforce learning progress.

There is no true blueprint for good schools. Good schools can be rural or city schools, large or small, with varying degrees of innovations. They may be public or private, affluent or non-affluent. No matter their location or affluence, no single set of recommendations can apply to all schools. Good schools can only be identified through common characteristics that lead to their effectiveness.

The research on **effective schools** lists common denominators and practices of effective schools. The research includes major aspects of school organization including **classroom characteristics and practices** and the **characteristics of the school** as a whole. In **effective classrooms,** instruction is guided by a preplanned curriculum, instructional groups are organized to meet the academic and affective needs of the students, learning time is used effectively, teachers set up routines that are smooth and efficient, and standards for classroom behavior are explicit and applied equitably and consistently. The learning that occurs in these settings is purposeful in an environment where teachers and students work together to develop concepts and skills. Students are carefully guided to the lessons and the instructor is clear and focused. Questioning is used to build both basic and higher level thinking and students receive feedback and reinforcement related to their learning process.

Additionally, teachers have high expectations of students and students receive incentives and rewards to promote excellence in learning. The interaction between teachers and students is always very positive and students' learning progress is closely monitored and assessed regularly. Finally, at-risk students and students with special needs are given the extra time and help they need to experience success.

The **quality of the school** can be measured well beyond the classroom in terms of the total climate in which education takes place. While the classroom can either enhance the work of the school, it can also detract from it. Therefore, the effectiveness of each classroom helps to provide the sum total quality and expectations held for the entire school. In **effective schools,** everyone emphasizes the importance of learning. All staff hold high expectations of children and they continually express the belief that all children can learn. The curriculum is based on clear goals and objectives, which are defined and displayed.

A clear relationship between goals, activities and students' assessment is established. Collaborative curriculum planning and decision making is the typical way of work. Curriculum continuity is built across grade levels, programs, and courses. Curriculum alignment is periodic, and staff, students, and parents know the priorities of the scope of the curriculum. The content of the curriculum is free from biases including gender, ethnic and racial biases.

Effective schools have strong leadership to guide the instructional program. Administrators involve teachers and together they strive for instructional effectiveness. Professional development is ongoing and learning is collegial. Administrators provide incentives and rewards to motivate students and staff. Parents and community members are invited and encouraged to become involved in the education of the children.

COMPETENCY H: Demonstrates knowledge of student performance evaluation.

Skill 1: Identifies appropriate practice for student performance evaluation.

Student performance evaluation is identified through test administration and scoring. **Test administration** is a key point in student performance because it is concerned with the **physical and psychological setting** in which the test takes place, as well as **cheating** and **time factor.** Test construction, while separate from test administration, may play a key role in test administration because of the impact of test items' arrangement on the test. Outside of reliability and validity in test item construction is the issue of clustering the items of a test by question and response type. For example, multiple choice questions should be clustered together and separated from true or false questions, just as established essay type responses should be separated from the former due to the length of the responses. This arrangement allows students to shift from one section to another rather than from one item to another. It also helps to group directions by sections and it makes it easy to score the responses (Airasian 1997).

The **physical setting for test taking** should be quiet, comfortable and free of interruptions. Interruptions can be avoided by ensuring test item ambiguity and typographical errors are identified and corrected prior to administering the test, but when errors are detected, they should be corrected for the whole class to avoid further student distractions. The teacher may state to the class for example: "item number three should read thus," correcting the error that was detected. Additionally, teachers should post a sign on the door to announce testing in progress to avoid disruptions from outside of the classroom. In the case of school-wide testing, the entire school should use the same precautions. The **psychological setting for test taking** should be anxiety-free and prompt by advanced notice for testing. Some teachers like the idea of pop quizzes which produce anxiety that affects student performance, while the effective teachers may select a day of the week for the spelling test or for the biweekly history quiz. Teachers should announce the test ahead of time and tell the students the general type of test that will be given as well as the content, to give students the opportunity to prepare.

Cheating is always an issue in test administration. Cheating should be avoided by establishing and discussing rules about cheating with the students. Teachers should arrange the physical setting to avoid cheating by separating the students' seating, making sure the desks are free of non-test items, prohiiting burrowing and sharing materials during testing, observing students during testing, and by simply enforcing the pre-established cheating rules. **Keeping track of time** helps students to self-monitor. A one-hour test time may have fifteen-minute intervals of time reminders with the last fifteen minutes consisting of three five-minute intervals of reminders to help student pace their time. To conform with **formative assessment process**, periodic reviews and frequent testing should be practiced.

Test taking skills will make up for poor teaching and a lack of study. It can help students to focus during testing, thus affecting student performance. Students must be familiarized with tests and response formats. They must learn exactly what is expected of them, no matter how simple the task may appear to an adult. Some specific strategies include learning to follow directions, learning how to self-pace and distribute time adequately across test items, planning and organizing essay responses before beginning to write, identifying the scoring approach in terms to maximize benefits, keeping track of answer sheet recording to make sure responses are marked in the correct places, and avoid cramming sessions prior to testing which might affect both physical and mental condition. Some **test-wiseness skills** may include careful analysis and elimination of items in which the stem does not attach smoothly to the response or choices contain grammatical or spelling errors and generally favoring items with words such as "some times," "often," or "a best indicator of" (Airasian 1997).

COMPETENCY I: Demonstrates knowledge of the main areas of a performance measurement system.

> **Skill 1:** Identifies the appropriate components of a performance measurement system which best describes a teacher performance problem.

Research on effective teaching performance gave origin to the **Florida Performance Measurement System or FPMS** which serves as the basis for teacher performance assessment in the system of public education in Florida. The Florida Performance Measurement System is organized into six domains of teaching. These domains include Planning, Management of Student Conduct, Instructional Organization and Development, Presentation of Subject Matter, Communications (verbal and nonverbal), and Testing which includes student preparation, administration, and feedback (Florida Department of Education 1993).

In the **Domain of Planning,** a course of action for teaching is formulated. The teacher organizes the subject matter to be taught, the materials to be used for instruction, the activities that will be implemented, and the method of assessing the learning outcome. Specific concepts included in this domain are content coverage, utilization of instructional materials, activity structure, goal focusing, and diagnosis. Effective indicators of planning included on the school district's formative assessment instrument may vary, but they will generally correlate with the selected concepts for the domain. For example, *"assesses students' needs before instruction"* might be used as an indicator of diagnosis, while *"presets goals for teaching"* might be used as an indicator of the concept of goal focusing

The domain of **Management of Student Conduct** is inclusive of teacher behavior that reduces probable student misconduct, ways of halting disruptive student behaviors once they occur, and ways of dealing with serious misconduct. The effective teacher knows that the misconduct of a student affects the behavior and learning of other students in the classroom. It is expected that the teacher will use appropriate techniques to stop a deviancy with minimal disruption to other children while using effective response to the misconduct. The effective teacher is aware that teacher behavior may also increase or decrease negative responses from students. The teacher is also aware of the need for appropriate teacher-student interaction. Specific concepts included in this domain are rule explication and monitoring, teacher with-it-ness, overlapping, quality of desists, group alert, movement smoothness, movement slowdown, and praise. Effective indicators of planning included on the school district's formative assessment instrument may vary, but they will generally correlate with the selected concepts for the domain. For example, *"stops misconduct while maintaining instructional momentum"* might be used as an indicator of movement smoothness.

The domain of **Instructional Organization and Development** includes the specific concepts such as efficient use of time, review of subject matter, lesson development, teacher treatment of student talk, teacher academic feedback, and management of seatwork/homework. A formative assessment instrument for teacher performance may use an indicator such as *"circulates and assists students"* to assess the concept of management of seatwork or *"recognizes responses, amplifies and gives corrective feedback"* to assess treatment of student talk.

The domain of **Presentation of Subject** focuses on the interaction with students as well as the treatment of the subject matter. Specific concepts included in this domain are presentation of interpretive (conceptual) knowledge, presentation of explanatory (law or law-like) knowledge, presentation of academic rule knowledge, and presentation of value knowledge which refers to statements about the worth of things. A formative assessment instrument for teacher performance may use an indicator such as *"develops concept, gives definition, attributes, examples and non-examples"* to assess the concept of presentation of interpretive or conceptual knowledge.

The domain of **Communications (verbal and nonverbal)** focuses on verbal and nonverbal skills to express information and establish personal relationships. Communication is based on the notions that while verbal interaction is important to successful teaching, body language and other nonverbal expressions are also crucial in establishing relationships and engaging students in meaningful learning. This domain includes the concepts of control of discourse, emphasis, task attraction, and challenge, speech, and body language. A formative assessment instrument for teacher performance may use an indicator to assess body language such as *"uses nonverbal expressions that show interest, such as smiles, gestures, etc."*

The domain of **Testing (student preparation, administration, and feedback)** addresses the environment in which students are tested, as well as the feedback they receive about their test performance. Administrators are seldom present during direct student assessment periods, which makes observation of classroom testing infrequent. Indicators for teacher testing competencies are usually initiated through the development of a school-wide plan for testing, but are individually assessed through conferences with teachers and feedback from parents and students.

"Of course I care about how you imagined I thought you perceived I wanted you to feel."

Directions: Read each item and select the best response.

1. Which of the following are best sources of curriculum?

    A. Textbooks and bibliographies

    B. Students and society

    C. Teachers and administrators

    D. Parents and community groups

2. Which theory group best represents a curriculum that emphasizes affective, rather than cognitive outcomes?

    A. Behaviorism

    B. Observation Learning

    C. Phenomenology

    D. Cognitive Development

3. Which of the following refers to the horizontal organization of the elements of the curriculum?

    A. The knowledge and skills students learn are useful in life situations

    B. The knowledge and skills that students learn at one grade level are relevant and useful as they progress to other grades

    C. Everything the student learns contributes to fulfillment

    D. What students learn in one class supports and reinforces what they learn in other classes

4. Which of the following refers to the vertical organization of the elements of the curriculum?

    A. Everything the student learns contributes to fulfillment

    B. The knowledge and skills that students learn at one grade level are relevant and useful as they progress to other grades

    C. What students learn in one class supports and reinforces what they learn in other classes

    D. The knowledge and skills students learn are useful in life situations

5. _____ refers to the linking of all types of knowledge and experiences contained within a curriculum plan.

   A. Scope

   B. Balance

   C. Integration

   D. Continuity

6. _____ is based on the clustering of subjects into categories of study.

   A. Process-centered curriculum design

   B. Subject-centered curriculum design

   C. Discipline-centered curriculum design

   D. Broad fields curriculum design

7. Which choice best represents balance in the curriculum?

   A. Equal time for each of the courses offered

   B. More time for reading and math because they are difficult subjects

   C. Concepts linked to continuity and integration

   D. Opportunities provided for the development of concepts and skills applied to real life experiences

8. Which statement best describes communication in and effective school?

   A. Top down formal and informal communication

   B. Bottom up formal and informal communication

   C. Lateral formal and informal communication

   D. Informal communication between teachers and between teachers and administration

9. **Effective teacher involvement in a new program is highly dependent on_____**

    A. Teacher satisfaction with the curriculum planners' background

    B. District office politics concerning program planning and development

    C. Teacher involvement in the planning process and in-service training

    D. Parent and community buy-in to the design of the program and evaluation process

10. **_____ the expressive form of communication that provides opportunity for non-verbal communication that enhances the message.**

    A. Lectures are

    B. Oral reports are

    C. Body language is

    D. Speeches are

11. **_____ is the process of gathering information to identify and define the problem before initiating a project or program.**

    A. Surveying

    B. Needs assessment

    C. Evaluation

    D. Aims and goals identification

12. **Which sequence best describes the order of a needs assessment?**

    A. Survey of needs, goals and objectives development, problem identification, implementation planning, process evaluation

    B. Problem identification, survey of needs, goals and objectives development, implementation planning, process evaluation

    C. Problem identification, survey of needs, goals and objectives development, process evaluation, implementation planning

    D. Survey of needs, problem identification, goals and objectives development, implementation planning, process evaluation

13. After identifying the curriculum phenomena, which sequence best represents the order of data gathering for program assessment?

    A. Reporting the information, collecting the information, organizing the information, recycling the information

    B. Collecting the information, organizing the information, recycling the information, reporting the information

    C. Collecting the information, reporting the information, recycling the information, organizing the information

    D. Collecting the information, organizing the information, reporting the information, recycling the information

14. A logical sequence in formulating goals is_____

    A. Philosophy, aims, goals, objectives

    B. Philosophy, goals, aims, objectives

    C. Aims philosophy objectives goals

    D. Philosophy, aims, objectives, goals

15. _____is the type of evaluation that is concerned with how to utilize the resources to attain the goals of the program.

    A. Input evaluation

    B. Content evaluation

    C. Process evaluation

    D. Product evaluation

16. Which of the following statements best describes process evaluation?

    A. It is concerned with the needs of the program

    B. It is concerned with the adequacy of resources to implement the program

    C. It is concerned with recording procedures and continuous monitoring

    D. It is concerned with the attainment of the goals for the program

17. Which of the following best illustrates an educational goal?

A. Provide good health and physical fitness

B. By the year 2000, the high school graduation rate will increase to at least 90%

C. Develop self-realization

D. The students will complete a reading comprehension examination within 30 minutes with 80% accuracy

18. Which of the following best illustrates a behavioral objective?

A. Students will be able to solve multiplication word problems at the rate of one problem per minute with 80% accuracy

B. Students will appreciate the originality of cultural music

C. 10% of the students will comprehend the implications of good health and physical fitness

D. By the year 2000, the literacy rate among all adults will increase to at least 90%

19. Which of the following is the best formative assessment practice for students?

A. Provide a comprehensive multiple choice test at the end of the chapter

B. Provide several teacher-made quizzes during the chapter

C. Provide guided practice during the unit

D. Provide a combination of test formats in the chapter test

20. Which of the following best describes the purpose of student assessment?

A. To analyze performance at various stages of goal attainment

B. To appraise curriculum goals and objectives

C. To determine outcome in terms of cost and achievement related to cost

D. To analyze various alternatives or program options

21. Which of the following statements best describes the need for formative evaluation?

A. A teacher wants to know to what extent the students have attained specific objectives at the end of the unit

B. A teacher wants to know how well a group of students in one part of the country compares to the students in another part of the country

C. A teacher wants information to identify problems before beginning a unit of study

D. A teacher wants to know well the students are doing at various points during the teaching of a unit of study

22. An example of reliability in testing is ____

A. The test was administered with poor lighting

B. Items on the test produce the same response each time

C. Items on the test measure what they should measure

D. The test is too long for the time allotted

23. _____ is a standardized test in which performance is directly related to the educational objective

A. Aptitude test

B. Norm-referenced test

C. Criterion-referenced test

D. Summative evaluation

24. Which of the following statements best represents a child who scored at the 75th percentile?

A. 25% of the normed group scored above the student who took the test

B. 25% of the normed group scored below the student who took the test

C. 75% of the normed group scored above the student who took the test

D. 75% of the normed group scored 75 points below the student who took the test

25. Which of the following is an indicator of instructional organization and development?

    A. The teacher stops misconduct

    B. The teacher discusses cause and effect and uses linking words to apply principles

    C. The teacher emphasizes important points

    D. The teacher recognizes responses, amplifies and gives feedback

26. Which of the following is included in the planning domain of the FPMS?

    A. Diagnosis

    B. Effective use of time

    C. Lesson development

    D. Preparation for testing

27. Which of the following is a change model that uses a vertical approach with an emphasis on teamwork to solve problems and maintain culture as part of the system as a whole?

    A. The educational Change Model

    B. The organizational Development Model

    C. The OCR Model

    D. Organizational Parts, Unit and Loops Model

28. Which of the following is an approach that sees the curriculum as emergent and concerned with cultivating the processes that allow for control of one's learning?

    A. Humanistic

    B. Reconceptualist

    C. Behavioral

    D. Managerial

29. Traditionalists are concerned with_____

A. Selecting, organizing, and sequencing curriculum content

B. Curriculum as an interactive system

C. Curriculum as dialogue

D. Curriculum as a child-centered endeavor

30. Which of the following is a major assumption of the technical scientific approach?

A. Curriculum development is dynamic and personal

B. Curriculum development is subjective

C. Curriculum development is rational

D. Curriculum development is transactional

31. Which statement does not describe the curriculum of an effective school?

A. The curriculum is planned with enough flexibility to address the changing needs of students

B. The curriculum is planned a year at a time and encompasses basic skills that are learned in the classroom

C. The curriculum is planned collaboratively with attention to basic skills and problem solving in the classroom and community

D. The curriculum is planned with clear goals and objectives along with instructional activities and student assessment

32. Which statement best describes the Discrepancy Evaluation Model?

A. Standards and performance are established for the old and new program

B. Standards and performance are normed

C. Standards and performance are compared to determine differences

D. Standards and performance differences are shared with parents and the community

33. **Which of the following models uses single and double loop learning to affect change?**

    A. The educational Change Model

    B. The organizational Development Model

    C. The OCR Model

    D. Organizational Parts, Unit, and Loops Model

34. **Change through professional growth and development is least supportive through_____**

    A. Intensive staff development over time

    B. Single day workshop with specific activities for the new program

    C. Project meetings to adopt new materials to the realities of the school

    D. Classroom assistance by resource personnel to assist with program implementation over time

35. **Which of the following is an indicator of appropriate procedure for effective classroom management?**

    A. Trust that the students will behave and allow them total freedom

    B. Allow enough time that while students make transition from one class to another they can have down time

    C. Use verbal private reprimand when using sarcasm

    D. Use verbal reprimand with calmness and in private

36. **During instruction, a group of students sitting in the back of the room are trading notes and making gestures. This indicates that the teacher lacks _____**

    A. Withitness

    B. Basic knowledge about how children learn

    C. Understanding about transition between activities

    D. Appropriate planning for instruction

37. **Which statement best describes effective classroom planning?**

    A. The teacher begins with the gathering of instructional materials to give meaning to the goals and objectives

    B. The teacher begins by gathering the best textbooks with sequential outlines to cover the subject matter

    C. The teacher begins by setting up the evaluation system with quizzes and tests to assess learning at the end of the chapter

    D. The teacher begins by specifying the instructional goals and objectives followed by the strategies for learning

38. **Which of the following <u>least</u> describes conditions for change?**

    A. The school uses a reactive approach rather than a proactive approach to solve problems

    B. Students' performance is at a decline

    C. The power structure at the school is unevenly distributed

    D. Someone has the knowledge base for a new idea that may benefit the school

39. **Which of the following best describes long-term planning?**

    A. Daily lesson plans

    B. Weekly lesson plans

    C. Semester unit plan

    D. Listing of activities

40. **Which of the following best represents the democratic leadership style in classroom management?**

    A. Students work in the classroom without constraints

    B. Students work in a friendly, caring, and sharing atmosphere

    C. Students comply without hesitation to the demands of the teacher

    D. Students respond diligently to pressures and criticism from the teacher

41. _____**increases achievement and interpersonal skills.**

    A. Ability grouping

    B. Cooperative grouping

    C. Tracking

    D. Homogeneous grouping

42. **Which phrase best describes long-term planning?**

    A. Concern with graphic organizers

    B. Concern with specific objectives

    C. Concern with guiding practice

    D. Concern with pacing the schedule for unit and topics

43. **Which statement best describes the effective classroom?**

    A. Classroom behavior standards are developed with student input and are written, taught, and practiced from the beginning of the school year

    B. Teachers give frequent general praise to all students to encourage and reward learning efforts

    C. The teacher grades the test given to students and provides valuable written feedback two weeks after the test

    D. Routines are established each week to promote change in the learning environment

44. **Which of the following represents best test taking practice?**

    A. The teacher tells the students: " Testing is just part of life and I am required to test you."

    B. The teacher tell the students: "Don't worry about the test. It has very little effect on your final grade."

    C. The teacher tells the students: "This test is your ticket for promotion from this class."

    D. The teacher tells the students: "I know you will do your best on this test."

45. **Which of the following statements will produce the least anxiety before testing?**

    A. The teacher announces a quiz for the following day and provides separate seating arrangement for students

    B. The teacher announces a quiz for the following day and scores the test to determine progress of each student

    C. The teacher announces a quiz for the following day and gives general information about the type of quiz the students will take

    D. The teacher announces a quiz for the following day and gives information about the content and type of quiz the students will take

ANSWER KEY (Subtest 2 – School Operations, Curriculum)

1.	B	36.	A
2.	C	37.	D
3.	D	38.	D
4.	B	39.	C
5.	C	40.	B
6.	D	41.	B
7.	D	42.	D
8.	C	43.	A
9.	C	44.	D
10.	C	45.	D
11.	B		
12.	D		
13.	D		
14.	A		
15.	A		
16.	D		
17.	B		
18.	A		
19.	B		
20.	A		
21.	D		
22.	B		
23.	C		
24.	A		
25.	D		
26.	A		
27.	B		
28.	C		
29.	A		
30.	D		
31.	B		
32.	C		
33.	D		
34.	B		
35.	D		

Bibliography

Airasian, P. (1997). *Classroom Assessment.* 3rd ed. New York: McGraw-Hill Companies, Inc.

Borman, S. Levine. J. (1997). *A Practical Guide to Elementary Instruction: form plan to delivery.* Needham Heights, MA: Allyn and Bacon.

Florida Association of School Administrators. (1997) *Florida Education Handbook 1997.* Tallahassee, FL: CMD Publishing, Inc.

Florida Department of Education. (1992). *Florida Performance Measurement System Domains: Knowledge Base of the Florida Performance Measurement System.*

Goodlad, John (1984). *A Place Called School: Prospects for the Future.* New York: McGraw-Hill Companies, Inc.

Lemleck, J. (1994). *Curriculum and Instruction Methods for the Elementary and Middle School.* 3rd ed. New York: McMillan Publishing Co.

Moore, K. (1995). *Classroom Teaching Skills.* 3rd ed. New York: McGraw-Hill Companies, Inc.

McMillam, J. (1997). *Classroom Assessment: Principles and Practice for Effective Instruction.* Needham Heights, MA: Allyn and Bacon.

McNell, J. (1996). *Curriculum: a Comprehensive Introduction.* 5th ed. New York: Harper Collins College Publishers.

Northwest Regional Educational Laboratory. (1990). *Effective Schools Practices: a Research Synthesis 1990 Update.* Portland, OR.

Ornstein, A and Hunkins, A. (1993). *Curriculum Foundations, Principles and Theory.* 2nd ed. Needham Heights, MA: Allyn and Bacon.

Pulliam, J. and Patten, J. (1995). *History of Education.* 6th ed. Needham Heights, MA: Allyn and Bacon.

Subtest 3 - School Management

6. School Finance

School finance provides you with information related to the principles of financing, managing, budgeting, accounting and reporting in the Florida public school system. It identifies current methods and practices governing the fiscal operation of schools.

COMPETENCY A: Demonstrates knowledge of Florida's funding plan for public elementary and secondary schools

> **Skill 1:** Identifies the requirements necessary for school district participation in the Florida Education Financial Program.

> **Skill 2:** Demonstrates knowledge of the Florida Education Finance Program regarding both child equity and taxpayer equity.

Early in the history of our nation, education became a local and state responsibility. The responsibility is granted to the legislature of each state through plenary power, which enables the enactment of laws it considers appropriate and desirable for education. Under this premise, the Florida legislature enacted the **FEFP (Florida Education Finance Program)** in 1973 to equalize the educational opportunities for every child in the state. Florida Statute section 236.012 defines its purpose as follows:

> "To guarantee to each child in the state of Florida public educational system the availability of programs and services appropriate to his educational needs which are substantially equal to those available to any similar student notwithstanding geographic differences and varying local economic factors."

Historically, until the early 1970s, previous formulas for public school funding were generally based on a school system's wealth, which took a ratio of school taxable property and allocated it equally to each child in the system. This resulted in either wealthy school systems or poor school systems. The higher the taxable property, the wealthier the school system became and conversely, the lower the taxable property, the poorer the school system became. To equalize the available resources to all children in Florida, the FEFP recognizes in its formula, the following components:
- varying local property tax bases
- varying program cost factors district cost differential
- differences in per student cost for equivalent educational programs due to sparsity and dispersion of student population

Each year the Florida Legislature determines the **minimum efforts of taxation** on district property tax rolls, as well as the program cost factors, to determine the base funding for each student. For participation in the state allocation of funds, each school board must levy the millage set for its required local efforts. Each district's share is determined by certification of the property tax valuations by the Department of Revenue and the Commissioner of Education. Assessment ratios are used to equalize the effects of the FEFP on differing levels of property appraisals in each county. **Millage rates** are also adjusted to ensure that the required local rates do not exceed 90% of the district total FEFP entitlement. Ultimately, the state's appropriation is used to fund the difference between the amount raised for each student through the required local millage times the property tax roll, plus the established base student allocation.

Since a key feature of the FEFP is based upon student participation in a particular educational program, the varying program cost factors set by the legislature are key to the formula when determining base funding. To better understand the formula, here are definitions to key terms:

FTE: A full-time equivalent student
Weighted FTE: An FTE multiplied by a program cost factor
Base student allocation: a fixed amount determined each year by the legislature

District cost differential: The Commissioner of Education annually averages each district's Florida Price Level Index for the last three years and applies the prices of salary on district operating cost to reduce its impact on the district.

The **base student funding** is calculated by multiplying the **full-time equivalent student (FTE)** by the **program cost factor,** which gives the weighted FTE. The weighted FTE is then multiplied by the base student allocation and the district cost differential to produce the base student funding as seen below.

FTE

X

program cost factor

=

weighted FTE

X

base student allocation

X

district cost differential

=

BASE STUDENT FUNDING

Other FEFP factors authorized by the Legislature are added to adjust and finalize the distribution of funds to each school district. These adjustments include declining enrollment supplement, sparsity supplement, safe school allocation, remediation reduction incentive, discretionary tax equalization, and hold harmless adjustment and disparity compression adjustment.

Outside of the FEFP formula, each district may levy discretionary millage, which is a level of additional discretionary taxes. This amount is authorized by the legislature with a proportion of it equalized with dollars from the state for **categorical funds** including instructional materials, student transportation, instructional technology and food services. Another categorical fund, outside of the FEFP formula, is preschool funding which comes from lottery proceeds. All of these considerations make the FEFP a model program for the equalization of educational opportunities for all children in the state of Florida.

To participate in the FEFP, every district must provide annual evidence of its efforts to maintain an adequate school program throughout the district and must meet at least the following requirements:

1. Maintain adequate and accurate records including a system of internal accounts for individual schools, and file with the department of Education, correct and proper form, on or before the date due, each annual or periodic report which is required by state Board of Education Rules.

2. Operate all schools for a term of 180 actual teaching days or the equivalent on an hourly basis. Upon written application, the State Board may prescribe procedures for altering this requirement.

3. Provide written contracts for all instructional personnel and require not less than 196 days of service for all members of the instructional staff.

4. Expend funds for salaries in accordance with a salary schedule or schedules adopted by the School Board in accordance with the provisions of the law and rules of the State Board.

5. Observe all requirements of the State Board relating to the preparation, adoption, and execution of budgets for the district school system.

6. Levy the required local effort millage rate on the taxable value for school purposes of the district. In addition, collect fees for adult education courses.

7. Maintain an ongoing systematic evaluation of the educational program needs of the district and develop a comprehensive annual and long-term plan.

COMPETENCY B: Demonstrates the ability to analyze the processes of planning, developing, implementing, and evaluating a budget.

Skill 1: Identifies the major funds of a school district budget.

Skill 2: Identifies the major categories of financial resources available to a district beyond the state allocation.

Skill 3: Identifies the interrelationship between the school individual budget and the district budget.

Skill 4: Selects, interprets, use, and/or detects the factors that cause change in the school operating budget.

Skill 5: Describes the purpose of a budget.

Skill 6: Demonstrates understanding of the purpose of internal funds and the need for proper accounting of those funds.

There are three major **sources of school funding** for the school districts in the State of Florida. Approximately 50% of the financial support comes from state sources, 42% from local sources and 7% from the federal government.

The **state support** for education comes from the state's general revenue funds (mainly from taxes), state school trust fund, Florida Lottery, and other funds that are appropriated to meet the needs of categorical programs and specific allocations. Other state funds come from proceeds from licensing of motor vehicles and gross utility taxes which support capital outlay, racing commission funds and other minor sources such as mobile home licensing.

Local support for education originates when the school boards levy the millage required for the local tax effort, which is determined by the state statutory process. Additionally, voters may approve other tax levies such as maintenance bonds and operation user fees. **Federal** funds to **support** education are administered by the Board of Education. These funds are provided to support federal mandates such as the National School Lunch Act, the Americans with Disabilities Act, and others.

Proceeds from the lottery are used to finance both district discretionary lottery funds and preschool projects. Education's share of the revenues is 38% which goes into the Educational Enhancement Trust Fund and is distributed at a rate of 70% for public schools, 15% for the community colleges, and 15% for universities.

Future resources for education are planned through student enrollment forecasts. This is a joint effort between the Florida Department of Education, the Governor's Office, the Legislature, and the school districts. The **forecast input** is essential for the FEFP appropriation, primarily because it is used to compute district allocation and make actual payments until the student membership can be finally determined through certified surveys. This process is defined by Florida Statute section 216.136(4).

From the appropriated funds, the district builds its budget. At this point, the **budget** becomes an important device for translating the educational plan into a financial plan. The budget is, in effect, the translation of prioritized educational needs into a financial plan, which is interpreted for the public in such a way that when it is formally adopted, it expresses the kind of educational program the community is willing to support financially and morally for a one-year period (Drake and Roe, 1994).

The budget must be managed through a **financial system of accounting**. In the state of Florida this system is predetermined for the school districts. This system is managed through the **Financial and Program Cost Accounting and Reporting for Florida Schools**, also known as The Red Book. It deals only with revenues and expenditures. Revenues are categorized by sources. Sources of revenues can be either federal, state or local. Expenditures on the other hand, are categorized by dimensions which include funds or account groups, objects, functions, facility, project, and reporting.

The funds or account groups are accounting entities with a self-balancing set of accounts that supports specific school activities to attain specific objectives. Therefore, funds or account can only be used for specified purposes. There are eight major funds or account groups: General Fund, Debt Services Funds, Capital Project Funds, Special Revenues Funds, Enterprise Funds, Internal Services Funds, Trust and Agency Funds, General Fixed Assets, and General-Long-Term Debt. Of all the funds, the General Fund is perhaps the most important to schools and school districts because it deals with the day-to-day operation of the school.

The budget of the district is generally made up of all of the account groups or funds established by the Red Book. Since many the accounts held by the district are not appropriate to the school operation, the school differs from that of the district. For example, most districts are responsible for salaries and benefits, utilities and services therefore, these accounts will not be included in the school-based budget.

At the school level the district allots a certain number of dollars based on a predetermined local formula to allow expenditures from General Fund related to the day-to-day operation of the school. Additionally, the school may have an Activity account and a School Internal account. The **Activity account** is derived from class fees, athletic contests and events, plays, yearly photos, and other special programs. While the proceeds belong to the school, they must be used for students' learning benefits such as award ribbons, trophies, and the like. These proceeds must be identified and accounted in the same manner as any other funds of the school.

The school **internal account** usually originates from vending machine sales in the teacher's lounge and from related faculty activities and must be used to benefit faculty and staff. Again, these proceeds must be identified and accounted for in the same manner as any other funds or accounts of the school.

COMPETENCY C: Demonstrates knowledge of, comprehension about, and the ability to apply school finance concepts.

> **Skill 1:** Demonstrates knowledge of, and makes inferences concerning model school finance plans of other states.

> **Skill 2:** Demonstrates knowledge of and discriminates among measures of school district fiscal capacity.

> **Skill 3:** Identifies measures of educational resource need.

> **Skill 4:** Identifies major sources of taxation used to support public education.

> **Skill 5:** Demonstrates knowledge of equity concepts tested in major school finance litigation.

> **Skill 6:** Identifies, interprets, classifies, and makes inferences concerning the contributions of education to the economy.

Every state has its own funding formula to allocate general distribution of funds to local districts to provide educational services to children. This formula can be complex because of the efforts of state legislatures to provide uniformity of support. While some public school programs are fully funded by the state, others may rely on flat grants, foundation programs or a variety of tax base equalization programs. The **Flat Grant Model** is a basic model that is very easy to compute. It is based on a fixed amount multiplied by the number of students enrolled in a school regardless of the **fiscal capacity** of the district and regardless of the needs of the students. This model has been the center of landmark court litigations because providing a per student allocation disregards the needs of students. It also assumes that the role of the state is to guarantee a minimum level of education to each student (Swanson and King 1997).

With **Foundation Grants,** on the other hand, the state defines the level of funding for basic education. The state and the school district in partnership provide the funds required for the educational programs. Unlike the Flat Grant Model, where the state alone provided per pupil funding, in the Foundation Program both the state and the districts act in partnership to determine the required level of local participation.

As of 1994-95 (Swanson and King 1997), only Delaware and North Carolina are utilizing the Flat Grant Model. Eighteen (18) states are utilizing the Foundation Program in which local support is not required, and twenty-three (23) states including Florida, Alabama, Alaska, Colorado, Mississippi, South Carolina, Tennessee, and others are using the Foundation Program in which local efforts are required. Hawaii and Washington are the only states with programs that are fully funded at the state level. In general, the blend of state and local revenues is important to the extent that they provide adequate support, recognition of fiscal responsibility of state district, and local capacity as defined by property valuation or personal income tax.

Major sources to support public education come from revenues generated from taxes. Property tax at the local level, sales tax at the state level, and income tax at the federal level constitute primary sources of revenues for education. From these sources approximately 50% of the financial support comes from state sources, 42% from local sources, and 7% from the federal government.

Legal provisions for funding public education come from the constitution. The lack of clear language and specificity of public school funding results in school funding litigations, which historically have led to major school finance reforms. Legislative enactment, regulations, decrees, or rulings are outgrowths of school finance litigations. These reforms originated from the basic values and beliefs of the citizens and leaders at the national, state, and local levels.

Early litigations of school finance alleged that the methods of financing education at the state level violated the equal protection for certain classes of people under our constitution. Allegations were also made that the reliance on local revenues to support a large portion of the total public school budget was unfair because of the disparity in property tax wealth among the school systems. There are four landmark court cases that build on each other to produce significant school financing reform.

In **McInnis v. Shapiro** –1969, the plaintiffs contended that the Illinois method of financing public education was inequitable because it permitted a wide variation in expenditures per student. This method of financing did not apportion funds according to the educational need of students. The court rejected the plaintiff contention stating that the controversy was unjustifiable because it lacked judicially manageable standards. The court further stated that equal expenditures per students were inappropriate as a standard. The court was ill prepared to provide advice on an equitable finance plan to public school because it lacked specific understanding of cost-effective analysis of such measurement. **Serrano v. Priest** -1971 emerged with the precedence set by the previous case. In this situation, the plaintiffs contended that the California school system of financing allowed substantial disparities between the various districts in the amount of revenues available for education

They further contended that this method denied equal protection of the laws under the constitution of the United States and the constitution of California. They also contended that this system required parents to pay taxes at a higher rate than taxpayers in many other districts in order to provide the same or lesser educational opportunities for their children.

In this landmark decision, the court contended that education is a constitutionally protected fundamental interest and that wealth was a suspect classification. The court established the **Standard of Fiscal Neutrality** as a measurement to determine whether or not a school finance program was constitutional. Under this standard, the quality of the child's education could not be based on the wealth of the local school district, but on the wealth of the state as a whole.

In **Rose v. The Council of Better Education** -1989, the plaintiffs contended that the system of financing schools by the Kentucky General Assembly was inadequate because it placed too much emphasis on local school board resources which result in inadequacies and inequalities throughout the state. This resulted in inefficient system of common school education, which violated the state constitution. The court ruled in favor of the plaintiffs. The court also appointed a committee to review relevant data, provide additional analysis, consult with financial experts, and propose remedies to correct the deficiencies in the present common school financing system.

Another landmark case in school finance is **San Antonio Independent School District v. Rodriguez** - 1973. The plaintiffs contended that the dual system of public school financing in Texas violated the equal protection clause of the Constitution of the United States and Texas. The initial ruling in 1971 held the state financing system of Texas unconstitutional under the equal Protection clause of the Fourteen Amendments. An appeal of this decision reversed the ruling because of unanswered questions concerning the constitution of Texas. But in the second ruling, the court found substantial **disparities among the districts' school expenditures**, which were largely attributed to the differences in the amounts of the dollars collected through property taxes. The court concluded that the dual system of public school finance in Texas indeed violated the equal protection clause.

Education is both a public and a private good because it enhances the individual as it brings important benefits to society (Swanson and King 1997). At an individual level, education provides the ability to enjoy a higher standard of living by earning more money and living a better quality of life, thus, making a contribution into the economy. Education supports the production of a skilled workforce for the efficient functioning of a society that is stimulated by economic growth and development.

COMPETENCY D: Demonstrates knowledge of the process of financial accounting, auditing and reporting.

Skills 1: Identifies methods or discriminates among the practices of cost reporting.

Skill 2: Identifies or discriminates among the practices, standards, and procedures of accounts used in school internal accounts audits.

Skill 3: Discriminates among components of the accounting classification structure used by school districts.

Skill 4: Identifies and differentiates among practices and procedures of fiscal control and accountability of school-based funds.

Methods for cost accounting and reporting are contained in the Florida Department of Education publication "**Financial and Program Cost Accounting for Florida Schools**" also known as The Red Book. The content of this publication also reflects the requirements of Rule 6A-1.001 of Florida Administrative Code and Sections 237.01 and 237.02 of Florida Statutes.

School administrators must be knowledgeable in basic **accounting principles** to provide appropriate **fiscal management** for the economic and efficient operation of the school. Accounting is the process used by administrators to **record, present, summarize,** and **interpret** accurate records of the financial data collected by the school through its daily operation. These basic accounting principles lead practicing administrators to the recognition of **revenues** and **expenditures** for the pre-established accounts of the school.

General principles of school cost accounting require the utilization of an **accrual basis for accounting** rather than a cash basis. This means that the financial transactions of the school must be recorded as **revenues** or **expenditures** at the time the transaction occurs and there should never be cash exchanged for goods or services. This generally accepted principle is called the accrual basis of accounting. In this process, revenues earned at the time of the transaction become **assets,** and **expenditures** become **liabilities,** regardless of when the cash receipt or reimbursement occurs. In this system of accounting assets are inventory, investments, accounts receivable, building and fixed equipment, furniture, motor vehicles, etc. while liabilities are salaries, benefits, accounts payable, construction contracts, etc. Unlike private enterprises for profit where there is owners' equity, schools are owned by the taxpayers. Therefore, balances are known as **fund equity,** which include reserves, retained earnings, contributed capital, and other fund equity.

Schools must adhere to specific rules governing their internal funds as prescribed by State Board Rules. All school organizations must be accountable for receipts and expenditures of funds obtained from the public. Additionally, sound business practices are expected for all financial transactions of the school. For example, in an effort to raise money to benefit programs of the school, fund-raising activities should not conflict with the programs administered by the school board.

All purchases from **internal funds** must be authorized by the principal or designee and district's pre-approved, serially numbered receipts forms must be used to record any cash received and to record the accounting transaction. Each school must have a bank checking account and each monthly statement must be reconciled as soon as it is received. Each account should have two authorized check signers, one being the principal. The principal should be never presign checks, under any circumstances. Monthly written financial reports must be made for the purpose of school decision-making, and annual reports must be made for the district's annual **financial statement**.

The sponsors of classes, clubs, or department student activities (such as athletic events, musical, and the like) are responsible for providing the **financial documents** and records to the principal or designee. The collection received must be deposited in the school internal fund in the respective classified account (athletics, music, art, Latin Club, and others). All disbursements by the club or organization must be made by check from internal funds. A financial report must be filed with the principal's office at the close of each fundraising activity.

Records and documents of school financial transactions used for its internal fund and accounts must be examined periodically through the **auditing process**. This auditing process, whether internal or external, provides an adequate safeguard to preserve the property of the public school system. This process secures evidence of propriety of completed transactions; it determines whether all transactions have been recorded, whether these transactions have been accurately recorded in the appropriate accounts, and whether the statements have been drawn from the accounts.

Good auditing reviews are the result of excellent accounting practices. Drake and Roe (1994) define the accounting cycle as continuous and inclusive of the processes of **documenting, analyzing, recording,** and **summarizing** financial information. **Documenting** includes recording all financial transaction including the authority or initiator of the transaction, ensuring that the debt incurred is within the limit of allotment, that every financial transaction is identified with a unit or fund, and that each fund is restrictive and limited in use. The process of **analyzing** requires that each transaction is analyzed and classified into debits and credits, and that each debit and credit is referenced to a specific account under the affected fund.

That a clear understanding is held of how a debit or a credit affects the balance in an account, and that budgetary accounts are restricted in purpose and amount of expenditure. The **recording** and **summarizing** processes requires that all transactions of a fund or account be recorded and that summaries be provided to allow comparisons and analyses of the changes that are taking place within the budget.

The school operation must be very conscious of its fiscal control to avoid over-expenditure and maintain a positive balance in each of its accounts. Therefore, an encumbrance system must be used to charge each purchase order, contract or salary to an appropriation. Once paid, these transactions are canceled and ceased to be an encumbrance as soon as the liability is recorded.

COMPETENCY E: Demonstrates the ability to explain the precedence for funding public elementary and secondary education.

> **Skill 1:** Identifies federal, state and local historical development in public school funding.

> **Skill 2:** Distinguishes among federal, state, and local purposes in the funding of public schools.

The U.S. Constitution does not include any mention of education. It is the **Tenth Amendment** that gives powers to the state in matters of education. This Amendment states, "The powers not delegated to the United States by the Constitution, nor prohibited by it to the States, are reserved to the States respectively, or to the people". This amendment clearly gives responsibilities to the states; yet, it does not prohibit the federal government from supporting public education for its citizens.

Since **colonial days**, schools have been the responsibilities of towns and cities. The earliest recollection goes back to 1647 when the Massachusetts Bay Colony enacted the **Old Deluder Satan Act**, which required towns of 50 or more families to hire a teacher for reading and writing, and towns of 100 or more families to hire a Latin teacher (Lemleck 1994). Towns became responsible for school buildings, levying taxes, and hiring teachers. Local support of schools preceded the federal government. Even with such traditions, upon becoming a nation, the federal government has always been involved in public education in some way. Tracing back to the land grant legislation when the northwest territory was divided into townships, which preceded the Constitution of the United States, Congress had the powers to tax for social purposes and general good which included education.

Historically, the role of the federal government and its relations with schools has evolved into a supporting relationship by using its resources to work directly with the state and local agencies to support the needs of all people. The role of the federal government has gone from separation of power between the federal government and the states to the government playing a greater role in education. During the first 150 years of education in this country, the founding fathers limited the federal government's involvement in education at all levels. During the time of **the Great Depression** emerged the period of **National Federalism** in which the economic climate and social circumstances created a greater need for federal involvement in education. This situation progressed with legislation such as the War on Poverty, the Civil Rights Act, and others (Lunenburg and Ornstein 1991). The period of New Federalism followed the National Federalism. It included the 1980s and 1990s which evolved into a dramatic shift with federal policy and programs reflecting the states taking a major monetary role and program responsibility for education. This new shift is characterized by deregulation, consolidation, and cutbacks from the federal government.

The federal government works through the **U.S. Department of Education** as its main agency to support education. Federal funds to support education have steadily declined because of the belief that during the 1980s and 1990s the federal government had become too involved in education. Additionally, through the tenth amendment of the Constitution, Congress was tasked with providing for the general welfare of the country. Therefore, it passes laws to support education. Among these laws are the Bilingual Education Act, American with Disabilities Act, National School Lunch Act, and the like.

Education is by law a **state function.** Each state has its own unique system of education which originates from the constitution of each state, but while there are differences there are also similarities in many of the systems of education. The states **delegate responsibility** to local districts for the day-to-day operation of schools. The states provide support to the local districts through legislative enactments that determine the level of funding and financial aid, minimum standards for training, certification standards, and other operational guidelines.

COMPETENCY F: Recognize the importance of external influences which impact upon the school.

> **Skill 1:** Identifies methods for the study of community power structure.
>
> **Skill 2:** Has knowledge of the types of power structure(s) in communities.
>
> **Skill 3:** Demonstrates understanding of the process of educational policy development at the state level.
>
> **Skill 4:** Demonstrates understanding of the process of educational policy development at the school district level

Schools operate in an Open System **Model** where **external influences** impact the effectiveness of the school-based administration and leadership. External influences provide input into the system of schooling in the form of people, policies, values, laws, technology, and other material resources. This input directly or indirectly affects not only school business decisions such as finance and purchasing, but also affects other functions of school operation such as the curriculum, pupil services, and the like.

It does not matter how efficient and knowledgeable the school-based administrator might be in the endeavors of managing the school if there is a lack of clear understanding of the **community power structures**, its strengths, and its effects on the operation of the school. Hudge, Anthony and Gayles (1996) suggest that understanding how **power** is distributed both **internally** and **externally,** as well understanding the political nature of organizations, are two crucial components to better understand the actions or inactions of organizations. To better understand the political nature of the school organization, administrators must clearly understand the difference between **authority** and **power**. Legal-rational organizations base their authority on formal policies and vests authority of command in specific individuals. Power, on the other hand, is the capacity to control or influence the behaviors of others (Hansen, 1996).

School administrators must be aware of the various **dimensions of educational politics** in school districts; among these politics of the community, politics of the state and the federal government, politics of the profession, politics of the local board of education, and politics of the bureaucracy (Kimbrough and Nunnery 1988). Perhaps the most important politics for school-based administrators are the politics of the community and its power structure, as well as identifying methods to analyze these structures and develop a plan to work with these groups.

Additionally, practicing administrators must understand the politics involved in the process of **educational policy development** at the state and district levels.

The school organizational structure is greatly affected by existing conditions in the local community such as customs, traditions, and value systems. These conditions affect the power that is exercised on the formal and informal decision making process at the school district and school building levels. The biggest challenge is to identify the main power brokers in the community and learn how to work with them. Kimbrough and Nunnery (1988) offer a **typology of community power structure** based on specific variables including structure of the groups. Leadership overlaps on different kinds of issues, degree of competition of decisions, membership among voting and interest groups, and kinds of issues in the school districts.

These variables lead to four types of power structures. **Monopolistic Structures** are dominated by a coalition of groups or a single group of leaders who dominate the decision-making process and community policies. **Multigroup Noncompetitive Structures** are typical of small towns or small school districts that are non-innovative and opposed to change in which several important power groups, with very little or no differences of opinion, make the decisions. **Competitive Elite System** is usually embroiled in ideological differences among its leaders. Finally, **Democratic Pluralism** includes a wide participation of people from the school community in an open process of decision-making.

Nunnery and Kimbrough describe how practitioners can make analyses that are usable to study the community power structure. Study the background materials about power structures; make special effort to obtain more information about the local problems, issues, and decisions; piece together information obtained from conversations and documents; record information obtained; observe leader behavior in community decisions; and participate in activities in the community.

Understanding the politics involved in the process of educational policy development at the state and district levels should be a concern for school administrators. The increase in government funding for education has paralleled the interest of educators in the nature of laws being considered or passed and policy development at the federal, state and local levels. Mandates and policies have direct implication for school level implementation of programs to meet the needs of children, especially when the level of funding is incongruent with the requirements of the law. State politicians constantly struggle to reduce **federal involvement** in the control over programs and return more control to state government, yet at times losing sight of the fact that the goal of the federal government's participation is constitutionally one of **equalizing funding** to provide an equal education for all children.

The hierarchy of state and local educational governance constitute a **political structure** that needs to be understood by school administrators. Each state in the union has a legal responsibility to support education as reflected in the **constitution of the state**. The **powers, authority, and methods** of school operation are also documented by provisions made by each state. In most states, there are three branches of governance, which include the executive branch represented by the governor, the legislative branch or state legislature, and the judicial or state court.

A main educational function of the governor of the state is to formulate budgetary recommendations for the legislature. In Florida, the Governor depends on his appointed advisors and the elected Commissioner of Education as his main support in policy discussion and recommendation. While the governor has many powers, the position holds some limitations in some personnel decisions. All Commissioners, the Secretary of State, and the Comptroller make up the Cabinet. The Cabinet approves State Board Rules. The Governor has only one vote along with all the other members of the Cabinet. In Florida, the governor does not appoint the Commissioner of Education. The citizens do, through the electoral process. The governor also has veto power which serves to discourage the state legislators from enacting laws considered detrimental to education.

The **governor** and **state legislators** are elected officials, who influence policies in education. In today's **political climate**, they invariably set an educational platform during the election campaign making promises that affect the **level of funding** for education. Candidates who are successful listen to various lobby groups, coalitions and educational administrative associations. Many districts currently appointed, salaried employees who serve as liaison with the state legislature to monitor the emergence of new laws before they take effect. These groups exercise tremendous **voting power** by influencing members of their organization and other **voting citizens** to support candidates who share their goal and views for education.

COMPETENCY G: Demonstrates knowledge of the components, stages, and appropriate application of macro and micro planning systems.

> **Skill 1:** Is able to specify long range and short range planning techniques.
>
> **Skill 2:** Cites and applies the logical stages of planning techniques to school-site endeavors.

The process of **financing schools** is a yearly process; yet it is a continuous process to appropriately review the strengths and weaknesses of the process so that meaningful and deliberate planning can take place to meet the need of students through appropriate programs.

School administration has evolved into an inclusive and cooperative endeavor with a structure that endorses a **participatory model** to include not only administrators and teachers, but also parents, business partners, and other interested citizens in the community. Therefore, the **planning** process must be ongoing and systematic to allow time for the development of **unity of purpose, methodology,** and **desirable outcome**.

Planning must be continuous at both the district levels, as well as the school building level, even though the process used at one level may overlap with the other. Planning methodologies and applications at both the **macro and micro planning** levels may also overlap.

The rationale approach to planning follows a very **logical sequence** to accomplish organizational goals. It begins with setting goals, which includes **articulating the mission** of the organization and clarifying specific goals to be attained. A plan of action that is long-term in nature and inclusive of general projections, along with the short-term plan with the details to carry out the actions deemed necessary. The action plan follows as the implementation tool for both the **short-term and the long-term** plans. The **evaluation process** provides feedback for improvement and the process is repeated, thereafter. While very useful to school administrators, the rational approach provides only general principles that are applicable to many areas of planning. School financial management requires specific budgetary techniques for appropriate fiscal accountability.

There are three commonly used techniques that apply to the budgetary process producing varying degrees of outcome. **Incremental budgeting** begins with the budget for the current term and examines each line item in relation to expected revenues in order to make decisions about the item. By addressing items and categories for expenditure, much is lost because of the failure to observe the impact of the budget as a whole and in reference to the goals of the organization and the needs of children. It also encourages a static state hindering creativity and change. **Zero-based budgeting** is another planning technique that produces similar outcomes as the incremental budgeting approach. It focuses on the current budgetary cycle and begins with zero dollars in all accounts to then justify the continuation of a program, activities, or expenditure.

The **Planning, Programming, Budgetary and Evaluation System** (PPBES) is the first approach to integrate long range planning with the resources provided through funded sources to achieve institutional goals to fund programs on the bases of annual fund allocation (Drake and Roe 1994). This process requires the periodic collection and analysis of data to inform the decisions to be made about programs to project needs to be met.

The evaluation component that is built into the process not only assesses the effectiveness of the goal, but it also measures the level of goal attainment over specific periods of time.

"When he leaves, I'm in charge."

Directions: Read each item and select the best response.

1. **The calculation of the base student allocation formula is best expressed in the following formula.**

    A. The FTE plus program cost factor, times base student allocation, times district cost differential

    B. The weighted FTE times base student allocation, times district cost differential

    C. The FTE times weighted FTE, times based student allocation, times district cost differential

    D. The weighted FTE times program cost factor, times base student allocation, times district cost factor

2. **Which of the following statements is not a requirement for school participation in the FEFP?**

    A. Operate all schools for a term of 180 teaching days or the equivalent on an hourly basis

    B. Provide a written contract for all instructional personnel and require at least 196 days of service

    C. Observe all requirements of the State Board related to the preparation, adoption, and execution of budgets for the district school system

    D. Maintain a ratio of classroom teachers and classroom related to the number of students

3. **Districts with higher non-tax exempt property tax base per FTE pay_____**

    A. More local support

    B. Less local support

    C. The same as the district with the lowest rate

    D. As much as the district with the highest rate

4. **A key feature of the FEFP is**

   _____

   A. The number of teacher participation at each school.

   B. The number of classrooms at each school in each district

   C. The number of students participating in particular educational programs

   D. The number of elementary students with specific needs versus secondary age students in the district

5. **Which of the following is a factor in the FEFP formula for equalization of funds to school districts?**

   A. Program FTE

   B. District cost factor

   C. Matching funds

   D. Varying local property taxes

6. **Which of the following best describes the purpose of budgeting?**

   A. A yearly and periodic task to defined and justify expenditure

   B. Financial plan to expend funds

   C. Continuous planning to put the educational goals into a financial plan

   D. A statement of anticipated revenues operate the organization

7. **Which of the following is not an adjustment in the FEFP formula**

   A. Declining enrollment

   B. Sparsity supplement

   C. Discretionary tax equalization

   D. Student transportation

8. **_____deals with the day-to-day operation of the school.**

   A. Internal Services Fund

   B. General Fund

   C. Debt Services Fund

   D. Special Revenue Fund

9. **Which of the following accounts are used by school principals?**

   A. PTA account

   B. Student activity account

   C. Employee benefits account

   E. Instructional staff account

10. **The district financial officer shared information about a fund that could be used for specific types of expenditures. He made reference to_____**

    A. A group of accounts

    B. A sum of money

    C. A cash balance

    D. A ledger

11. **The largest category of local funds to support education comes from _____**

    A. Motor vehicle licensing

    B. Mobile home licensing

    C. Ad valorem taxes

    D. Racing Commissioners fund

12. **If a millage represents one thousandth of a dollar, which of the following statements represents a tax rate of 25 mills?**

    A. $250 for every $1,000 of assessed property value

    B. $2.50 for every $1,000 of assessed property value

    C. $25 for every $1,000 of assessed property value

    D. $0.25 for every $1,000 of assessed property value

13. **_____administers federal funds received by the state.**

    A. The governor of the state

    B. The commissioner of education

    C. The local school board

    D. The board of education

14. **At the end of the budget term a school district finds that there is an excess of assets over liability. Which of the following describes what the district has?**

    A. Revenues

    B. Working capital

    C. Owners' equity

    D. Fund balance

15. **Which of the following formulas best describe public school accounting?**

    A. Assets = Liability + Owners' equity

    B. Assets = Liability – Fund equity

    C. Assets = Liability + Fund equity

    D. Assets = Liability - Owners' equity

16. **Which of the following best describes liabilities in the equation of accounting?**

    A. Taxes receivable

    B. Inventory

    C. Salaries and benefits

    D. Retained earnings

17. **Which of the following best describes the cycle of public school accounting?**

    A. Documenting, analyzing, recording, summarizing

    B. Documenting, summarizing, analyzing, recording

    C. Documenting, summarizing, recording, analyzing

    D. Summarizing, analyzing, documenting, recording

18. **Early methods of financing public education violated the constitutional equal protection clause expressed in the _____**

    A. X Amendment

    B. XIV Amendment

    C. XV Amendment

    D. VIII Amendment

19. **Which statement best expresses the basis for early school finance litigations?**

    A. Some assessed property values were much higher than others

    B. Taxpayers carried too much of a burden in funding public education

    C. There was disparity between taxable wealth among the local districts

    D. There was disparity among wealthy school districts

20. **A school funding model that requires a certain level of participation from the state, and local district with a local option to levy additional millage is _____.**

    A. Matching grants

    B. Foundation programs

    C. Flat grants

    D. Guaranteed tax base

21. This court case established the standard of fiscal neutrality.

A. Serrano v. Priest

B. McInnis v. Shapiro

C. Rose v. the Council of Better Education

D. San Antonio Independent School District v. Rodriguez

22. Fiscal neutrality is best described as

A. A measurement that determines the quality of a child's education could not be based on the wealth of the local district, rather on the wealth of the state

B. A measurement that determines the quality of a child's education could not be based on the wealth of the state, rather on the wealth of the local district

C. A measurement that determines the quality of a child's education could not be based on the wealth of the parents but of the local district

D. A measurement that determines the quality of a child's education could not be based on the wealth of the local district, but on the wealth of the families in the local district

23. District fiscal capacity refers to

A. The expenditure per pupil

B. The level of support per student

C. The tax rate that is applied to the value of property

D. Resources held by the district that are available for taxation

24. Collecting and expending school's Internal Fund Accounts must be done in accordance to

A. Rules set by the principal

B. Rules set by the State Board of Education

C. Rules set by the PTO

D. Rules set by the superintendent

25. It was decided that the coaches would be compensated for sponsoring athletic competitions. The compensation should come from

A. Collections after the most productive games of the year

B. Collections from home games

C. A check by district payroll department

D. A check from internal account

26. **Which of the following is not a principle of school accounting?**

   A. Revenues and expenditures are recorded as the transaction occurs

   B. An accrual basis is used for transactions

   C. A cash basis is used for transactions

   D. Revenues earned are recorded as assets and expenditures are liabilities

27. **Which of the following is not a part of the auditing process?**

   A. Secure evidence of propriety of completed transactions

   B. Secure evidence of transactions appropriately recorded

   C. Safeguard the property of the school district

   D. Record the financial transactions of the school

28. **Dual signatures of school financial transactions exist for the purpose of**

   A. Recognizing the authority of the principal

   B. Avoiding collusion at the school

   C. Making sure there are balances in the accounts

   D. Making sure the financial institution recognizes at least one of the signatures

29. **A fund is _____**

   A. A group of self-balancing accounts designated for a specific purpose

   B. A sum of money used for activities

   C. A group of self-balancing accounts used for any school related activities

   D. Excess assets over liability.

30. **The _____ gives responsibility to the states in matters of education.**

   A. X Amendment

   B. XIV Amendment

   C. XV Amendment

   D. VIII Amendment

31. The _____ is the earliest legal enactment of the states' responsibility to education.

    A. Land Grant Legislation

    B. War on Poverty Act

    C. Old Deluder Satan Act

    D. Civil Rights Act

32. The _____ marked a change in the role of the federal government from separation of power to more involvement in the education of the people.

    A. Period of National Federalism

    B. Colonial Period

    C. Modern Era

    D. Period of expanding America

33. The day-to-day operation of the school is regulated by mandates from _____

    A. The Commissioner of Education

    B. The federal government

    C. The State Legislature

    D. The Governor

34. In the Open System Model in which the school operates, internal and external forces affect the operation of the school. Which of the following has the least effect at the local level?

    A. Laws and enactments

    B. Policies and procedures

    C. Values and organizational culture

    D. Curriculum

35. Which of the following statements describe the difference between power and authority?

A. Power is the capacity to influence the behaviors of others while authority is the capacity to control the behaviors of others

B. Power is the capacity to influence and control the behaviors of others while authority is based on formal policies that are vested in the command of designated individuals in the organization

C. Power is the capacity to influence the behaviors of others while authority is the capacity to influence policy changes to control the behaviors of others

D. Power is the capacity to influence the behaviors of others while authority is the capacity based on informal organizational structures to control the behaviors of others

36. Within the structure of the community power groups, which of the following variables is the least significant?

    A. The degree of competition and decision-making

    B. Membership among voting and interest groups

    C. Leadership on different types of issues

    D. Residential location

37. Which of the following statements best describe the competitive elite power structure?

    A. Group or groups of leaders who dominate community policies

    B. A group that is non innovative and opposed to change

    C. A group concerned with ideological differences

    D. A group that embraces an open process of decision-making

38. Which of the following statements best describes the monopolistic community power structure?

    A. A group or groups of leaders who dominate community policies

    B. A group that is non-innovative or opposed to change

    C. A group concerned with ideological differences

    D. A group that embraces an open process of decision-making

39. Which statement best represents the role of the Governor?

    A. Approve State Board of education rules

    B. Appoint the Commissioner of Education as a partner in school matters

    C. Make laws that directly benefit schools

    D. Formulate budgetary recommendations to the state legislature

40. Which of the following best describes the process of school planning?

A. The visionary principal who knows about the needs of the school, developing the school plan

B. Principal, teachers, parents, business partners , and other community members developing the school plan

C. Principals, teachers and parents developing the school plan

D. A visionary team of teachers and administrators developing the school plan

41. Which of the following statements best describe zero based budgeting process?

A. It examines each item in relation to expected revenues

B. It begins with empty accounts to then justify the continuation of the expenditure

C. It begins with accounts for the past three years and looks at the history of spending to justify new expenditures

D. It integrates long-range planning with the resources provided to meet specific needs

42. Which of the following should mark the initial stages of school-based planning?

A. Developing a plan of action

B. Evaluating the process

C. Clarifying and articulating the mission and goals

D. Analyzing the plan of action

43. Which of the following statements is <u>not</u> a benefit of planning a budget?

A. It establishes a plan for the coming year

B. It recognizes coordination throughout the organization

C. It establishes a system of management control

D. It serves as a ledger to record anticipated financial transactions

44. Which of the following statements best describe the Incremental Budgeting process?

A. It integrates long-range planning with the resources provided to meet specific needs

B. It begins with empty accounts to then justify the continuation of the expenditure

C. It begins with accounts for the past three years and looks at the history of spending to justify new expenditures

D. It examines each item in relation to expected revenues

45. Which of the following best describes the purpose of the evaluation component in the process of budgeting?

A. To determine the attainment of goals, the effectiveness of cost and benefits and new needs over a period of time

B. To justify new expenditures and needed revenues

C. To decrease or increase a line item in the budget

D. To keep abreast of unit or program cost

ANSWER KEY (Subtest 3 – School Operations, Finance)

1.	B	23.	D
2.	A	24.	B
3.	A	25.	C
4.	D	26.	C
5.	D	27.	D
6.	C	28.	B
7.	D	29.	A
8.	B	30.	A
9.	B	31.	C
10.	A	32.	A
11.	C	33.	C
12.	C	34.	A
13.	C	35.	B
14.	D	36.	D
15.	C	37.	C
16.	C	38.	A
17.	A	39.	D
18.	B	40.	B
19.	C	41.	B
20.	B	42.	C
21.	A	43.	D
22.	A	44.	A
		45.	D

BIBLIOGRAPHY

Alexander, K. and Salmon, R. (1995). *Public School Finance*. Needham Heights, MA: Allyn and Bacon.

Bracy, Gerald (November 1995). "Debunking the Myths about Money for Schools." *Educational Leadership*, pp. 65-69.

Burrup, p. Brimley V. and Garfield, R. (1996). *Financing Education in a Climate of Change*. 8th ed. Needham Heights, MA: Allyn and Bacon.

Drake, T. and Roe. W. (1994) *School Business Management Supporting Instructional Effectiveness*. Needham Heights, MA: Allyn and Bacon.

Dickerson, B., Campsey, B.J. and Brigham, E. (1995). *Introduction to Financial Management*. 4th ed. Forth Worth, TX: The Dryden Press.

Florida Association of School Administrators (1997). *Florida Education Handbook 1997*. Tallahassee, Florida: CMD Publishing, Inc.

Florida Department of Education (1994). *Financial and Program Cost Accounting and Reporting for Florida Schools* ("The Red Book").

Florida Department of Education (1996-97). *Florida education finance program: statistical report*. Tallahassee, Florida.

Florida Department of Education (1994-95). *Analysis of district expenditures and program cost factors. Florida education finance program*. Tallahassee, Florida.

Florida Department of Education (1996). *Profiles of Florida school districts 1994-95 financial data. Statistical report*. Tallahassee, Florida.

Hansen, E. (1996). *Educational Administration and Organizational Behavior*. 4th ed. Needham Heights, MA: Allyn and Bacon.

Hanushek, E. (November 1995). "Moving Beyond Spending Fetishes." *Educational Leadership*, pp. 60-694.

Hodge, B.J., Anthony, W. and Gales, L. (1996). *Organizational Theory: a Strategy Approach*. 5th ed. Needham Heights, MA: Allyn and Bacon.

Johns, R. and Morphet, E. (1975). *The Economics and Financing of Education. A Systems Approach*. Englewood Cliffs, NJ: Prentice-Hall.

Kimbrough, R. and Nunnary M. (1983). *Educational Administration: an Introduction.* 3rd ed. New York, NY: Macmillan Publishing Co.

LaMorte, M. (1996). *School Law: Cases and Concepts.* 5th ed. Needham Heights, MA: Allyn and Bacon.

Lemleck, J. (1994). *Curriculum and Instructional Methods for the Elementary and Middle School.* 3rd ed. New York, N.Y: Macmillan Publishing Co.

Lunenburg, F. and Onrstein, A. (1991). *Educational Administration: Concepts and Practices.* Belmont, CA: Wadsworth Publishing Company.

Molnar, Alex (November 1996). "School Funding: the Right Issue, the Wrong Logic." *Educational Leadership,* pp. 65-69.

State of Florida (1996). *Florida Statutes.* Tallahassee, Florida.

Swanson, A. and King, R. (1997) *School Finance : Its Economics and Politics.* 2nd ed. White Plains, NY: Longman Publishers.

Subtest 3 - School Operations

7. School Law

Introduction

One of first things that students of educational administration ask during the first class meeting of school law classes is "Why do we have to know law?" And invariably, the last thing they exclaim at the end of the class is "Why didn't we have this information before? We needed this as teachers!" These students are reacting to the fundamental nature of the American educational system: that it is anchored in the legal policies of the nation and the states. State and/or federal policy impact every administrative aspect of the school leadership role. After all, public school systems are state governmental entities.

School law is a dynamic area. In order for educational administrators to keep up with the constant changes in state and federal statutes and regulations as well occasional changes in state constitutions, they should make every effort to understand the broad legal concepts and the relationships among those concepts. Once they acquire this type of understanding they will be able think their way through situations and make informed decisions. School law courses are designed to help administrators recognize problematic situations.

Some basic concepts that are essential to studying school law include an understanding of the sources of law, the organization of the American court system, and a sense of differentiation between state and federal roles and responsibilities. Sources of law at both the federal and state levels include constitutions and amendments, statutes, case law, executive orders and attorney general opinions. The courts establish case law when a decision is made and a precedent is established. Under the doctrine of *stare decisis*, courts in the same jurisdiction may use the precedent to settle subsequent cases of similar fact (LaMorte, 1996, p. 10). At the state and local levels, board and district policies have the force of law.

The federal court system has three levels with the Supreme Court positioned at the highest level. The lowest level, the district courts, are courts of original jurisdiction (LaMorte, 1996, p. 16) or trial courts. Courts of Appeals and the Supreme Court hear cases only on appeal for the lower courts. Higher courts can also choose to review a case from a lower court a *certiorari*. The Supreme Court is the highest court in the land; its decisions are not subject to appeal. It is the only court overtly established by the federal Constitution (Valente, 1994).

The organization of state courts often replicates the federal system, but some variations do exist. Each state has the authority to develop its court system under its own state constitution. Despite the variations, the state systems will include trial courts (courts of original jurisdiction) and courts of appeals. Whether the court jurisdiction in a particular situation will be in the state of federal courts will be determined by the source of the law in question (state or federal) and the geographical setting.

This chapter will attempt to provide some organization and clarity to the legal concepts that will help school administrators avoid legal faux pas and recognize situations that will require thought and additional support.

COMPETENCY A: Know federal constitutional provisions that apply to public education.

Although "education" is not specifically mentioned in the federal constitution, the federal government's role in education does indeed have roots in specific articles and amendments to the constitution.

Article I, Section 8. [1] The General Welfare Clause empowers Congress to perform whatever actions are necessary to "provide for the common defense and general welfare of the United States...." Early in the establishment of the United States, the founding fathers determined that an educated citizenry was essential for the survival of the democracy. Thus, the federal government's involvement in public education, although indirect, has been significant over the history of the nation.

Article I, Section 8. [3] The Commerce Clause regulates commerce with foreign nations, among states and within the Indian tribes. The term "commerce" has been defined in the broader context to incorporate the interchange of ideas and the concept of social discourse.

Article I, Section 10. [1] States are prohibited from passing any legislation that impairs the obligations of contracts. This article has implications for many the contractual agreements that are established in the operation of any school system.

Article III. This clause establishes the Federal Court System. The judicial power of the United States is vested in a Supreme Court with the provision that other inferior courts can be established as needed. The jurisdiction of the federal courts and the terms for the judicial service and compensation are established. Jurisdiction of the federal courts is also clearly delineated.

Article VI. In the Supremacy Clause, the Constitution, the laws of the United States and treaties made under the authority of the United States are designated as the "law of the land." These laws bind judges in every state, and all public officials are bound oath to support the Constitution.

Skill 1: Identifies judicially recognized individual right guaranteed by the First Amendment.

The First Amendment contains three of the most powerful clauses in the Constitution: the Free Speech Clause, the Establishment Clause, and the Free Exercise Clause.

Free Speech: This clause prohibits congress from passing any law that might abridge freedom of speech or freedom of the press. Administrators are regularly faced with situations that have potential free speech significance for teachers, staff, and students. The Supreme Court opened the door to free speech analysis for students in *Tinker v. De Moines*. It determined that students did not shed their constitutional rights at the schoolhouse door. The concept of symbolic speech is also spelled out in this case. Although the courts have supported free speech in school settings for teachers and students, that personal freedom has been balanced against the state's compelling interest to maintain an educational environment that is free from disruption. The disruption test weighs free speech against the interference with other individuals, school property, school activities, and school discipline. Thus, even a teacher's right to free speech about a public concern might be overshadowed by the state's compelling interest in a school environment that is free from disruption. The balance is constantly weighed. A review of the cases cited below will provide insights into a wide range of free speech issues such as symbolic free speech, faculty's protected speech, and free speech related to student publications.

<u>Freedom of Speech.</u> *Tinker v. Des Moines, Bethel School District v. Fraser, Pickering v. BOE, Mt. Healthy v. Doyle, Hazelwood School District v.Kuhlmeier, Cox v. Dardenelle Public School District, Goetz v. Ansell, Lipp v.Morris.*

The Establishment and Free Exercise Clauses: These two clauses of the First Amendment set up a natural tension (Valente, 1994, p.86) and are sources of on-going litigation. The Establishment Clause states that Congress shall make no law respecting the establishment of a religion. This phrase has been broadly interpreted through the years to encompass not only the establishment of a religion, but also the perception that one religion might be sanctioned by the "state" over and above any other religion. This broader interpretation of the Establishment Clause undergirds the Supreme Court's decision to prohibit the reading of scripture from the Bible as a required exercise in the schools. The requirement has the effect of placing one religion (Christianity) in the position of being sanctioned by the "state" to the exclusion of other religions.

The Free Exercise Clause prohibits Congress from passing any law that might keep an individual from exercising the religion of his/her personal choice. In Wisconsin v. Yoder, the state brought charges against the Yoder family for breaking the state's compulsory attendance law. Although the compulsory attendance statute was a state statute, the case was brought into the federal courts under the Free Exercise Clause of the First Amendment. The Supreme Court ruling in this case is informative on several points. The court acknowledged the states compelling interests in seeing that its citizens receive an adequate education. Yet the court weighed the state's compelling interest against the family's free exercise right to raise their children according to their religious tenets. In the analysis of the situation, the court considered the history of the Yoder's Amish community and the its religious tenets to determine that in this particular case, the family's right to free exercise overshadowed the state's compelling interest.

The tension that is set up by these twin clauses places the state in the position of retaining neutrality in the area of religion. The classic rule for determining the neutrality of a policy is provided by the three prongs of the Lemon Test: (1) Does it have a clearly secular purpose? (2) Does it have a primary effect that neither advances nor inhibits religion? (3) Does it require an excessive entanglement between the government and religion? If the consideration of the policy in question yields a positive response to any of the three prompts, the policy probably will not withstand First Amendment scrutiny in the area of religion.

Religion has an impact on all of the major areas of education. The most obvious areas include things like Bible reading and school prayer. Yet more subtle issues are imbedded in the life of the school. School calendars have historically revolved around the Christian holidays of Christmas and Easter. Displays and activities that have become a part of the American way of life often have roots in religious origins. Textbooks and courses often touch on issues that have religious significance (e.g. evolution in biological science courses). Other areas of education that bring the church and the state into contact are special student services that are funded by state and federal governments, the use of school property by religious groups, and teachers' religious practices and garb.

The Establishment Clause. *Engle v. Vitale, Abbington v. Schempp, Lemon v. Kurtzman, Wallace v. Jaffree, Edwards v. Aguillard.*

The Free Exercise Clause. *Wisconsin v. Yoder.*

Skill 2: Identifies judicially recognized Fourth Amendment rights.

The Fourth Amendment Right to Privacy covers a wide area of concerns for both teachers and students and protects them from unreasonable search and seizure, with emphasis on "unreasonable." In situations where an individual has no expectation of privacy, no right to privacy exists. Although the traditional standard required for search and seizure is "probable cause," the courts have upheld the lesser standard of "reasonable suspicion" for school administrators. The reasoning seems to be that administrators have a compelling interest in maintaining a safe environment that is conducive to learning.

Searches of lockers, desks and other areas supplied by the school for student and teacher use can be searched if the authorities have reasonable suspicion the school rules or laws have been violated. The use of dogs to search lockers and areas of the school is permissible and not considered a search. The use of dogs to search individuals is problematic; such a situation requires a heightened and individualized level of justification.

In the areas of privacy rights in the public work place and in providing medical information, the rulings vary. Again, the individual's personal rights are balanced against the state's interests. In employee search situations where the employer is not state related, the interest of the employer and existing organizational policies are considered. Strip searches and mandatory blood and urine analyses are excessively intrusive and the factors that would lead to such searches should be of significant a nature as to warrant such intrusion.

Freedom from Illegal Search and Seizure. *Conner v. Ortega, New Jersey v. T.L.O, Horton v. Goose Creek Independent School System*

> **Skill 3:** Identifies judicially recognized individual right guaranteed by the Fourteenth Amendment.

The Fourteenth Amendment represents one of the most powerful of the constitutional amendments. First, it prioritizes the order of citizenship by stating that "all persons born or naturalized in the United States and subject to the jurisdiction thereof, are citizens of the United States and of the state wherein they reside." It further asserts that no state "shall abridge the privileges or immunities of citizens of the United States." That has the effect of giving national citizenship priority over state citizenship. The amendment then presents two significant clauses: the Due Process Clause and the Equal Protection Clause.

The Due Process Clause indicates that no state can deprive any person of life, liberty, or property without due process of law. Liberty and property have been broadly defined to refer to a wide range of substantive rights. For example, educators' contracts provide them with a property interest and expectation of employment for the terms of the contract. Tenure provides an expectation of future employment and so endows the individual who has tenure with a property interest. Liberty interest has been defined to encompass a wide range of personal freedoms. The courts have described liberty as fundamental rights that are "essential to the orderly pursuit of happiness by free men." The due process clause declares that no STATE can deprive a citizen of the United States of a substantive right WITHOUT according that citizen due process of the law.

This clause has major implications for educators for several reasons. It makes the earlier amendments applicable to the states. Prior to the Fourteenth Amendment, the earlier amendments applied to the federal government only. Another important factor lies in the nature of public education; it is a state governmental function. When educators are acting in their professional capacities, they are "the state". So, when administrators interact with teachers and students, they must be sure that they are functioning in a way that does not deprive an individual of his/her substantive rights. In addition to the substantive interests cited above, the freedoms identified in the earlier amendments are considered substantive. For example, if a teacher is fired from his/her position for speaking out on an issue of public interest in the middle of the school year, the teacher could bring legal action in the federal courts, because the state (the school system) deprived him/her of free speech rights. The teacher would also have to be accorded procedural due process because of the property interest in the remainder the annual contract. In another example, before a student can be suspended for a significant period of time, he/she must be accorded procedural due process, because the right to an education accrues to the student as a property interest through the state constitution. The sources of substantive rights are multiple and varied, but regardless of the source, the due process clause of the Fourteenth Amendment will protect them. The major elements of procedural due process are notice, a hearing, and an impartial tribunal.

Due Process. *Goss v. Lopez, Perry v. Sinderman*

The Equal Protection Clause of the Fourteenth Amendment indicates that no state shall deprive any person within its jurisdiction of equal protection of the laws. In other words, if a person resides within the boundaries of a state, that person has equal access to the protections and the benefits of the laws that state. When state laws stipulate that a state will provide free and adequate public education for all persons who reside in the state who are between ages 6 and 18 years, then to deny any person who meets those criteria such an education would deny that person equal protection of the laws of the state.

Equal Protection of the Law. *Brown v. Board of Education, San Antonio v. Rodriguez, Keyes v. Denver, Debra P. v. Turlington, United States of America v. State of South Carolina*

COMPETENCY B: Know federal statutory and regulatory provisions that influence public education.

>   **Skill 1:** Identifies judicially recognized interpretations of the purpose and intent of federal statutes prohibiting discrimination in public schools.

Title VI, The Civil Rights Act of 1964, extends protection against discrimination on the basis of race, color, or national origins in any program or activity receiving federal financial assistance. *Clark v. Huntsville, Tyler v. Hot Springs*

Title VII, The Civil Rights Act of 1964, states that it is unlawful for an employer to discriminate against any individual with respect to compensation, terms, conditions, or privileges of employment because of an individual's race, color, religion, sex, or national origin. Some exceptions are noted in this statute. It does not apply to religious organizations that seek individuals of a particular religion to perform the work of that organization. Where suspect classifications (those classifications having no basis in rationality) represent bona fide occupational qualifications, they are permitted. Classifications based upon merit and seniority are also acceptable under this statute. *Ansonia BOE v. Philbrook*

Title IX, The Educational Amendments of 1972, states that no individual shall be excluded from participation in, be denied the benefits of, or be subjected to discrimination under any educational program or activity that receives or benefits from federal assistance on the basis of sex. This statute covers the areas of admission, education programs and activities, access to course offerings, counseling and the use of appraisal and counseling materials, marital or parental status and athletics. *Marshall v. Kirkland*

Section 504, The Rehabilitation Act of 1973 indicates that "No otherwise handicapped individual... will be excluded from the participation in, be denied the benefits of, or be subjected to discrimination under any program or activity receiving federal financial assistance solely because of his/her handicap. *School Board of Nassau Co v. Arline*

The Age Discrimination Act of 1967 states that it shall be unlawful for an employer to fail or refuse to hire or to discharge any individual or otherwise discriminate against any individual with respect to his/her employment because of an individual's age. This statute does allow an employer or employment to consider age as a bone fide occupational qualification (bfoq). *Geller v. Markham*

Skill 2: Identifies educational entitlements and related rights under federal statutes.

The Family Rights and Privacy Act of 1964 (FERPA) [Buckley Amendment] states that no funds will be made available under any applicable program to any state or local educational agency, any institution of higher education, any community college, any school, agency offering a preschool program, or any other educational institution which has a policy of denying parents of students the right to inspect and review any and all official records, files, and data directly related to their children. This includes material incorporated into the student's cumulative folder such as identifying data, academic work completed, level of achievement, attendance date, testing results, health data, family background information, teacher or counselor ratings and observations, and verified reports of serious or recurring behavior problems. Each educational organization must establish appropriate procedures for granting access requests within a reasonable period of time (not to exceed 45 days).

- Parents have an opportunity for a hearing to challenge the record's contents, to ensure the record's accuracy, and to provide corrected or rebuttal information.
- Educational organizations must require written consent of the parent in order to release identifying information to external individuals and organizations.

The state specifies exceptions.

- All persons, agencies or organizations seeking access to a student's record must sign a written form that must be included in the student file.
- Students who are 18 years of age or attending a post-secondary educational institution acquire the right of consent formerly held by the parent. "Directory information" can be released without consent. Such information includes the following: student's name, address, telephone listing, date and place of birth, major field of study, participation in officially recognized activities and sports, weight and height of members of athletic teams, dates of attendance, degrees and awards of attendance, degrees and awards received, and the most recent educational agency or institution attended by the student.

Individuals with Disabilities Education Act (IDEA)[The Education of All Handicapped Children Act] requires that states adopt policies that assure all children with disabilities receive a "free and appropriate public education." The statute requires that each student's unique needs are addressed through an "individualized educational plan (IEP) and that extensive procedural requirements are put into place. Requirements allow for the withholding of federal financial resources to states that fail to comply with the statute. *Honig v. Doe, Hendrick Hudson Board of Education v. Rowley*

The Equal Access Act of 1985 states that is will be unlawful for any public secondary school which receives federal financial assistance and which has a limited open forum to deny equal access or a fair opportunity to or discriminate against any students who wish to conduct a meeting within that limited open forum on the basis of the religious, political, philosophical, or other content of the speech at the meetings. A limited open forum exists whenever a school grants an opportunity for one or more non-curriculum-related student groups to meet on the school premises during non-instructional time. The criteria for a fair opportunity provide that

- the meeting is voluntary and student initiated;
- there is no sponsorship by the school, the government, or its agents or employees;
- school agents or employees are present at the meetings only in a non-participatory capacity;
- the meeting does not substantially interfere with the orderly conduct of educational activities within the school;
- non-school persons may not direct, conduct, control or regularly attend activities of student groups.

This statute does authorize the school, its agents or employees, to maintain order and discipline on the school premises, to protect the well-being of students and faculty, and to assure that the attendance of the students at the meeting is voluntary. *Board of Education of Westside Community Schools v. Mergens*

The federal constitutional amendments cited above all contain powerful clauses and educators must be careful to ensure that a balance is struck between the individual's constitutional freedoms and the state's compelling interest (e.g. to provide an appropriate educational environment).

Court cases that arise out of the federal constitution and/or federal statutes come under the jurisdiction of the federal court system. As noted earlier, when school administrators, teachers and school employees act in their official capacities, they represent the state. This has significant implications for analyzing actions performed in the course of official duties that could breach the constitutional and statutory rights of students, parents, teachers, and staff members.

The Congress of the United States and state legislatures have the authority to attack discrimination by passing statutes that codify constitutional intent and even surpass that intent as long as the statutes do not violate the equal protection rights of others. Congressional statutes provide broader equal opportunity rights and remedies by linking the observation of those rights to federal dollars, by prohibiting acts that are not covered by the Constitution, and by creating remedies that are not available under the Constitution. The evidentiary requirements to establish statutory discrimination are lower than those required for constitutional discrimination. (Valente, 1994, p.336).

COMPETENCY C: Know of state constitutional, statutory, and regulatory provision governing Florida's public schools

>   **Skill 1:** Identifies the statutory powers and duties of Florida's State Board of Education, Commissioner of Education, local school boards, superintendents, and principals.

F.S. 228 Public Education: General Provisions sets forth the plan and scope of the state public education system. It includes definitions of terms, the rules and objectives for specialized schools and programs that operate through the public education system. The "Florida Equity Act" that covers issues concerning discrimination against students and employees is spelled out. Other provisions set forth in this statute cover the handling and retention of records, test security, and school food service.

F.S. 229 Functions of State Education Agencies consists of three parts. Part I outlines the key information about the State Board of Education: composition, operating procedures, powers, and its role and responsibility in handling resources. Part II describes the duties and powers of the commissioner, educational management procedures, school improvement processes, powers and duties of the commission, implementation of the school-to-work transition accountability, the career education program, educational partnerships, international education, and the school readiness pilot program.

F.S. 230 District School Systems specifically lays out the scope, authority and operational procedures for district school systems. It provides clear guidelines for the management, control, operation, administration, and supervision of the school district.

F.S. 231 Personnel of School Systems spells out personnel qualifications, selection processes, certification processes, the operation of the Education Standards Commission and the Education Practices Commission, leave policies, contractual and termination procedures.

>   **Skill 2:** Identifies the standards and procedures of Florida administrative law, public disclosure and record keeping.

F.S. 120.50-.73 Administrative Procedures Act specifies the administrative operations of government units. The units affected by the statute are defined and their duties and responsibilities regarding meetings, rulemaking, decision-making, and hearings are explained.

F.S. 119.10-.15 Public Records states the penalties for violation of the public records statute, describe the victim protection procedures, the guidelines for accelerated hearing, and the assessment of attorney's fees. The "Open Government Sunset Review Act of 1995" is a part of this statute.

F.S. 228.092-.093 Student Records details the rules for the retention of records of students attending nonpublic schools. Definitions, transfer procedures, Department of Education responsibilities and intent are provided. The procedures for compliance with FERPA are included in this statute.

F.S. 231.29-.291 Assessment Procedures and Criteria Personnel Files provides specific criteria and procedures involved in the assessment process. The hearing process for is outlined. The criteria for personnel file contents are presented and the procedures for accessing and maintaining the files are described.

> **Skill 3:** Identifies state statutory criteria applicable to certification, selection, evaluation, dismissal, reprimand, and non-renewal of professional employees.

F.S. 231 Personnel spells out personnel qualifications, selection processes, certification processes, the operation of the Education Standards Commission and the Education Practices Commission, leave policies, contractual and termination procedures. It is a key statute because it provides the a detailed description of every aspect of the professional personnel area.

> **Skill 4:** Identifies standards and procedures applicable to state statutory provisions for minimum competencies, compulsory school attendance, curriculum, facilities, and finance.

Florida Constitution, Article IX, Uniform System of Public Schools focuses specifically on education and contains six sections. The first section states that "adequate provision shall be made by law for a uniform system of free public schools..." Section 2 describes the makeup of the State Board of Education; section 3 states the terms of service for appointive board members. Section 4 identifies the scope duties of school districts. Section 5 states the manner in which, superintendents come to office and the terms of office. Section 6 identifies the use of the income from the state school fund.

F.S. 229.565 Educational Evaluation Procedures sets up student performance standards in the various program categories and grade levels. The standards apply to language arts, mathematics, science, social studies, the arts, health and physical education, foreign language, reading, writing history, government, geography, economics, and computer literacy.

F.S. 232 Compulsory School Attendance covers all areas pertaining to the enrollment and attendance in the Florida public schools. Attendance policies, school health and immunization policies, truancy, transfer, graduation and issues of child welfare are included.

F.S. 233 Courses of Study sets forth the instructional programs that are to be offered, the guidelines for their implementation, and the duties of school personnel in providing the instructional program.

F.S. 235 Educational Facilities provides inclusive information regarding the acquisition and maintenance of physical facilities, the role of the Department of Education and the local boards, funding information, building code guidelines, contract information, and other related information. This statute is known as the "Educational Facilities Act."

F.S. 236 Finance and Taxation details the finance and taxation issues for all aspects of the Florida education system. The specifics of the Florida Education Finance Program (FEFP) are spelled out. Fund allocation and distribution and taxation requirements are also included in detail.

COMPETENCY D: Know of tort and contract liability as related to the operation of Florida's Public Schools.

> **Skill 1:** Identifies legislative and/or judicial elements of tort law liability applicable to Florida school districts:

Negligence: Negligence constitutes the failure to exercise ordinary prudence and foresight that results in injury to another person, specifically, another person to whom some duty is owed. This has implications for educators because of the nature of the relationship between the educator and the student. The level of that relationship rises to the level of "in loco parentis," by its very nature, implies a heightened duty of care. The facts of each situation must be analyzed to determine negligence. The elements of that analysis to determine a valid cause of action for negligence are (1) a legal duty to conform to a standard of conduct for the protection of others, (2) a failure to exercise an appropriate standard of care, (3) a causal connection (proximate cause) between the conduct and the resultant injury, and (4) actual loss or damage as a result of the injury. An actionable case for negligence requires a positive response to each of the elements. The defenses for negligence include the demonstration that the elements are not present. Other defenses include contributory negligent and assumption of risk. *Rupp v. Bryant, Collins v. SB of Broward, Donohue v. Copiaque Free Union SD*

Intentional torts: A tort is a civil wrong. Assault and battery are the most common intentional tort that educators experience. Battery is the unpermitted and unprivileged contact with another person. Actual harm is not necessary. Assault is the placing of someone in apprehension of immediate harm; physical contact is not part of the definitions (LaMorte, 1996, p.389). *Heff v. Ploetz, Vinson v. Linn-Mar Community SD*

Statutory liability:
F.S. 231.17 Official Statements of Eligibility and Certificates provides specific requirements for official statements of eligibility and certificates. It describes the application process for statements of eligibility, the temporary certificate, and the professional certificate. Exceptions for the issuance of certificates, the demonstration of professional competence, examination requirements, and certificate denial are also addressed.

F.S. 232.50 Child Abuse and Neglect Policy states the requirements for all schools regarding the child abuse and neglect policy. Notice must be posted that all employees or agents of the district school board have an affirmative duty to report all actual or suspected cases of child abuse or neglect. It also stipulates that the superintendent or a designee will act as a liaison to the Department of Health and Rehabilitative Services and child protection team.

F.S. 236.0811 Educational Training provides for the development and maintenance of an educational training program in all districts. Classroom teachers and guidance counselors are required to participate in inservice training for child abuse and neglect prevention, alcohol and substance abuse prevention education, and multicultural sensitivity education.

F.S. 415.501, .5015, 504, .509, .513 Protection from Abuse, Neglect, and Exploitation addresses the guidelines for educators regarding the prevention of abuse and neglect of children. The protective services for abused and neglected children are also outlines.

Federal tort: Title 42, Section 1983 of the Civil Rights Act of 1871 (statutory liability) provides for liability if a "person" operating under the color of the states violates another person's "rights, privileges, or immunities secured by the Constitution, and laws...." The federal courts have addressed the liability of school officials and school districts under this federal statute (42 U.S.C. s 1983) and have determined the extent of resultant damages. *Wood v. Strickland, Carey v. Piphus, Monell v. Dept. of Social Services*

> **Skill 2:** Identifies legislatively and/or judicially recognized standards applicable to contracts for goods and services.

F.S. 237 Financial Accounts and Expenditures for Public Schools describes that guidelines for uniform record keeping and the handling of accounts. It sets forth the procedures for establishing budgets, levying taxes, incurring indebtedness, the obligation to eliminate emergency conditions, handling school funds, and auditing procedures.

"Are we there yet?"

Directions: Read each item and select the best response.

Competency A

1. The Lemon Test provides a rubric for analyzing educational policies and practices to determine their constitutionality. The constitutional issue that the Lemon Test addresses is

    A. Free speech

    B. Search and seizure

    C. Establishment of religion

    D. General welfare

2. A student nominated a classmate at a school assembly describing the classmate in terms that had sexual overtones. The student had been informed prior to the assembly that the comments were not appropriate, but he made the presentation anyway. Which of the following rulings should the school administration include in its consideration?

    A. A student may not be punished for exercising First Amendment free speech rights

    B. A student may be disciplined for speech which is lewd, indecent or obscene. A student can be held liable for a defamatory statement

    C. A student loses First Amendment rights to free speech once inside the public school classroom.

3. The reader adopted for the third grade classes this year contains a unit of stories that focus on heroes. One of the stories recounts the tale of David and Goliath. The parents of two students have complained about the use of this story in reading class. As the senior administrator, you should

    A. Provide alternative reading materials for the students

    B. Cut the story out of all of the textbooks

    C. Exercise the procedures of the Religious Freedom Restoration Act

    D. Encourage the parents to allow the students to participate in the reading lesson that includes the David and Goliath story.

4. **The Fourth Amendment requires that "probable cause" precede a search of a person. The Supreme Court has interpreted this provision for school administrators to mean "reasonable suspicion." Identify the precedent court case from which this ruling emerged.**

   A. Pierce v. The Society of Sisters

   B. New Jersey v. TLO

   C. Rodriguez v. San Antonio

   D. Aguilar v. Felton

   Competency B

5. **Free appropriate education, the individual education program, procedural safeguards, and least restrictive environment: identify the legislation represented by these elements.**

   A. Americans with Disabilities Act

   B. The Equal Access Act

   C. The Individuals with Disabilities Education Act

   D. Title VI, The Civil Rights Act of 1964

6. **As chair of a personnel committee considering applicants for an administrative position in the central office, one member of the committee advises the principal that the superintendent has expressed difficulty in working with female administrators. What action should you take?**

   A. Advise the committee member to introduce this consideration into the committee's deliberations

   B. Advise the committee member that consideration of the superintendent's expressed difficulty in working with women should not influence the selection of an applicant

   C. Advise the committee member that the superintendent's expressed difficulty in working with women should be weighed in the selection process

   D. Advise the committee member that the superintendent's expressed difficulty in working with women should be a primary consideration in determining the applicant to be recommended

7. Once special education experts have determined that a student has a disability, the parents' rights include

A. None

B. The right to unilaterally pace the child in a private school at the school district's expense

C. The right to review and reconsideration of the diagnosis, access to student records, and representation in a hearing

D. Limited rights while the child is placed in a self-contained class for the emotionally handicapped

Competency C

8. Which of the following criteria would be most difficult to establish as grounds for unsatisfactory teacher performance that would justify dismissal?

A. Inability to maintain classroom order and discipline

B. Lack of student progress toward instructional goals

C. Failure to construct and utilize proper lesson plans

D. Failure to vary teaching method in response to needs of the learners

9. Which of the following statutory bases for teacher dismissal requires repeated acts to establish good cause for dismissal under Florida law?

A. Immorality

B. Reduction in force

C. Insubordination

D. Incompetence

10. Under Florida law, a professional contract teacher is

A. Entitled to remain in a position without the necessity of annual nomination and reappointment.

B. Granted tenure and a right to a position in the school district until the age of mandatory retirement

C. Subject to annual review of performance

D. Granted renewal for 10 years

11. Florida's compulsory school attendance law requires that

A. Students who are married or become pregnant shall be prohibited from attending school

B. A child who attains the age of sixteen during the school cannot be required to attend school beyond that date

C. No child can be admitted or promoted to the first grade in a public school unless he or she has successfully completed kindergarten in a public school

D. No special education service be provided to children over the age of sixteen

Competency D

12. A pupil's or student's name, address, telephone number (if it is a listed number), date and place of birth, major field of study, participation in officially recognized activities and sports, weight and height of member of athletic teams, dates of attendance, degrees and awards received, and the most recent educational agency or institution attended by the pupil or student: these elements constitute

A. Privileged information

B. Directory information

C. Suspect classifications

D. Exempt information

13. Federal and state laws that govern record keeping in school districts are

A. The Equal Protection Clause and the Sunshine State Standards

B. The Family Education Rights and Privacy Act (FERPA) and F.S. 228.093

C. The Age Discrimination Act and the Craig Dickson Act

D. Title IX and the Education Accountability Act

14. Parents and students have specific rights regarding educational records. Those rights include all EXCEPT

A. The right of access

B. The right of waiver of access to confidential letters or statements

C. The right to remove objectionable but accurate information

D. The right to privacy

15. According to Florida law, if a person is to be employed in an instructional capacity, she/he must hold a certificate or license issued under state rules. That person must also

A. Have lived in Florida for 3 years

B. Have had 3 years of prior teaching experience

C. File a set of fingerprints for a background check

D. Consent to teach in Florida for 5 years

16. The phase(s) of the Florida certification process are the Statement of Eligibility and

A. The Temporary Certificate

B. The Professional Certificate

C. Student teaching eligibility

D. A and B

17. Some information included in students' folders is subject to review and, when appropriate, eliminated when it is no longer useful. That information would be classified as

A. Category B information

B. Exempt information

C. Directory information

D. Transcript information

18. What law requires the Medical Services of the Department of Health to participate and fully cooperate in the development of a state plan at both local and state levels for the mandated reporting of child abuse or neglect and includes the "Child Abuse Prevention Training Act"?

A. F.S. 827

B. F.S. 415

C. F.S. 229

D. I.D.E.A.

19. A six year old student in Mrs. Brack's first grade class has exhibited a noticeable change in behavior over the last month. The child was usually outgoing, alert, and happy in the classroom, but she has become quiet and withdrawn and appears to be unable to concentrate on her work. Yesterday, bruises were evident on the child's arms and her right eye. Mrs. Brack should

A. Ignore the situation

B. Provide extra remedial work

C. Immediately report the suspected abuse to the Department of Children and Families

D. Call the girl's parents

20. **During a noon recess where no supervision was provided, two high school students engaged in "slap fighting," a form of boxing that employs the use of open hands. The incident resulted in the death of one of the students. The court found the school system to be negligent in this incident. Identify the element of negligence that best supports the court's judgement.**

    A. Duty of care

    B. Standard of care

    C. Proximate cause

    D. Actual loss or injury

21. **When school personnel make a report of suspected child abuse, they are required by statute to**

    A. Submit a written report

    B. Provide the name of school principal

    C. Provide support for the other children in the class

    D. Provide their own name

22. **After resolving a disciplinary matter involving one of your students, you prepare a written report of the situation and forward it to your superintendent. The student's parents demand to see a copy of your report. As principal, you should**

    A. Give the parents a copy

    B. Direct the parents to the superintendent

    C. Refuse the request because this correspondence was confidential and privileged

    D. Inform the parents of what was in the correspondence but deny them a copy of the report

23. A former student in the high school claims that he is unable to fill out a standard employment application. The former student contends that the district was negligent in that it graduated him without adequate training in basic skill. The principal is aware that

A. Failure to properly educate school children has resulted in legal liability for negligence in school districts throughout the United States

B. Parents have sole responsibility and liability for the provision of adequate education for their children

C. A former student who lacks adequate educational skill is contributorily negligent and barred from any recovery for educational malpractice

D. Legal claims of education malpractice have been rejected by courts as contrary to public policy and outside the scope of a negligence remedy

24. Which of the following statements best reflects the liability of Florida public school teachers for acts of negligence?

A. Teachers can be held liable for negligent acts committed within the scope of employment

B. School districts have statutory immunity from liability for negligent acts of their employees

C. School districts can be held liable for the negligence of employees but employees cannot be held liable for negligence when their behavior is in conformity with board rules as long as excessive force or cruel and unusual punishment are not present

D. School districts and employees can be held jointly liable for negligence under Florida's "comparative negligence" standard

25. The Equal Access Act requires that public secondary schools grant equal access to student groups who wish to meet for religious political purposes if the school allows any non-curriculum-related group to meet. When applying the Act, a school administrator must understand three fundamental principles. Which of the following is not one of those principles?

A. The Act protects religious speech that is student initiated and student led

B. The Act protects religious speech that is state initiated, school sponsored, or teacher led

C. The Act in no way diminishes the authority of school officials to maintain order and discipline in the schools

D. The Act requires equal access, not preferential treatment, for religious, political or philosophical speech

26. The legal concept that had its origin in English common law principle that the "king can do no wrong" protects the state the state from being sued is ____.

A. Sovereign immunity

B. Equal protection

C. Due process

D. Equal opportunity

27. Which article of the Federal Constitution that vests the judicial power of the United States in the Supreme Court?

A. Article I

B. Article II

C. Article III

D. Article VI

28. Sources of law are

A. Constitutions

B. Statutes

C. Administrative rules

D. All of the above

29. The Copyright Act of 1976 allows educators to make copies of copyrighted material for classroom use through

A. Primary process

B. Imminent domain

C. Equal access

D. Fair use

30. Although the courts upheld the right of the state to prescribe curriculum for its public schools, the Supreme Court ruled that a state law making it illegal for a teacher to teach evolution was unconstitutional in

A. Epperson v. Arkansas

B. Wisconsin v. Yoder

C. Pierce v. The Society of Sisters

D. Mills v. Board of Education

31. Compulsory attendance can fulfilled by attending public school, private school, parochial school and home school. The case that set this precedent was

A. Swann v. Charlotte-Mecklengurg

B. McCollum v. Board of Education

C. Pierce v. Society of Sisters

D. Lau v. Nichols

32. The doctrine that holds the ultimate employer liable for tortious acts of its employees even if the employer was not at fault is _____.

A. Caveat Emptor

B. A Certiorari

C. Respondeat superior

D. Mandamus

33. The intent to place another in reasonable apprehension of imminent bodily harm or offensive contact is _____.

A. Battery

B. Libel

C. Slander

D. Assault

34. When separation of races occurs by law, it is known as

A. Critical

B. De jure

C. Judiciable

D. De facto

35. Which Supreme Court case authorized mandatory busing to achieve desegregation?

A. Swann v. Charlotte-Mecklenburg Board of Education

B. Brown v. Board of Education

C. Grove City College v. Bell

D. Martinez v. Bynum

36. **When the Department of Education makes the decision to deny a certificate to an applicant, the decision to deny the certificate is subject to review by**

   A. The State Board of Education

   B. The state attorney general

   C. The local board of education

   D. The Education Practices Commission

37. **When a school district develops and maintains an approved alternative certification program, that program must require each applicant to**

   A. Have expertise in the subject area for certification

   B. Complete training in only those competency areas in which deficiencies are identified

   C. Complete the program and demonstrate professional education competence with 2 years after initial employment as a member of the districts instructional staff

   D. All of the above

38. **Each person who seeks certification will receive which of the following within 90 days of submitting a completed application, the appropriate fees, and social security number?**

   A. A contract

   B. An official statement of eligibility for certification

   C. A certificate covering the classification, level, and area for which the applicant is deemed qualified

   D. B or C

39. **Each person who is employed and enters services as an athletic coach in any public school in any district of Florida must**

   A. Demonstrate collegiate participation in the sport that s/he will coach

   B. Hold a valid part-time, temporary, or professional certificate

   C. Hold a degree in health and physical education

   D. Coach a minimum of two sports

40. The duties required of members of the instructional staff of the public schools include

A. Earning an advanced degree

B. Providing individualized tutoring for students

C. Using prescribed materials and methods

D. Participating in all school-related functions

41. The Commissioner of Education, the members of the State Board of Education, the superintendent of schools and member of the school board are

A. Certified personnel

B. Instructional personnel

C. School officers

D. Administrative personnel

42. A district school board may decrease the minimum 180 days of instruction for 12th grade pupils for the purposes of graduation without a proportionate reduction in funding up to

A. 10 days

B. 8 days

C. 5 days

D. 4 days

43. The parameters of the school fiscal year:

A. Begins July 1st, ends June 30th

B. Begins January 1st, ends December 31st

C. Begins October 1st, ends September 30th

D. Begins September 1st, ends August 31st

44. Regular school attendance under Chapter 232.02 of the Florida School Laws can be fulfilled by a pupil's attendance in

A. A religious, denominational school

B. Regular conferences with certified teachers

C. Co-curricular activities sponsored by the local school district

D. A public school for 6 weeks out of each academic year

45. Florida's school attendance statute requires that, except as provided by law, all children are required to attend school regularly during the entire school term if

A. They have attained the age of 6 years by February 1st of any school year

B. They have not attained the age of 16 years

C. They have attained the age of 16 years

D. A and B

Answer Key (Subtest 3 – School Operations, Law)

1. C

The Lemon Test was described in *Lemon v. Kurtzman* and is used to analyze policies and practices in regard to the Establishment Clause of the First Amendment. The test has three parts; if a policy or practice violates any one of the three parts, than the policy or practice violates the Establishment Clause. The three parts of the Lemon Test are (1) Does the policy have a secular purpose? (2) Does the policy advance or inhibit religion? (3) Does the policy allow an entanglement between religion and the state (school)?

2. B

In *Bethel v. Fraser* the courts ruled that although students do have free speech rights in the school context, the school has a compelling interest in maintaining an atmosphere that is conducive to learning.

3. C

The Religious Freedom Restoration Act provides that any law or policy of general applicability that substantially burdens a person's free exercise of religion MUST further the state's compelling interest. If the state cannot prove a compelling interest in requiring participation in that particular reading lesson, the state (school) is legally required to excuse the students from the lesson.

4. B

5. C

The Individuals with Disabilities Education Act (IDEA) requires that all states receiving federal funding to educate handicapped children provide mandatory education programs. P.L. 94 -142 was reenacted as IDEA and the elements listed represent its key concepts.

6. B

Title VII, The Civil Rights Act of 1964, Section 703(a) specifically states that "It shall be unlawful employment practice for an employer ...to discriminate against any individual ... because of such individual race, color, religion, sex, or national origin..."

7. C

The Individuals with Disabilities Education Act (IDEA) spells out clear procedural rights for parents.

8. B

Although lack of student progress toward instructional goals can be established, it is the most complex and difficult to demonstrate in comparison to the other choices.

9. C

Chapter 229.71 of the Texas's Statutes lists the behaviors that constitute "just cause" from removal. A pattern of gross insubordination must be established to rise to the level of "just cause."

10. C

Chapter 231.36 provides the contract renewal process for instructional staff members who hold the professional contract.

11. B

Chapter 232 of the Texas Statutes provide the specific requirements for the fulfillment of the compulsory attendance laws.

12. B

The noted elements are directory information; under FERPA and F.S.228.093, these elements can be released without parental/student consent.

13. B

14. C

FERPA and F.S. 229.093 provide clear guideline to parental/student rights.

15. C

Sections 231.001 and 231.10 of the Texas Statutes spell out the qualifications for certification. A person must be of good moral character and have attained 18 years of age. That individual must also hold a certificate or license and file a set of fingerprints for a background check.

16. D

17. A

Information contained in education records is classified as "permanent" (Category A) or "temporary" (Category B) under F.S. 230.331. Permanent information has been verified and is such educational importance that it is retained in perpetuity. Temporary information is subject to frequent review and is eliminated when it is no longer useful.

18. B

F.S. 415 covers major aspects of child abuse prevention. F.S. 827 is the general law on abuse of children. F.S. 229 cover the functions of state educational agencies. I.D.E.A. is the federal statute that addresses student disability issues in the educational setting.

19. C

F.S. 415.504 mandates the reporting of child abuse or neglect by any person and specifically by a school teacher or other school official.

20. B

The standard of care that educators must exercise to avoid liability is defined as that of the reasonable and prudent educator charged with similar duties under similar circumstances. The standard of care varies according to such factors as age of student, the child's mental capacity, and the environment and circumstances under which the injury occurred. Since adolescent high school students are not adults, they should not be expected to exhibit the degree of discretion associated with mature adults. The school was negligent in not having a schedule of supervision assignments with appropriate instructions.

21. D

Reporters of suspected child abuse in certain occupational categories that are designated by F.S. 415.51 are required to provide their names to the hotline staff. The category "school personnel" is one the designated categories.

22. A

The guidelines of FERPA and chapter 228.093 of the Texas Statutes outline the access rights of parents and students 18 years of age and older.

23. D

The courts have not upheld claims for educational malpractice. Many factors are involved in the learning process, and thus, the courts have been reluctant to lay all of the blame for failure to learn at the door of public education. In *Peter W. v. San Francisco Unified School District,* the court contended that failure of educational achievement was not an injury within the meaning of tort law.

24. C

Chapter 232.275 of the Texas Statutes provides the criteria.

25. B

The Act specifically states that although school personnel can be present at the meeting, they cannot participate, lead or initiate activities in the meeting. Their presence is required to insure safety and adherence to school policy.

26. A

Sovereign immunity protects the state from being sued without its consent. Many states, including Texas, have waived sovereign immunity by statute.

27. C

Article III vests the judicial power of the United States in the Supreme Court and defines the jurisdiction of the Supreme Court. The qualifications for Supreme Court judges are also given.

28. D
Although constitutions and statutes are the most commonly recognized forms of law, administrative rules by governmental agencies also have the force of law. In fact, even board policy has the force of law.

29. D
The Copyright Act states that "fair use of copyrighted work for purposes such as criticism, comment, news reporting, teaching (including multiple copies for classroom use), scholarship or research is not an infringement on copyright."

30. A

31. C

32. C
In this situation, the tortious act must be committed with the scope of the employee's professional duties.

33. D
The apprehension in this situation must be of the form that would be aroused in a reasonable person.

34. B

35. B

36. D
Chapter 231.17 (10) outlines the procedure for an applicant to appeal the denial of a certificate. The applicant must file a written request within 20 days after the receipt of the notice of denial.

37. D

38. D

Review Chapter 231.17 (1).

39. B

40. C
Review Chapter 231.09.

41. C
Review Chapter 228.04 (8).

42. D
Review Chapter 228.04 (16).

43. A
Review Chapter 228.04 (17).

44. A
Review Chapter 232.02.

45. D
Review Chapter 323.01.

Bibliography

Alexander, K. & Alexander, M.D. (1984). *Law of Schools, Students and Teachers in a Nutshell.* St. Paul, MN: West.

Alexander, K. & Alexander, M.D. (1992). *American Public School Law* 3rd ed. St. Paul, MN: West.

Aquila, F.D. & Petzke, J.J. (1994). *Course Outline: Education Law.* Santa Monica,CA: Casenote Publishing Co., Inc.

Fischer, L. & Sorenson, G.P. (1996). *School Law for Counselors, Psychologists, and Social Workers.* White Plains, NY: Longman Publishers.

Florida School Laws (Current Edition). Tallahassee, FL: Florida Department of Education.

Florida Education Handbook (1998). Tallahassee, FL: Florida Association of School Administrators.

Imber, M. & van Geel, T. (1995). *A Teacher's Guide to Education Law.* New York: McGraw-Hill.

Journal of Law and Education. Columbia: University of South Carolina.

LaMort, M.W. (1996). *School Law: Cases and Concepts.* Boston: Allyn and Bacon.

O'Reilly,R.C. & Green, E.T. (1992). *School Law for the 1990s: A Handbook.* New York: Greenwood Press.

Osborne, A.G., Jr. (1996). *Legal Issues in Special Education.* Boston: Allyn and Bacon.

Thomas, G. T., Sperry, D.J. & Del Wasden, F. (1991). *The Law and Teacher Employment.* St. Paul, MN: West.

U.S. Supreme Court Education Cases 3rd ed. (1993). Rosemont, MN: Data Research, Inc.

Valente, W. (1987). *Law in the Schools.* Columbus, OH: Merrill.

Walston-Dunham, B. (1990). *Introduction to Law.* St. Paul, MN: West.

Sub-test 3 – School Operations

Technology

Computer technology has changed our way of life and how we work. Computers have utility in school environments when they are applied to administrative functions and instructional objectives. The roles of computer technology are expanding as more and more school tasks are being accomplished using computers. An understanding of the capabilities and the limitations of technological devices and how they can be integrated into the business operations of a school to support its instructional mission is a challenge and opportunity to create effective and efficient school organizations.

COMPETENCY A: Evaluates various computer hardware components which are appropriate to the management of schools and describes their use.

> **Skill 1**: Identifies the major components of a computer system.

> **Skill 2:** Demonstrates the ability to select compatible computer hardware equipment for use in a school setting.

The 1980s witnessed a number of electronic devices' debut in America's public schools. These devices were grouped under the heading of technology. Each of these devices, however, has particular capabilities and advantages, that when applied in the interactive experience of teaching and learning, makes the process stimulating, relevant, and constructive. As well, when these electronic tools are applied to administrative tasks, they yield results specific to administrative goals.

Given the assortment of technology available to schools and the range of capabilities of specific devices, a challenge facing school administrators is to identify the capabilities of technological devices and make a determination regarding the utility of that technology in the school environment and its ability to ultimately accomplish school objectives.

It is rarely useful to have technology in a school but not able to apply it to solving school problems. Since technology is expensive to acquire and maintain, it is important that the introduction of given technological devices be related to addressing specific school goals and objectives. Very little benefit, if any at all, accrues students, teachers, and administration when technology is idle in the school's educational process.

There are a number of administrative tasks in schools to which technology can be applied to make a time-saving and organizational difference. Some of the task areas are scheduling, accounting, purchasing, inventory, attendance, grading, testing and library automation. The appropriate use of technology in these areas can make a difference in personal productivity, efficiency, and time expenditure. An administrator's ability to identify the capabilities of technological devices available in the marketplace and to subsequently match that technology with the needs, goals, and objectives of the school's curriculum and administrative functions is a primary skill.

A computer is an electronic device that processes information, usually numeric data, according to a body of instructions. A computer system is a collection of components that includes the computer and all the devices that people use with a computer. A computer by itself is limited in relation to what it can accomplish in a work or other productivity related environment. For a computer to actualize its potential and demonstrate its capabilities requires it to operate in relation to a number of other elements. When the computer and other hardware are combined, the result is a computer system.

A computer system consists of hardware and software. The hardware component of a computer system is defined by the physical components. The software component of a computer system consists of the program applications that tell a computer what to do. In effect, a computer system is delineated by the software which provides instructions to the computer and the hardware which executes the commands.

In a computer system, various components accomplish certain tasks. There are certain functions and operations that cannot be conducted when certain components are missing from a computer system. And like a computer, if a particular component of a computer system stands by itself, it cannot accomplish its designated function.

School administrators need to be aware of the components that make up a computer system. This is because a collection of some components will allow certain productivity operations to occur, while a collection of other components will not permit an objective to be realized. The appropriate computer system must be used to accomplish specific tasks. Understanding the components of a computer system and the capabilities of those components allows administrators to determine the kind of technological devices needed in a school environment to accomplish specified objectives. Computer technology, like other tools applied to work situations, will only accomplish that which they are designed to do.

COMPETENCY B: Evaluates various types of computer software which are available for assisting in the management of a school and demonstrates an understanding of their proper selection and use.

> **Skill 1:** Selects appropriate software for automating a specified school management task which is currently accomplished through manual system.

> **Skill 2:** Demonstrates knowledge of legal and illegal practices involved with the use and maintenance of software.

> **Skill 3:** Demonstrates knowledge of appropriate software or procedural safeguards necessary to secure and limit access to school records stored on computer media.

As the information age enters the third decade, more and more organizations are relying on computer systems to accomplish the bulk of the organizational work. Schools too, have found the utility of computer systems to automate its tasks and can even be transformed by its capabilities. Computer technology is having a profound impact on the administrative functions of schools. The popularity of computers is reinforced by their ability to get tasks completed in less time and with greater efficiency. It is the software part of the computer system that is to be recognized for accomplishing certain tasks with this efficiency.

The acquisition of software is an expensive proposition. Therefore, it is not something to engage in lightly. Mistakes can be made, and mistakes have been made, in the selection and purchase of software programs intended to accomplish certain school-related objectives. Software evaluation is a critical skill for administrators. The following are several steps to keep in mind when selecting software for administrative use. **One,** identify the objectives that are to be accomplished by introducing the software in the school environment. **Two,** determine if the features and capabilities of the software match administrative goals and objectives. **Three,** determine if the software actually does what it describes and if what it does is what is needed. **Four,** be sure to ascertain that the software is compatible to the computer system in operation at the school.

In school administration, the right application must be selected and applied to the appropriate task. Seldom can curriculum applications be applied to school administrative functions with desirable results. And likewise, seldom can administrative software be applied to the curriculum. The efficiency and effectiveness of the accounting software to handle school budget matters does not translate to the teaching and learning environment of the classroom.

Lack of knowledge about how to use technology is common in the educational world (Kearsley & Lynch, 1994). It is important for the school administrator to distinguish between software designed for accounting, scheduling, information management, and communication purposes. An administrator needs to be aware of what software programs can and cannot do. A leadership role in technology requires an ability to describe major hardware and software components and to be a role model for teachers.

In an effort to protect the interests of originators, producers, and distributors of original works of art, information, and now technology, governments enact copyright laws. Copyright laws protect the originator from unlawful infringement upon a creation and specifies the conditions under which a work or idea may be copied (Heinich, Molenda, Russell, & Smaldino, 1996).

In 1976, Congress enacted the most recent copyright law. It included provisions for technological developments. Guidelines regarding computer software and television broadcasts were included in the 1976 version of the copyright law. Both criminal and civil penalties are a part of the copyright law. In 1990, Congress amended the copyright law which, in effect, took away a public institution's immunity from being sued. An employer can be held liable as well as the employee who infringed upon the copyright. Educators who intentionally and deliberately violate copyright law are subject to criminal penalty which can be a fine up to $1000.00 and a year in jail.

The information age brings with it considerations of privacy and confidentiality of group and individual information. Who has access to certain records and who should not have access to certain records are important determinations to make. The question of security is always an issue when significant amounts of information are stored in one location. Not only are enormous amounts of information stored on computers, but that information is often of a sensitive nature, meaning not everyone needs to have access to it. Information can be used in inappropriate ways especially if that information is student data. A breach of professional ethics occurs when student data is disseminated publicly to those who do not have a need for the information. The confidentiality of school records is a paramount issue. In this time of computer hackers, the security and safeguard of school records becomes a high priority. Access to computers with school records engenders another problem also, that of computer viruses. Vigilance must be exercised regarding access to prevent the possibility of a virus and, hence, the destruction of school records.

Because information can be used for inappropriate purposes, it is important for school administrators to limit access to that information and to also safeguard school data. The ways in which this can be accomplished by a school administrator are an important part of the professional repertoire of skills the administrator needs.

COMPETENCY C: Determines the appropriate application of technology in the learning process.

> **Skill 1:** Identifies the most significant barrier(s) to the adoption of technology in the learning process.

> **Skill 2:** Describes the appropriate use of computers in the design and delivery of learning systems. Differentiates among various types of computer-assisted instructional strategies.

> **Skill 3:** Describes the appropriate use of computers in the design and delivery of learning systems. Given a computer-assisted instruction strategy, selects a learning task for which it would be appropriate.

> **Skill 4:** Describes the appropriate use of computers in the design and delivery of learning systems. Demonstrates a knowledge of appropriate applications of programs to be used by students as "tools of learning."

> **Skill 5:** Identifies the characteristics of various video technologies.

Technology, especially computer technology is viewed by many as an advantage in achieving a school's stated learning objectives. The use of technology in achieving the learning objectives is not as widespread as should be. Few of America's 2.8 million teachers are using technology in their teaching (Hancock, 1993; Office of Technology, 1995). What accounts for slow pace of technology's diffusion and integration into teachers' practice? Kearsley and Lynch (1994) concluded that teachers and administrators are not prepared to advance and manage technology in schools.

One can attribute the lack of adoption of technology in the teaching and learning environment to a number of causes. These causes can be characterized under the headings of organizational factors and individual factors (Hope, 1997). Organizationally, integration of technology is hampered by a lack of specific plans. Incorporating technology into the teaching and learning process requires access to the technology that is to be used in the teaching environment. Because technology is expensive, teachers often do not have access to the technology. As well, teachers need training in the use of technology. The lack of effective training opportunities for teachers to visualize the capabilities of technology impedes its use in classrooms.

Leadership is an important ingredient in adopting technology and using it in the teaching and learning process. Without leadership from principals, teachers are often reluctant to introduce new methodology into the learning process. Because teachers are familiar with the processes and methodologies of earlier generations of teaching, and technology is a recent phenomenon, many do not have the background for using technology in the classroom. Teachers resist integrating technology into the teaching and learning process when they have not been exposed to the advantages technology affords beyond the methodologies they presently use.

The thrust to use technology in the learning environment is not likely to abate in the near future. So, for school administrators, it is important to recognize the capabilities of technology and the advantages it brings to the classroom, as well as becoming an advocate for using technology. A major responsibility falls on the school leader to model technology use and to also provide access and training for teachers to use technology.

The use of technology in schools by teachers and students is contingent upon an understanding of the capabilities of various technology and an ability to integrate these capabilities into the curriculum framework of a school. The application of technology to curriculum goals and objectives is an important function of school leadership. Involving students in learning sequences that utilize technology provides a new and motivating context to learning. Proponents of technology assert a significant role for technology in the teaching and learning process. They view technology as an ingredient with potential to transform the relationship between students and teachers and the dynamics that take place in the classroom. Computer technology offers teachers and students a constructivist learning environment. That is, opportunity exists for students to engage in hands-on learning.

The placement of computers in individual teacher's classrooms offers the most benefit. This placement maximizes both teacher and student access to technology. Computers can be used in schools for achieving a number of instructional objectives. They can be used for remediation, drill and practice, and to simulate real world activities. Effective teaching utilizing technology is available. Understanding the appropriate application of technology to specific curriculum and learning objects is a key administrative skill. Knowing which applications of technology advance student learning is necessary.

Educational technology evidences itself in many forms in schools. By far, however, the computer and various software applications predominate as the technology of choice in the teaching and learning environment. In an era of constructivist thinking in classrooms, where students take charge of their own learning, computer technology is perceived as an advantage to students' working independently, learning to think critically, and using computer technology as a productivity tool.

Technology should support the curriculum of a school. It should be utilized to obtain the objectives and outcomes desired by school leaders, the community, and ultimately the nation. Determining how best to incorporate computer technology into the curriculum should be a process that not a little time is spent on. In fact, the appropriate design and integration of computer technology into a schools curriculum is a major undertaking.

Integrating computers into school curriculum takes on the character of more than the aspect of fun. Computers can be significant in the teaching and learning process when the advantages and applications are carefully thought out and implemented. There are traditional uses of computers in classrooms like drill and practice, games, and remediation. However, the capabilities of computers and software applications make it a versatile teaching tool with potential beyond traditional computer use. Computer technology can be used to support students in analysis, creative thinking, and problem solving. Specifically, information management, writing, and mathematical concepts can all be taught to students using the computer.

Video has a powerful potential for education (Maurer & Davidson, 1998). Video formats have the potential for being the most creative educational applications developed thus far (Picciano, 1998). Moving images have an advantage over still visuals in the teaching and learning process. Video can be used in the learning environment for both affective and cognitive learning. Video technology comes in a variety of formats. These are videodisc, videocassette, (U-matic and VHS), videocassette (8 millimeter), and compact disc. Videodisc and videotape are common media being used in the instructional process in schools today.

Each of these formats presents advantages and disadvantages in the instructional environment. Video technology can be used to analyze human interactions, mastery of skills through repeated observations, and the shaping of attitudes (Heinich, Molenda, Russell, & Smaldino, 1996).

COMPETENCY D: Demonstrates a knowledge of the use of technology in instructional design.

    Skill 1: Identifies appropriate technologies for a given learning experience.

    Skill 2: Understands the use of technology in the evaluation of learners and managing learning systems.

Using technology to support student learning is not a new concept in education. Technology in various forms has been introduced into the educational environment over the decades. Technology can be seen in the form of books, radio, television, and duplicating machines. The advent of the computer, however, affords perhaps the greatest opportunity for students to engage in learning through an interactive medium. Computer technology provides and interactive environment in which students can respond and receive feedback.

Computer Assisted Instruction (CAI) describes a way in which the computer can be used as a tool to instruct students. The software used in CAI is categorized into five categories. Those categories are tutorials, simulations, drill-and-practice, educational games, and exploratory environments (Grabe & Grabe, 1996). Each of these provides meaningful learning experiences in the classroom and address specific teaching objectives.

Educators must consider the kinds of learning outcomes to be derived from instructional experiences. Matching the appropriate technologies to the desired behavioral objectives requires an understanding of the characteristics of the given technologies. Bringing to bear the capabilities of technology to the needs of the learners and tailoring the advantages of that technology to objectives are important in taking advantage of technology. Understanding what is being asked of students and then identifying the best technology available to deliver a solution is important in the educational environment.

COMPETENCY E: Demonstrates the ability to make policies and decisions which appropriately govern the use of the technological resources of a school.

> **Skill 1:** Determines the items missing from a list of specifications for a laboratory which will house various "high technology" equipment.

> **Skill 2:** Identifies the characteristics of the impact of high technology curriculum as a learning environment.

One of the major impediments to establishing successful computer-based applications in schools is the lack of careful and extensive planning (Picciano, 1998). Kearsley (1995) wrote that the role of leadership in schools requires the ability to identify how computers can improve the efficiency of school operations. He continues, stating that a school leader must adjudicate computer use so that it serves the interests and needs of all school constituents. Specific lists of competencies are associated with school leaders' ability to make policy and decisions governing the use of technological resources. A school leader must have a knowledge of computer terminology, a knowledge of instructional and administrative applications, and an understanding of the impact of technology in the school environment.

An essential ingredient of good administration is planning. A school leader must plan for all aspects of integrating technology in a school. The determination of hardware and software are essentials in the process. The identification of goals and objectives for the introduction of technology is important. Missing components from a computer system that is expected to be implemented thwarts the ability of technology to be used to its potential. To ensure that computer implementation proceeds unhindered from problems, it is important to have policy statements and procedures governing technology.

The introduction of technology in a learning environment should not be based on technology for technology's sake, but rather on a calculated and planned agenda to which technology will be used to address identified needs. Will the introduction of technology address productivity, administrative functions, or will its introduction address student achievement? In each of the situations, a different set of resources, policies, and decisions regarding the implementation will need to occur. An administrator's depth of understanding regarding salient issues in each area is required to make informed decisions.

The classroom environment, in many instances, is characterized by teachers being at the center of attention, performing, and students acting as passive vessels, consuming knowledge and information. A learning environment characterized by technology, however, offers a much different scene, and, of course, a very different mode of instruction and interaction. When technology is a part of the learning process, a different model of teaching and learning unfolds. It is a student-centered, constructivist model, where students are challenged to engage in higher order thinking skills, interact with technology at their own level, and learn what interests them.

Jonassen (1996) discusses how computers in the classroom become powerful tools for learning when they are applied in the learning process. Specific applications, like databases and spreadsheets, become key elements of the learning process, allowing students to integrate and interrelate content ideas (Jonassen, 1996).

COMPETENCY F: Demonstrates a knowledge of the definition, function, and application of common computer software/hardware terminology.

> **Skill 1:** Identifies and describes the basic function of specified computer hardware and software.

Five categories of hardware are needed to make a computer system. Those categories are the computer, input devices, output devices, firmware (extra memory, video cards, and audio cards), and cables and connectors (Simonson & Thompson, 1997). When combined, these elements can have a significant influence on the method and manner in which work in a school can be accomplished. Knowing what hardware is needed to accomplish specific tasks and the software required to instruct the hardware is a responsibility of school leaders seeking to improve the efficiency of operations in a school. There are multiple manufacturers and multiple brands of hardware with varying capabilities. Selection of hardware and software is an important task. Standardization and compatibility are significant issues to be addressed in selection and subsequent purchase of computer technology.

Technology is changing teaching roles and administrative roles. In order to understand how technology can assist and support administrative functions and curriculum goals and objectives requires an understanding of the functions and features of a specific computer hardware and software. Not to be aware of the capabilities of given technologies is to be unable to apply them to the tasks of administration and instruction. Computer technology can facilitate changes in the way work is accomplished in the school setting. In order to take advantage of what technology offers, however, requires a familiarization beyond mere recognition.

School districts and schools are investing significant amounts of money to bring technology into schools. The costs associated with technology, however, require and understanding of the capabilities of the technology that is being introduced in a school environment. Not all technology is applicable and appropriate for use in schools, depending upon the identified needs and objectives. An application can seemingly perform miracle like work, but whether it has utility in the school environment must be explored and a determination made.

An understanding of the capabilities of technology to be used in schools for administrative and/or instructional purposes is key to fulfilling the promise of technology transforming the educational process. The identification of the goals and objectives to be accomplished and the matching of those to technology is an important function of leadership. Wanting to be able to accomplish certain tasks but not having the appropriate tools to do so is frustrating. When it involves technology, an understanding of the capabilities of hardware and software provides the ability to match goals and objectives with the resources that can perform the task

"First, They do an on-line search."

Directions: Read each item and select the best answer.

1. The major input devices in a computer system include

   A. Keyboard, modem, mouse, and scanner

   B. Diskettes, hard disks, magnetic tape, and CD-ROM

   C. Applications, peripherals, programs, and software

   D. CRT's, monitor, printer, and plotters

2. The physical components of a computer system are called

   A. Peripherals

   B. Software

   C. Devices

   D. Hardware

3. The letters CPU stand for

   A. Computer program user

   B. Cathode pixel unit

   C. Current program user

   D. Central processing unit

4. The most common output device in a computer system is the

   A. Printer

   B. Microphone

   C. Modem

   D. Drive bay

5. The main types of printers are

   A. NLQ, LQ, and Photo Realistic

   B. Dot-matrix, ink-jet, and laser

   C. Typeset, black and white, and color

   D. Okidata, Panasonic, and HP

6. The floppy disk is a

   A. Magnetic storage medium

   B. Non-magnetic storage medium

   C. Tape storage medium

   D. Digital storage medium

7. An administrator wants to create a file with the names, addresses, and phone numbers of faculty at a school. The application best used in this situation would be a _____ program.

   A. Spreadsheet

   B. Database

   C. Communication

   D. Word processor

8. An administrator wants to organize the school's daily schedule using a software application. Which of the following would best complete the task?

   A. Communications

   B. Word processor

   C. Database

   D. Spreadsheet

9. The following are advantages presented by computerized databases except

   A. Flexible access

   B. Practice and feedback

   C. Amount of information

   D. Ease of manipulation

10. An example of software piracy is

    A. When teachers remove needed software from school computer labs

    B. Reselling copies of computer programs purchased by one school to another school

    C. The illegal duplication of software

    D. Running software applications at MHZs they are not designed to run at

11. Which of the following is an illegal practice?

    A. Making a back-up copy of school- owned software to keep on file

    B. Installing a school owned copy of a program on several computers

    C. Posting signs in a computer lab informing lab users that copying may be illegal

    D. Two or more people using the same copy of a program

12. **According to law, you may do which of the following regarding software?**

    A. Make multiple copies of a copyrighted program

    B. Make multiple copies of an adaptation of a copyrighted program even for use within a school or school district

    C. Adapt a copyrighted program to meet local needs

    D. Sell a locally produced adaptation of a copyrighted program

13. **Access to a student information system and the privileges accompanying that access are important considerations for school districts. The best solution to this problem is to**

    A. Limit access to one system operator who will provide information upon request.

    B. Provide read-only access to most personnel and capability to enter or change records to key individuals

    C. Locate the student information system in schools and provide access to all school personnel but appoint a system manager

    D. Combine the student information system with the school library circulation system with the librarian as overall system manager

14. **School districts maintain databases containing confidential information. The best way to prevent unauthorized access to the databases is through a**

    A. Set of keys

    B. Template

    C. Password

    D. Control of typography

15. Which of the following is not a physical or procedural safeguard for computer hardware and software?

A. Locking hardware to desks or tables

B. Supervising students when they are using computers

C. Using back-up copies of programs while the master copy is in a secure location

D. Allowing teachers and staff to take computers home for training purposes

16. Although the number of teachers using computers has doubled in the past five years, students rarely use computers for content-area learning tasks. Which of the following is a plausible explanation for this situation?

A. Lack of planning time, teacher training, and scheduling difficulties

B. Lack of leadership

C. Students desire to focus on other learning activities

D. Schools are still undergoing restructuring.

17. Your school was given money to purchase computer systems and content software for all teachers. The equipment and software has been installed in all classrooms. Three months have passed and minimal instruction using computers has taken place. What explanation can be given to explain this situation?

A. Students lack interest in using computers

B. Administration shows little interest in teachers using computers

C. Teachers are afraid they may infringe upon copyright laws

D. The software does not match the curriculum of the district and school

18. You are interested in teachers using computers in the teaching and learning process. To effect this, you have moved all computers to a central computer lab which is managed by a technology teacher. After several months you notice that teachers are not using the lab as you had intended. What explanation can be offered for this situation?

A. There is a problem with scheduling

B. The technology teacher relieves the classroom teacher of the teaching responsibility in the computer lab

C. Students prefer to be taught by a technology teacher

D. Teachers do not feel comfortable teaching in the computer lab

19. The Lily Pad is a program that allows students to dissect a frog. Student's traverse a frog's anatomy using a surgical instrument. Organs at certain points called operation rooms are highlighted. At these points, the surgical instrument can be used to perform an operation. This type of computer program is called

A. Drill and practice

B. Simulation

C. Tutorial

D. Game

20. A computer program called Decisions Decisions asks students to determine the most appropriate response to a crisis situation. The program has predetermined answers to various crises. Students engage in decision making to provide a response. Students are given three opportunities to approximate the predetermined answer. An analysis of the students' response is provided. A computer program of this type is known as

A. Problem-solving

B. Tutorial

C. Simulation

D. Drill and practice

21. When using this type of computer program, students are tested and placed at the appropriate level. They then proceed through successive levels mastering the content as they go. The program keeps track of students' progress. This type of program is known as

A. Simulation

B. Tutorial

C. Drill and practice

D. Problem-solving

22. The functions of justification, deletion, insertion, and edit are all features of which of the following application software (program)?

A. Communication

B. Word processing

C. Authoring tools

D. Html

23. The basic parts of this application software (program) can be described in terms of three levels: fields, record, and files. This application software is known as

A. Communication

B. Word processing

C. Database

D. Spreadsheet

24. Preparing the schools' annual budget is one of the most important tasks a school administrator performs. Which application is best suited to accomplish this task?

A. Sysop

B. Relational database

C. Uniform Resource Locator

D. Spreadsheet

25. Which technology is capable of holding 30 minutes of motion video images per side, or more than 50, 000 still images, or a mix of motion and still images?

A. Cassette

B. Videodisc

C. Videotape

D. Video encyclopedia

26. Which of the following statements gives a correct description of a video tape?

A. This medium is round with two sides capable of holding images

B. The medium permits viewing step through frame by frame images, which can be played at various speeds

C. This medium comes in two formats and is self-contained and self-threading

D. This medium is 4.72 inches in diameter, low in cost and easy to use

27. Today, video technologies allow "time-shift and place-shift" instruction that occurs away from a live teacher. A popular term used to describe this event is

A. Non-formal education

B. Computer conferencing

C. Wide area network (WAN)

D. Distance education

28. The teacher gives a lecture to the class on the history of the middle east. The class is informed that they will have an opportunity to organize their notes using the computer. Identify the application most appropriate for this activity.

A. Word processor

B. Video tape and VCR

C. Online database

D. Tutorial

29. A class has been studying the countries of the world. Students' notes contain information on population, languages spoken, agricultural products, land area, per capita income, literacy rate, type of government, and resources. What application is most appropriate for students to use in organizing this information?

A. Content database

B. Collaborative thinking model

C. Content spreadsheet

D. Semantic network tool

30. Mrs. Lancaster, a biology teacher, requires students to learn the internal parts of a worm. Given that there are no worms available for dissection, which of the technologies listed below will provide the student the opportunity to approximate dissecting a worm?

A. A videotape on worm dissection

B. A movie showing a worm being dissected

C. A computer simulation program titled Worm Dissection

D. Role playing

31. A teacher is in the process of determining students' grades for the grade reporting period. Students grades will be determined by averaging numerical scores derived from varying weights assigned to tests, quizzes, homework, projects, and class participation. Which of the following would be the most efficient method to determine students' grades?

A. Using a hand-held calculator

B. An electronic grade book program

C. Paper and pencil calculations

D. A linked processor

32. This educational technology usually includes a pretest, diagnosis of the learner's ability level, assignment of appropriate lesson, a post-test, and if needed, reinforcement lessons. It allows students to work at their own pace, provides feedback, and does not criticize. The term applied to this educational technology is

A. LOGO

B. Integrated Learning System

C. Hypermedia

D. Role playing

33. Computer-managed instruction includes a category of tool applications that assist teachers and administrators in managing the instructional process. CMI applications are used to collect, store, update, retrieve, and analyze information on student performance and progress. Which of the following is an example of a CMI application?

A. Tutoring

B. Simulation

C. Test generation

D. Problem solving

34. The school district's technology coordinator has made plans to update the computer laboratory at your school. You have obtained a copy of the plans which specify the hardware, software and other products designated for purchase. Included in the coordinator's plans are computers, printers, a scanner, modems, furniture, locks and alarms, and wiring. From the list select the most important item missing from the coordinators plans.

A. A LAN

B. Surge protectors

C. New chalk boards

D. Mouse pads

35. Your proposal for an Integrated Learning System containing 31 stations has been approved. Except for one item, all other items to make the ILS functional have been installed. Select the item that has not been installed that would make the ILS operational.

A. Storage room for software

B. An overhead projector panel

C. File server

D. An electronic alarm

36. The computer lab has been equipped with the latest technological devices. All necessary hardware and software and other equipment is operational. You are excited about the prospect of students going online to access information and complete assignments for teachers. When a _____ has been secured, students will be able to access the Internet. Select the item from the list that needs to be secured.

A. An internet service provider (ISP)

B. A modem

C. A service contract

D. URL (Uniform Resource Listing)

37. **Using a computer to perform tasks offers several advantages. Which of the following describes an advantage of using a computer?**

    A. Reduces class size

    B. Time savings

    C. Multiple operations

    D. Fun

38. **Computer simulations are most appropriate for**

    A. Replicating key elements of real-world environments

    B. Mastering basic facts

    C. Emphasizing competition and entertainment

    D. Providing motivational feedback

39. **One-on-one teacher-student tutoring is recognized for its academic benefits to the student. One-on-one teaching experiences are time consuming and unsustainable over time. A computer, however, can spend an unlimited amount of time with a student providing instruction. Computers in schools have been successful when employed for purposes of**

    A. Gender equity

    B. Resolving individual differences

    C. Remediation

    D. Artificial intelligence

40. **ROM which stands for Read Only Memory is**

    A. Changeable

    B. Permanent

    C. Temporary

    D. Used only on start up

41. Select the statement that best describes the term virus.

A. An infection that is introduced to a computer through a keyboard

B. A microscopic organism that invades a computer when it is not operating

C. A code that attaches itself to modem messages

D. A program that infects other programs by modifying them to include a version of itself

42. From the list of definitions shown, select the one that most appropriately describes operating system.

A. The master control program for a computer

B. A symbolic notation that identifies a location or address for a command

C. Handling, manipulation, and storage of data or information

D. The window that allows a user to choose commands appropriate to a specific function

43. This device converts the output of a computer into a visible image on a cathode ray tube.

A. Scanner

B. Monitor

C. LCD panel

D. VCR

44. A fixed disk is the same as a

A. Floppy disk

B. Hard drive

C. 1.44 drive

D. 3.4" diskette

45. Copying software to multiple computers (multiple loading) and allowing several users to simultaneously use the program is a copyright violation unless there is a special agreement called

A. Public domain

B. Cumulative effect

C. Software prerogative

D. Site license

Answer Key Subtest 3: School Operations, Technology

1. A		21. C	
2. D		22. B	
3. D		23. C	
4. A		24. D	
5. B		25. B	
6. A		26. C	
7. B		27. D	
8. D		28. A	
9. B		29. A	
10. C		30. C	
11. B		31. B	
12. B		32. B	
13. B		33. C	
14. C		34. B	
15. D		35. C	
16. A		36. A	
17. D		37. B	
18. B		38. A	
19. B		39. C	
20. A		40. B	
		41. D	
		42. A	
		43. B	
		44. B	
		45. D	

Bibliography

Editorial Projects in Education. (1997). "Technology Counts: Schools and Reform in the Information Age." *Education Week*, 17(11), 6-94.

Durost, R. (1994). "Integrating computer technology: Planning, training, and support," *NASSP* 78(563), 49-54.

Grabe, M. & Grabe, C. (1996). *Integrating Technology for Meaningful Learning.* Boston: Houghton Mifflin Company.

Heinich, R. , Molenda, M., Russell, J. & Smaldino, S. (1996). *Instructional Media and Technologies for Learning.* Englewood Cliffs, NJ: Merrill/Prentice Hall.

Hodas, S. (1995). *Technology Refusal and the Organizational Culture of Schools.* Unpublished Manuscript.

Hope, W. (1996). "Factors facilitating teachers use of computer technology." *The Clearing House* 70(2), 106-107.

Hope, W. (1997). "Teachers, Computer Technology, and the Change Process." *The Clearing House,* 70(4), 191-193.

Hope, W. (1997). "Why Technology Has Not Reached its Potential in Schools: A Perspective." *American Secondary Education,* 25(4), 2-9.

Hope, W. (1997). "Resolving teachers' concerns about microcomputer technology." *Computers in the Schools,* 13(3/4), 147-160.

Jonassen, D. (1996). *Computers in the Classroom: Mindtools for Critical Thinking.* Englewood Cliffs, NJ: Merrill/Prentice Hall.

Kearsley, G. (1995). *Computers for Educational Administrators: Leadership in the Information Age.* Norwood, NJ: Ablex Publishing Corporation.

Kearsley, G. & Lynch, W. (1994). *Educational Technology: Leadership Perspectives.* Englewood Cliffs, NJ: Educational Technology Publications, Inc.

Kinnaman, D. (1990). "Staff Development: How to Build Your Winning Team." *Technology and Learning,* 11(2), 24-26.

Lockard, J., Abrams, P., & Many, W. (1994). *Microcomputers for Twenty-first Century Educators* 3rd ed. New York: Harper-Collins.

Maurer, M., & Davidson, G. (1998). *Leadership in Instructional Technology.* Columbus, OH: Merrill/Prentice Hall.

Means, B. ed. (1994). *Technology and Education Reform: The Reality Behind the Promise.* San Francisco: Jossey-Bass Publishers.

Merrill, P., Hammons, K., Tolman, M., Christensen, L., Vincent, B., & Reynolds, P. (1992). *Computers in Education.* Boston: Allyn and Bacon.

Office of Technology Assessment (1995). *Teachers and Technology: Making the Connection.* Washington, DC: US Government Printing Office, 1995.

Picciano, A. (1998). *Educational Leadership and Planning for Technology.* Columbus, OH: Merrill/Prentice Hall.

Thomas, L. & Knezek, D. (1991). "Providing technology leadership for restructured schools." *Journal of Research on Computing in Education* 24(2), 265-279.

Simonson, M. & Thompson, A. 1997. *Educational Computing Foundations.* Columbus, OH: Merrill/Prentice Hall.

Wiebe, J. (1995). "The Need to Teach People about Computers." *Journal of Computing in Teacher Education* 11(3), 2-3.

"Never, ever, think outside the box."

"Relax, honey ---- change is good."

"Sometimes it's important to stop whatever break you're taking and just do the work."

"Mrs. Hammond, I'd know you anywhere from little Billy's portrait of you."

"Gosh, now we've seen everything!"